WHICH
BIBLE
?

BOOKS BY DAVID OTIS FULLER

Which Bible?
True or False?
Counterfeit or Genuine?
Treasury of Evangelical Writings

WHICH
BIBLE
?

Edited by

DAVID OTIS FULLER, D.D.

Fifth Edition

Grand Rapids International Publications
Grand Rapids, Michigan 49501

Library of Congress Catalog Card Number 70-129737
ISBN 0-8254-2612-X

First edition 1970
Second edition, revised and enlarged 1971
Third edition, revised and enlarged 1972
Fourth edition 1974
Fifth edition with Alphabetical, Scriptural
and Chronological Indexes by
Thomas R. Steinbach 1975

Printed in the United States of America

DEDICATION

This book, being a book about the Holy Bible, is reverently dedicated to Him Who is the Chief and all glorious Subject of the Sacred Book, Who alone could say of the Holy Scriptures —
"They are they which testify of ME."

ACKNOWLEDGMENTS

The writers of some of the articles quoted in this book are now with the Lord, having faithfully served Him in their generation as earnest contenders for "the faith once delivered to the saints." The compiler acknowledges the help derived from their writings and also from some who continue in the battle at this present time.

Zane C. Hodges, A.B., Th.M., Assistant Professor of New Testament Literature and Exegesis, Dallas Theological Seminary.

E. F. Hills, A.B., (Yale), Th.D., (Harvard), author of *The King James Version Defended, Believing Bible Study,* etc.

The Reverend Henry W. Coray, pastor of the Orthodox Presbyterian Church, Glenside, Pennsylvania. Author of the biographies in my book *Valiant for the Truth,* now published as *A Treasury of Evangelical Writings.*

The Reverend Terence H. Brown, Secretary of the Trinitarian Bible Society, London, England, who contributed the chapter entitled "The Learned Men."

Jasper James Ray, who kindly permitted quotations from his excellent book, *God Wrote Only One Bible* (Eye Opener Publishers, Box 77, Junction City, Oregon 97448).

The Reverent David Fountain, M.A., (Oxford), pastor of the Spring Road Evangelical Baptist Church, Sholing, Southampton, England.

Miss Betty Wood, my efficient secretary, who helped to collect the material and prepared the typescript.

Quoted material beginning on page 9 is from *MASADA: Herod's Fortress and the Zealot's Last Stand,* by Yigael Yadin, copyright © 1966 by Yigael Yadin. Reprinted by permission of Random House, Inc.

The individual contributors are responsible only for their respective articles and are not necessarily in agreement with every point in the other articles.

CONTENTS

WHY THIS BOOK?

David Otis Fuller

In many important matters everyone recognizes the need for an authority — a supreme "court of appeal" higher than which no one can go. In the realm of supernatural things there is only *One Authority* recognized by Christian people. This is not the church, nor the "infallible" words of men, nor one's own ego, nor a hierarchy of Roman "priests," Protestant ministers, or Jewish rabbis. All such are fallible and prone to error and prejudice. The Bible makes high claims to Divine inspiration, inerrancy and authority; and if it is true that the Sovereign God of the universe has condescended to reveal Himself supernaturally in His Book, even as He has revealed Himself naturally in the material universe, then man — even in a world ruined by sin — has a firm foundation on which to build for time and eternity.

That the Sovereign God of creation has done this in the Holy Scriptures is acknowledged by many earnest Christians, but a question arises which demands a clear answer: "Which Bible do you mean?" A generation or two ago this question would have had but one answer — the King James Version; but now many new translations demand recognition and prominence — the Revised Version, the American Standard Version, the Revised Standard Version, the New

1

English Bible, the Knox Version, the Anchor Version, the Berkeley Version, etc., etc.

Jasper James Ray, missionary and Bible teacher, in the splendid book, *God Wrote Only One Bible,* says — "A multiplicity of differing Bible versions are in circulation today, resulting in a state of bewildering confusion. Some versions omit words, verses, phrases and even chapter portions which are well known to be included in a number of the ancient manuscripts. In some of these new versions words and phrases have been added which have no corresponding basic expression in authentic copies of the Hebrew and Greek. Among these you will not find the Bible which God gave when "holy men of God spake as they were moved by the Holy Ghost" (II Peter 1:21; II Timothy 3:16).

Those who favor the modern versions claim that they are based upon the oldest and best manuscripts, but oldest and best do not necessarily go hand in hand. Mr. Ray's book makes this clear — "Within the first hundred years after the death of the Apostles, Irenaeus said concerning Marcion the Gnostic, 'Wherefore also Marcion and his followers have betaken themselves to mutilating the Scriptures, not acknowledging some books at all, and curtailing the gospel according to Luke and the Epistles of Paul, they assert that these alone are authentic which they themselves have shortened.' "[1] Epiphanius in his treatise the *Panarion* describes no less than eighty heretical parties, each of which planned to further its own ends by the misuse of the Scriptures.[2]

Those who were corrupting Bible manuscripts said that they were correcting them, and corrupted copies were so prevalent that agreement between them was hopeless. The worst corruptions to which the New Testament has ever been subjected originated within a hundred years after it was composed. The African fathers and the whole Western, with a portion of the Syrian Church, used far inferior manuscripts to those employed by Erasmus or Stephanus

---

[1] *Ante-Nicene Fathers* (Grand Rapids, 1953), Vol. 1, pp. 434-435.

[2] G. T. Fisher, *History of Christian Doctrine,* p. 19.

thirteen centuries later when molding the Textus Receptus. Many of the important variations in the modern versions may be traced to the influence of Eusebius and Origen — "the father of Arianism."

Eusebius was a great admirer of Origen and a student of his philosophy. J. J. Ray quotes from Dr. Ira Price's *Ancestry of the English Bible*,[3] "Eusebius of Caesarea, the first church historian, assisted by Pamphilus, or vice versa, issued with all its critical remarks the fifth column of Origen's *Hexapla* with alternative readings from the other columns, for use in Palestine. The Emperor Constantine gave orders that fifty copies of this edition should be prepared for use in the churches." It has been suggested that the Codex Vaticanus may have been one of these copies. Many modern textual critics regard this document as the oldest and best representative of the original text of Holy Scripture. The object of the following chapters is to demonstrate that this appraisal is fundamentally wrong, and that the Majority Text or Traditional Text — sometimes called the Received Text — underlying the King James Version more faithfully preserves the inspired revelation.

There have been many attempts to adulterate and to destroy the Holy Scriptures, and every age has witnessed such assaults. As early as the second century such writers as Irenaeus describe the attempts of heretics to corrupt the inspired records, and during periods of Roman persecution imperial decrees demanded the surrender and destruction of the copies cherished by many of the Lord's people.

In the Reformation period the Church of Rome sought to maintain its dominant position by burning not only the copies of the Bible, but also those who recognized the supreme authority of God's Word. Tyndale was burned at the stake at Vilvorde outside Brussels in Belgium on August 6, 1536. His great offense was that he had translated the Scriptures into English and was making copies available against the wishes of the Roman Catholic hierarchy. His prayer was heard before he died, — "O Lord, open the eyes of the King of England." His prayer

---

[3] J. J. Ray, *God Wrote Only One Bible*, p. 70.

was heard and answered; and in less than a year King Henry VIII, who had ordered Tyndale's death, gave his permission for the Bible to be placed in the parish churches, and the people of England rejoiced to have the Word of God in their own tongue.

Ray asserts that while the true Christian religion puts the inspired Word of God above everything else, the false system puts something above the Bible or places human tradition in a chair of equal authority with it. At the Council of Trent in 1546 fifty-three prelates made a decree declaring that the apocryphal books together with un-written tradition are of God and are to be received and venerated as the Word of God. In the primitive church the only authentic Scriptures recognized were those given by the inspiration of God (II Peter 1:21). These are the true Word of God, and through His gracious providence and infinite wisdom the stream of the life-giving water of God's inspired Word has come to us crystal clear.

The "god of this world" directs his attack first on the character and Person of the Son of God, the Lord Jesus Christ, the Incarnate Word, and then on the integrity and accuracy of the written Word of God — the Bible. From the beginning there has been no pause in the assault on God's Son and God's Word. The first Gospel promise in Genesis 3:15 had hardly been uttered when Satan sought to erase the "Seed of the woman" from the scene. There came a time when a six-month-old baby was the only one left of the royal line following a massacre by the wicked Queen Athaliah (II Chronicles 22:10-12). When Jesus was but a baby He, with His foster father Joseph and mother Mary, was forced to flee into Egypt from the wrath of Herod the Great, who secured and kept his throne by crimes of unspeakable brutality, murdering even his own wife and two sons. It was this Herod who slew the children of Bethlehem in an effort to kill the Christ.

In the days of His earthly ministry three times they sought to stone Him to death; once they hustled Him to the brow of a hill overlooking Nazareth and were going to cast Him down headlong, "But he passing through the midst of them went his way" (Luke 4:30). True, they

4

finally crucified Him, but only by His permission; for it is written, "Therefore doth my Father love me, because I lay down my life, that I might take it again" (John 10:17). In all these, and in many other ways the hatred of Satan toward the Son of God was manifested.

In the second arena, that of the Word of God written, Satan is more than ever active today. From the very outset, when he cast doubt upon God's Word in the garden with the question, "Yea, hath God said . . .?" he has sought to corrupt or destroy that which God has caused to be written. The power and providence of God are displayed in the history of the preservation and transmission of His Word, in fulfillment of the promise of the Son of God, "For verily I say unto you, Till heaven and earth pass, one jot or one tittle shall in no wise pass from the law, till all be fulfilled" (Matthew 5:18). Our Lord was not given to exaggeration, and God's holy Law was not confined to the commands of Sinai but is set forth in all that He inspired His prophets and apostles to write.

The whole realm of created things is ordered and sustained by the over-ruling providence of God, Who upholds all things by the word of His power. The Scriptures make it quite clear that He is also well able to insure the providential preservation of His own Word through the ages, and that He is the Author and Preserver of the Divine Revelation. The Bible cannot be accounted for in any other way. It claims to be "Theopneustos," "God-breathed." "All scripture is given by inspiration of God" (II Timothy 3:16). Without impairing or destroying their individual personalities and style, the Spirit of God "carried along" those inspired writers of His words, so that they did in fact record the very words of God — "Not in words which man's wisdom teaches, but which the Holy Spirit teaches." Those who reject this as impossible would reduce the Almighty to the stature of a fallible man, but "with God all things are possible."

The compiler of this book, and the able writers whom he quotes, all contend that the Bible is the inspired, inerrant and authoritative Word of God and that there has been a gracious exercise of the Divine providence in its preservation and transmission. They are also deeply convinced that the inspired text is more faithfully represented by the Majority Text — sometimes called the Byzantine Text, the Received Text or the Traditional Text — than by the modern critical editions which attach too much weight to the Codex Vaticanus, Codex Sinaiticus and their allies. For this reason the reader is encouraged to maintain confidence in the King James Version as a faithful translation based upon a reliable text.

Many ancient copies of the Scriptures have perished, but the Divine revelation has been preserved. In countless instances the old and well-worn copies were deliberately destroyed when new copies had been made from them. In this way the ancient text has been perpetuated in less ancient copies. Some very ancient copies have escaped decay and destruction for the simple reason that they were not regarded as accurate enough for copying purposes or for common use. Dr. E. F. Hills draws attention to this in his scholarly little book, *The King James Version Defended.* The author received his A.B. from Yale University and his Th.D. from Harvard. He also pursued graduate studies at Chicago University and Calvin Seminary. Dr. Hills is entitled to a hearing because of his scholarship and scientific research, which qualify him to evaluate the facts.

The following extracts are taken from his book, pages 42, 43 and 69.

"Kirsopp Lake, a brilliant liberal critic of the Scriptures, began his study of the Byzantine manuscripts with the expectation of finding many cases in which one of the manuscripts examined would prove itself to be a direct copy of one of the other manuscripts. But to his amazement he could discover no such cases of direct copying. He summarized this surprising situation in the following manner: 'The Ferrar group and family 1 are the only reported cases of the repeated copying of a single archetype, and even for the Ferrar group there were probably two archetypes rather than one. . . . Apart from these two there seem to be no groups of manuscripts which are conceivably descendants of a single lost codex. . . . Taking this fact into consideration along with the

6

negative result of our collation of manuscripts at Sinai, Patmos, and Jerusalem, it is hard to resist the conclusion that the scribes usually destroyed their exemplars when they had copied the sacred books.'[4]

"But this hypothesis which Lake advanced as something new and startling was essentially the same as that for which consistently Christian scholars, such as J. W. Burgon (1813-1888), Dean of Chichester, had contended long before. According to Burgon,[5] there once were many ancient manuscripts containing the Byzantine text, manuscripts much older than B[6] or ALEPH. But they were read so constantly and copied so frequently that finally they wore out and perished. This is why only a few ancient Byzantine manuscripts are extant today, none of which is as old as B or ALEPH. And conversely, the reason why B, ALEPH, and other non-Byzantine manuscripts have survived to the present day *is because they were rejected by the Greek Church as faulty and so not used.*

"Burgon's contention was universally rejected in his own day by naturalistic critics. It is interesting, therefore, to see it confirmed forty-five years later by a leading representative of the naturalistic school. For if Lake was right in supposing 'that the scribes usually destroyed their examplars when they had copied the sacred books,' then many ancient Byzantine manuscripts could have perished in this manner, and certainly B, ALEPH, and other ancient non-Byzantine manuscripts now extant would have so perished *had they contained an acceptable text.*

"Naturalistic New Testament critics seem at last to have reached the end of the trail. Westcott and Hort's broad highway, which appeared to lead so quickly and smoothly to the original New Testament text, has dwindled down to a narrow foot path and terminated finally in a thicket of trees. For those who have followed it, there is only one thing to do, and that is to go back and begin the journey

---

[4] *Harvard Theological Review,* Vol. 21 (1928), pp. 347-349.

[5] *The Revision Revised* (London, 1883), p. 319.

[6] The 4th century Codex Vaticanus and Codex Sinaiticus, by which misguided critics have attempted to correct the New Testament text.

all over again from the consistently Christian starting point; namely, the divine inspiration and providential preservation of Scripture.

"Those who take these doctrines as their starting point need never be apprehensive over the results of their researches in the New Testament text. For the providence of God was watching over this sacred text even during the first three centuries of the Christian era. Even during this troubled period a sufficient number of trustworthy copies of the New Testament Scriptures was produced by true believers under the guidance of the Holy Spirit. These were the manuscripts to which the whole Greek Church returned during the fourth and fifth centuries, again under the leading of the Holy Spirit, and from which the Byzantine text was derived."

Dr. John Warwick Montgomery, author of the penetrating and incisive book, *The Suicide of Christian Theology,* makes this comment on page 38: "The historical value of the New Testament records about Christ is, when considered from the objective standpoint of textual scholarship, nothing less than stellar. Writes Sir Frederic G. Kenyon, formerly director and principal librarian of the British Museum: 'The interval . . . between the dates of original composition and the earliest extant evidence becomes so small as to be in fact negligible, and the last foundation for any doubt that the Scriptures have come down to us substantially as they were written has now been removed. Both the *authenticity* and the *general integrity* of the books of the New Testament may be regarded as finally established.' "[7]

Dr. Yigael Yadin is the author of a most unusual book, *Masada,* the momentous archaeological discovery revealing the heroic life and struggle of the Jewish Zealots. Dr. Yadin at the time of Israel's struggle for independence and during the War of Liberation in 1948, became Chief of Operations of the Israeli Defense Forces and later Chief of the General Staff.

----

[7] *The Suicide of Christian Theology,* ©1970 Bethany Fellowship, Inc.

In 1952 he resigned from the army to resume his research and joined the Hebrew University in Jerusalem where he is now professor of archaeology. In 1955 and 1958 he directed the excavations at Hazor, and in 1960 and 1961 he led the explorations of the Judean Desert Caves where Bar-Kochba documents were discovered. He has done much research work on the scrolls from the Dead Sea area and has written numerous papers in archaeological and scientific journals. In 1956 he was awarded the Israel prize in Jewish studies and in 1965 the Rothschild prize in humanities. The following are extracts from his book.[8]

"About three feet away from the shekels the first scroll was found. All the details of this discovery are sharp in my mind. In the early hours of the afternoon, while I was in one of the northern storerooms, Shmaryahu Guttman came running to me, followed by some of the volunteers working with him, and flourished before me a piece of parchment. It was so black and creased that only with difficulty could one make anything out. But a quick examination on the spot showed us immediately that here was a fragment from the Book of Psalms, and we could even identify the chapters: the section ran from Psalm 81 to Psalm 85.

"A little while later we also found another part of the scroll, which completed the top part of the first fragment. . . . This discovery is of extraordinary importance for scroll research. It is not only that this is the first time that a parchment scroll has been found not in a cave, and in circumstances where it was possible to date it without the slightest doubt. It could not possibly be later than the year 73 AD, the year Masada fell. As a matter of fact, this scroll was written much before — perhaps twenty or thirty years earlier; and it is interesting that this section from the Book of Psalms, *like the other Biblical scrolls which we found later,* is almost exactly identical (except for a few minor changes here and there) to the text of the biblical books *which we use today.* Even the division into chapters

8 Yigael Yadin, *MASADA: Herod's Fortress and the Zealots' Last Stand.* Copyright © 1966 by Yigael Yadin. Reprinted by permission of Random House, Inc.

and psalms is identical with the traditional division" (pp. 171-172).

"On the very first day of the second season, early in the afternoon, it fell to a young lad from a *kibbutz* in Western Galilee to discover in the western corner of the court in front of the large wall, fragments of a scroll scattered among the ruins. This discovery provoked great excitement and was taken as a happy omen for our future work. Parts of the fragments had been eaten away, but those that were undamaged were very well preserved and we could immediately identify them as several chapters from the Book of Leviticus, chapters eight to twelve, and to note that this scroll too was *absolutely identical with the traditional text of Leviticus.* . . . How this scroll reached this location we shall never know. Maybe it was blown here by the wind during the destruction of Masada and was buried among the ruined debris; or perhaps it was thrown here by one of the Roman soldiers. At all events, its discovery here might be called an archaeological 'miracle' " (p. 179).

"Within a few hours he [Chief Petty Officer Moshe Cohen, from the Israeli Navy] had reached almost to the bottom of the pit and there his groping hands found the remains of a scroll. Though the parchment was badly gnawed, we could immediately identify the writing as chapters from the Book of Ezekiel; and the parts that were better preserved than others, and which we could easily read, contained extracts from Chapter 37 — the vision of the dry bones.

"As for the rolled scroll discovered in the first pit, it was found on opening — which had to be done with great care in the laboratory in Jerusalem — to contain parts of the two final chapters of the Book of Deuteronomy. But the tightly rolled core of the scroll, on which we had pinned much hope, turned out to our dismay to be simply the blank end 'sheets' of the scroll. They had been sewn to the written 'sheets' to facilitate rolling and unrolling. It need hardly be added at this stage that these two scrolls, too, are *virtually identical with the traditional Biblical texts.*

There are only a few slight changes in the Ezekiel scroll" (pp. 187-189).

In the following pages though there is language that is technical and difficult for the average layman to grasp, there is also much that anyone may comprehend and greatly profit from. May God, the Blessed Holy Spirit, use the pages of this book to inspire and challenge the hearts of believers who have been bought with the precious blood of the Son of God. Let us be willing to stand against what is erroneous and ready always to give a reason for the hope that lieth in us in meekness and fear.

THE LEARNED MEN

Terence H. Brown

The Rev. Terence H. Brown has been Secretary of the Trinitarian Bible Society of London, England for a number of years and is a scholar in his own right. God is increasingly using the TBS around the world, with branches being formed recently in Canada and the United States.

"There were many chosen that were greater in other men's eyes than in their own, and that sought the truth rather than their own praise."[1]

Advocates of the modern versions often assume that they are the product of scholarship far superior to that of the translators of the King James Version of 1611, but this assumption is not supported by the facts. The learned men who labored on our English Bible were men of exceptional ability, and although they differed among themselves on many matters of church order, administration and doctrine, they approached the task with a reverent regard for the Divine inspiration, authority and inerrancy of the Holy Scriptures. To them it was "God's sacred Truth" and demanded the exercise of their utmost care and fidelity in its translation.

---

[1] Miles Smith, *The Translators to the Reader.*

The most learned men in the land were chosen for this work, and the complete list shows a high proportion of men with a profound knowledge of the languages in which the Bible was written. Of the fifty-four who were chosen, a few died or withdrew before the translation was started and the final list numbered forty-seven men. They were divided into six companies, and a portion was assigned to each group. Everyone in each company translated the whole portion before they met to compare their results and agree upon the final form. They then transmitted their draft to each of the other companies for their comment and consent. A select committee then went carefully through the whole work again, and at last two of their number were responsible for the final checking.

The six committees were to meet at Westminster, Oxford and Cambridge. The first Westminster Committee was attended by:

1. Dr. Lancelot Andrewes, Fellow of Pembroke, Cambridge, where he took his B.A., M.A. and divinity degrees, later became Dean of Westminster, Bishop of Ely and then of Winchester.
2. Dr. John Overall, Fellow of Trinity and Master of St. Catharine's, Cambridge, became Dean of St. Paul's and successively Bishop of Coventry and Lichfield and Norwich. He took his D.D. in 1596 and became Regius Professor of Divinity at Cambridge.
3. Dr. Adrian Saravia, Professor of Divinity at Leyden University in 1582, became Prebendary of Canterbury and Westminster. In the controversies of that period he is often referred to as "that learned foreigner." His Spanish descent and residence in Holland qualified him to assist the translators with his first-hand knowledge of the work of Spanish and Dutch scholars.
4. Dr. John Layfield, Fellow of Trinity, Cambridge in 1585 and Greek lecturer in 1593, was specially skilled in architecture; and his judgment was relied on regarding passages describing the Tabernacle and Temple.
5. Dr. Richard Clarke, Fellow of Christ's College, Cambridge, D.D.

6. Dr. William Teigh, Archdeacon of Middlesex, Rector of All Hallows, Barking-by-the-Tower, described by Wood as "an excellent textuary and profound linguist."

7. Dr. F. Burleigh, B.D. 1594, D.D. 1607. Fellow, King James' College, Chelsea.

8. Richard Thomson, M.A., Fellow of Clare College, Cambridge, described by Richard Montagu as "a most admirable philologer . . . better known in Italy, France and Germany than at home."

9. William Bedwell, M.A., St. John's College, Cambridge, had established his reputation as an Arabic scholar before 1603 and is recognized as "the Father of Arabic studies in England." He was the author of the *Lexicon Heptaglotton* in seven folio volumes, including Hebrew, Syriac, Chaldee and Arabic. He also commenced a Persian dictionary and an Arabic translation of the Epistles of John (now among the Laud MSS in the Bodleian Library).

10. Professor Geoffrey King, Fellow of King's College, Cambridge, and Regius Professor of Hebrew. Lively, Spalding, King and Byng held this professorship in succession.

The second Westminster Committee included another seven scholars:

1. Dr. William Barlow, St. John's, Cambridge, B.A. in 1583, M.A. in 1587, Fellow of Trinity in 1590, B.D. in 1594, D.D. in 1599. He represented the "Church Party" at the Hampton Court Conference and wrote *The Summe and Substance of the Conference,* which the Puritans criticized as being biased against their cause. He was made Bishop of Rochester in 1605, "one of the youngest in age, but one of the ripest in learning" of all those that had occupied that position. He later became Bishop of Lincoln.

2. Dr. Ralph Huchinson, President of St. John's College, Oxford, B.A. in 1574, M.A. in 1578, B.D. in 1596, and D.D. in 1602.

3. Dr. T. Spenser, President of Corpus Christi College, Oxford.
4. Dr. Roger Fenton, Fellow of Pembroke, Cambridge, D.D., one of the popular preachers of the day.
5. Mr. Michael Rabbet, Rector of St. Vedast, Foster Lane.
6. Mr. Thomas Sanderson, Rector of All Hallows.
7. Professor William Dakins, Fellow of Trinity, Cambridge, M.A. in 1594, B.D. in 1601, Greek Lecturer at Trinity, and Professor of Divinity at Gresham College in 1604.

The Oxford Old Testament Committee enrolled:

1. Dr. John Harding, President of Magdalen College and Regius Professor of Hebrew. He presided over this committee.
2. Dr. John Reynolds, Merton College, Oxford, moved to Corpus Christi and became Fellow in 1566. He took his D.D. in 1585 and became Regius Professor of Divinity. After several years as Dean of Lincoln he was made President of Corpus Christi College in 1598. He represented the Puritans at the Hampton Court Conference at which he suggested that a new translation of the Bible should be undertaken. His reputation as a Hebrew and Greek scholar was sufficient warrant for his inclusion among the translators, and Hall relates that "his memory and reading were near to a miracle." He worked on the translation of the Prophets until his death in 1607. During this period the Oxford translators met at his residence once a week to compare and discuss what they had done.
3. Dr. Thomas Holland, Balliol and Exeter Colleges, Oxford, B.A. 1570, M.A. 1575, B.D. 1582, D.D. 1584. Master and Regius Professor of Divinity, 1589. He achieved so much distinction in many fields of learning that he was not only highly esteemed among English scholars but also had a good reputation in the universities of Europe. Like Apollos, he was mighty in the Scriptures, and like the Apostle, he was faithful in explaining them. His example went hand in hand with

his precepts, and he himself lived what he preached to others. Among the translators he was probably the most strongly opposed to Rome, and it is recorded that whenever he went on a journey away from his college he would call the men together and "commend them to the love of God and to the abhorrence of popery."

His biographer writes — "He loved and he longed for God, for the presence of God, and for the full enjoyment of Him. His soul was framed for heaven, and could find no rest till it came there. His dying prayer was — 'Come, O come, Lord Jesus, Thou Morning Star! Come, Lord Jesus; I desire to be dissolved, and to be with Thee!' "

4. Dr. Richard Kilbye, Lincoln College, Oxford, B.A. 1578, M.A. 1582, B.D. and D.D. in 1596 and Regius Professor of Hebrew in 1610. Author of a work on Exodus prepared from Hebrew commentators. An interesting story is found in Walton's biography of Bishop Sanderson illustrating the truth of the old proverb, "a little learning is a dangerous thing." Dr. Kilbye, an excellent Hebrew scholar and Professor of this language in the university, also expert in Greek and chosen as one of the translators, went on a visit with Sanderson, and at church on Sunday they heard a young preacher waste a great amount of the time allotted for his sermon in criticizing several words in the then recent translation. He carefully showed how one particular word should have been translated in a different way. Later that evening the preacher and the learned strangers were invited together to a meal, and Dr. Kilbye took the opportunity to tell the preacher that he could have used his time more profitably. The Doctor then explained that the translators had very carefully considered the "three reasons" given by the preacher, but they had found another thirteen more weighty reasons for giving the rendering complained of by the young critic.

5. Dr. Miles Smith, M.A., D.D., Corpus Christi, and

Brasenose and Christ Church, Oxford, Bishop of Gloucester in 1612. He provided more evidence of his contribution than any of the others, as it was left to him to write the long Translators' Preface — "The Translators to the Reader," which used to be printed at the beginning of most English Bibles. His knowledge of the oriental languages made him well qualified for a place among the translators of the Authorized Version of the Bible. He had Hebrew at his fingers' ends; and he was so conversant with Chaldee, Syriac, and Arabic, that he made them as familiar to him as his native tongue. He persisted in this task from its commencement to its completion and was himself the last man engaged in the translation.

The work of the whole company was revised and improved by a small group selected from their number, and was then finally examined by Bilson and Miles Smith. The latter then wrote the famous preface, beginning — "Zeal to promote the common good. . . ."

6. Dr. Richard Brett, Fellow of Lincoln College, Oxford, D.D., well versed in classical and Eastern languages, Latin, Greek, Hebrew, Chaldee, Arabic and Ethiopic.

7. Mr. Fairclowe, Fellow of New College, Oxford.

The Oxford New Testament Committee includes:

1. Dr. Thomas Ravis, Christ Church, Oxford, B.A. 1578, M.A. 1581, B.D. 1589, D.D. 1595, Vice Chancellor 1597. He was one of the six deans who attended the Hampton Court Conference in 1604 and was made Bishop of Gloucester in that year.

2. Dr. George Abbot — began his university studies at Balliol College, Oxford in 1578 and soon became known for his strong Calvinism and puritanism. In 1593 he took his B.D., in 1597 his D.D., and in the same year became Master of University College at the age of thirty-five; and a few years later he was Vice Chancellor. He very strongly opposed the Romanizing influence of Laud and was very severe in his denuncia-

tion of anything which savored of "popery." Nevertheless he accepted some high offices in the Church of England and in 1609 became Bishop of Lichfield and Archbishop of Canterbury in 1611. He was regarded as the head of the Puritans within the Church of England, and he vigorously opposed the King's declaration permitting sports and pastimes on the Lord's Day. He encouraged James to request the States General to dismiss Vorstius from his professorship at Leyden because of his Arminianism.

3. Dr. R. Eedes, Dean of Worcester.
4. Dr. Giles Thompson, Dean of Windsor, Bishop of Gloucester, a man of high repute as scholar and preacher.
5. Sir Henry Saville, Brasenose College, Oxford, Fellow of Merton College in 1565 and Warden in 1585, Provost of Eton in 1596, Tutor to Queen Elizabeth I. He was a pioneer in many branches of scholarship and the founder of the Savillian Professorships of Mathematics and Astronomy at Oxford. His works include an eight volume edition of the writings of Chrysostom.
6. Dr. John Perin, Fellow of St. John's College, Oxford, Canon of Christ Church and Professor of Greek.
7. Dr. Ralph Ravens, Fellow of St. John's College.
8. John Harmar, M.A., New College, Oxford, Professor of Greek in 1585. He was well read in patristic and scholastic theology and a noted Latinist and Grecian. His works include translations of Calvin's sermons on the Ten Commandments, several of Beza's sermons, and some of the Homilies of Chrysostom.

The first Cambridge Committee also numbered eight scholars:

1. Edward Liveley, Trinity College, Cambridge, B.A. in 1568, M.A. and Fellow in 1572, Regius Professor of Hebrew in 1575, enjoyed the reputation of an acquaintance with the oriental languages unequalled at that period.

2. Dr. John Richardson, Fellow of Emmanuel College, D.D., Master of Peterhouse and later Master of Trinity.

3. Dr. Laurence Chaderton, Fellow of Christ's College, D.D., Master of Emmanuel. Chaderton entered Christ's College in 1564 and embraced the Reformed doctrines. He had been brought up as a Roman Catholic, and his father offered him an allowance of thirty pounds if he would leave Cambridge and renounce Protestantism — "Otherwise I enclose a shilling to buy a wallet — go and beg." He acquired a great reputation as a Latin, Greek and Hebrew scholar and was also proficient in French, Spanish and Italian. For fifty years he was Afternoon Lecturer at St. Clement's, Cambridge, and forty of the clergy said they owed their conversion to his preaching.

   He was a noted Puritan; but he did not join the cry against "prelacy," although he never accepted a bishopric himself. He was one of the three representatives of the Millenary Plaintiffs at the Hampton Court Conference. This faithful preacher and teacher lived to be 94 (one of his biographers says 104), and almost to the time of his death he was able to read his small type Greek New Testament.

4. Francis Dillingham, Fellow of Christ's College, Cambridge, M.A. in 1590 and B.D. in 1599. According to Fuller, he was "an excellent linguist and subtle disputant." His works include *A disswasive from Poperie, containing twelve effectual reasons by which every Papist, not wilfully blinded, may be brought to the truth.*

5. Dr. Roger Andrewes, Fellow of Pembroke, Master of Jesus College, D.D., brother of Dr. Lancelot Andrewes.

6. Dr. Thomas Harrison, St. John's College, Cambridge, B.A. in 1576. Fellow, Tutor and Vice-Master of Trinity, D.D., noted Hebraist and chief examiner in Hebrew. He was a convinced Puritan.

7. Professor Robert Spalding, Fellow of St. John's College, Cambridge, succeeded Edward Liveley as Professor of Hebrew.

8. Professor Byng, Fellow of Peterhouse, Cambridge, and Hebrew Professor.

The second Cambridge Committee included the following scholars:

1. Dr. John Duport, Jesus College, M.A. and Fellow before 1580. D.D. in 1590, Master of Jesus College, four times Vice-Chancellor of the University.
2. Dr. William Brainthwaite, Fellow of Emmanuel and Master of Gonville and Gaius College.
3. Dr. Jeremiah Radcliffe, Fellow of Trinity College, Cambridge.
4. Dr. Samuel Ward, Emmanuel College, Cambridge, D.D., Master of Sidney College, and Margaret Professor. His correspondence with Archbishop Ussher contains treasures of diversified learning, especially concerning Biblical and oriental criticism.
5. Professor Andrew Downes, St. John's, Cambridge, B.A. 1567, Fellow 1571, M.A. 1574, B.D. 1582, Regius Professor of Greek 1585. Downes and Boys revived the study of Greek at St. John's. These two men joined Miles Smith on the sub-committee which subjected the whole translation to a final careful process of checking and correction.
6. John Boys, Fellow of St. John's, Cambridge, and Greek lecturer there. He was born in 1560 and at a very early age showed an unusual interest in languages. He began to read Hebrew at the age of five years and was admitted to St. John's College, Cambridge, when he was fourteen. There he very soon distinguished himself by his knowledge of the Greek language, which he sometimes studied in the library from 4 a.m. until 8 p.m.

   When he was elected Fellow of his college he was suffering from smallpox, but he was so anxious not to delay his career that, at some risk to himself and fellow-scholars, he persuaded his friends to wrap him in blankets and carry him in. After studying medicine for some time he gave up this course and applied himself to the study of Greek. For ten years he was the chief Greek lecturer in his college. At four in the morning he voluntarily gave a Greek lecture in his own room which was frequented by many of the Fellows.

After twenty years of university life he became Rector of Boxworth in Cambridgeshire, and while he was there he made an arrangement with twelve other ministers that they should meet each Friday in each other's homes in turn and share the results of their studies.

When the translation of the Bible was begun he was chosen to be one of the Cambridge translators, and eventually he not only undertook his portion but also the part allotted to another member of the committee. When the work was completed John Boys was one of the six translators who met at Stationers' Hall to revise the whole. This took them about nine months, and during this period the Company of Stationers made them an allowance of thirty shillings each per week.

After a long life of profitable study, ministry, translating and writing he died at the age of eighty-four, "his brow without wrinkles, his sight quick, his hearing sharp, his countenance fresh and his body sound."

7. Dr. Ward, Fellow of King's College, Cambridge, D.D., Prebendary of Chichester.

Lancelot Andrewes, a member of the Westminster Committee, had his early education at Coopers Free School and Merchant Taylors School, where his rapid progress in the study of the ancient languages was brought to the notice of Dr. Watts, the founder of some scholarships at Pembroke Hall, Cambridge. Andrewes was sent to that College, where he took his B.A. degree and soon afterwards was elected Fellow. He then took his Master's degree and began to study divinity and achieved great distinction as a lecturer. He was raised to several positions of influence in the Church of England and distinguished himself as a diligent and excellent preacher, and became Chaplain to Queen Elizabeth I. King James I promoted him to be Bishop of Chester in 1605 and also gave him the influential position of Lord Almoner. He later became Bishop of Ely and Privy Counsellor. Toward the end of his life he was made Bishop of Winchester.

It is recorded that Andrewes was a man of deep piety and that King James had such great respect for him that in his presence he refrained from the levity in which he indulged at other times. A sermon preached at Andrewes' funeral in 1626 paid tribute to his great scholarship — "His knowlege in Latin, Greek, Hebrew, Chaldee, Syriac and Arabic, besides fifteen modern languages was so advanced that he may be ranked as one of the rarest linguists in Christendom.

"A great part of five hours every day he spent in prayer, and in his last illness he spent all his time in prayer — and when both voice and eyes and hands failed in their office, his countenance showed that he still prayed and praised God in his heart, until it pleased God to receive his blessed soul to Himself."

No reasonable person imagines that the translators were infallible or that their work was perfect, but no one acquainted with the facts can deny that they were men of outstanding scholarship, well qualified for their important work, or that with God's blessing they completed their great task with scrupulous care and fidelity.

It is remarkable that the literary style of individual members of the company of translators was generally inferior to that of the version which they jointly produced. The explanation of this is that they exercised their wisdom in leaving undisturbed the simple style and vocabulary of the earlier translators. If they had cast the translation in the mold of the more ornate style of their own period, it is doubtful whether their work would have triumphed for so long as it has. They made many thousands of small changes, most of which improved the rhythm, clarified the meaning, or increased the accuracy of the translation.

They were indeed "learned men" — and their scholarship was accompanied by a deep conviction of the Divine origin of the records which they were translating. Learning and faith went hand in hand to open the storehouse of God's Word of Truth for the spiritual enrichment of millions from generation to generation, over a period of more than three hundred and fifty years.

THE GREEK TEXT OF THE KING JAMES VERSION

Zane C. Hodges

This article is reproduced with the kind permission of Prof. Z. C. Hodges and Dr. J. F. Walvoord, Editor of *Bibliotheca Sacra,* published by the Faculty of Dallas Theological Seminary and Graduate School of Theology. Prof. Hodges is Assistant Professor of New Testament Literature and Exegesis, Dallas Theological Seminary.

The average well-taught Bible-believing Christian has often heard the King James Version corrected on the basis of "better manuscripts" or "older authorities." Such corrections are often made from the pulpit as well as being found in print. If he has ever inquired into the matter, the Bible-believing Christian has probably been told that the Greek text used by the translators of 1611 is inferior to that used for more recent translations. He has perhaps also been told that the study of the Greek text of the New Testament (called textual criticism) is now a highly developed discipline which has led us to a more accurate knowledge of the original text of the Bible. Lacking any kind of technical training in this area, the average believer probably has accepted such explanations from individuals he regards as qualified to give them. Nevertheless, more than once he may have felt a twinge of uneasiness about the whole matter and wondered if, by any chance, the familiar King James Version might not be somewhat better than its detractors think. It is the purpose of this article to affirm that, as a matter of fact, there are indeed grounds for this kind of uneasiness and — what is more — these grounds are considerable.[1]

By way of introduction, it should be pointed out that a very large number of Greek manuscripts of the New Testament survive today. A recent list gives these figures: papyrus manuscripts, 81; majuscules (manuscripts written in capital letters), 267; minuscules (manuscripts written in smaller script), 2,764.[2] Of course, many of these are fragmentary and most of them do not contain the entire New Testament. Nevertheless, for an ancient book the available materials are massive and more than adequate for our needs providing they are properly handled by scholars. It is also well known among students of textual criticism that a large majority of this huge mass of manuscripts — somewhere between 80-90% — contain a Greek text which in most respects closely resembles the kind of text which was the basis of our King James Version.[3] This piece of information, however, may come as a surprise to many ordinary Christians who have gained the impression that

---

[1] The body of the article which follows is written so that it may be understood by the general reader. More technical information, for those who may want it, will be found in the footnotes.

[2] The figures are those of Prof. Kurt Aland, to whom scholars have committed the task of assigning official numbers to Greek manuscripts as they are found. In addition to the totals given above, Aland also lists 2,143 lectionaries (manuscripts containing the Scripture lessons which were read publicly in the churches), so that the grand total of all these types of texts is 5,255. Kurt Aland, "The Greek New Testament: Its Present and Future Editions," *Journal of Biblical Literature,* LXXXVII (June, 1968), 184.

[3] According to Aland, the percentage of minuscules belonging to this type of text is about 90% (say, 2,400 out of 2,700), while its representatives are found also among the majuscules and later papyri. Cf. Kurt Aland, "Die Konsequenzen der neueren Handschriftenfunde für die neutestamentliche Textkritik," *Novum Testamentum,* IX (April, 1967), 100. Among 44 significant majuscules described in Metzger's handbook, at least half either belong to or have affinities with this text form. Bruce M. Metzger, *The Text of the New Testament: Its Transmission, Corruption, and Restoration,* pp. 42-61. The low figure of eighty per cent is, therefore, likely to be a safe estimate of the percentage of witnesses to this text from among papyri, majuscules, and minuscules taken together.

the Authorized Version is supported chiefly by inferior manuscripts, but have never realized that what contemporary textual critics call inferior manuscripts actually make up a huge majority of all manuscripts.

The question therefore naturally arises on what grounds scholars have set aside this large majority of manuscripts which contain a Greek text very much like that used by the translators of the AV in 1611. Why do they prefer other manuscripts with differing texts? What arguments do they advance for their views? Needless to say, it would be impossible in the short compass of this discussion to consider every ramification of modern textual theory. It must suffice to set forth three basic arguments which are used against the type of Greek text which underlies the King James Version. This kind of text will henceforth be referred to as the Majority text.[4] The arguments against it are arranged in the order of ascending importance.

I. The Oldest Manuscripts Do Not Support the Majority Text

This argument is the one most likely to impress the ordinary person. Yet it is almost a truism in textual research that the oldest manuscript does not necessarily contain the best text.[5] Still, the argument from "old manuscripts" can be presented in a way that sounds impressive.

No extant Greek manuscript which can be dated in the fourth century or earlier contains a text which can be

---

[4] For this very excellent name we are indebted to Prof. Aland who informs us that the siglum M will represent the Majority text in the forthcoming 26th edition of the *Nestle-Aland* text. Cf. Aland, *Journal of Biblical Literature,* LXXXVII (June, 1968), 181. The familiar term "Byzantine text" was never descriptively accurate nor was it entirely free from pejorative overtones.

[5] Recently this has been reaffirmed by Aland in these words: "But we need not mention the fact that the oldest manuscript does not necessarily have the best text. P[47] is, for example, by far the oldest of the manuscripts containing the full or almost full text of the Apocalypse, but it is certainly not the best." Kurt Aland, "The Significance of the Papyri for Progress in New Testament Research," *The Bible in Modern Scholarship,* ed. J. Philip Hyatt, p. 333.

clearly identified as belonging to the Majority text. What is more, the papyrus finds of the last thirty to forty years have yielded manuscripts which more or less support the kind of Greek text used in more modern translations (like the ASV or RSV). Particularly striking is the discovery of the papyrus manuscript known as P[75] containing large portions of Luke and John. This new find, which is dated around 200 A.D., has a type of text substantially the same as that found in the famous Codex Vaticanus (B) of the fourth century. More than any other manuscript, Codex B had long been regarded as an extremely valuable witness to the New Testament text. By many it was regarded as the most valuable of all. The modern editions of the Greek New Testament and the translations made from them leaned heavily on the evidence of B. Now, thanks to P[75] , there is proof that the kind of Greek text found in B was in circulation in the latter part of the second century and, no doubt, even earlier.[6] All of this, it may be said, tends to support the general rejection of the Majority text by modern critics.

Such arguments, however, have only a superficial plausibility. In the first place, all of our most ancient manuscripts derive basically from Egypt. This is due mainly to the circumstance that the climate of Egypt favors the preservation of ancient texts in a way that the climate of the rest of the Mediterranean world does not. There is no good reason to suppose that the texts found in Egypt give us an adequate sampling of texts of the same period found in other parts of the world. One might just as well affirm that to sample the flora and fauna of the Nile valley is to know the flora and fauna of Greece, or Turkey, or Italy. It is, therefore, most likely that the text on which our modern translations rest is simply a very early Egyptian form of the text whose nearness to the original is

---

[6] "Since B is not a lineal descendent of P[75], the common ancestor of both carries the Alexandrian type of text to a period prior to A.D. 175-225, the date assigned to P[75]." Bruce M. Metzger, "Second Thoughts: XII. The Textual Criticism of the New Testament," *Expository Times,* LXXVIII (1967), 375.

open to debate.[7] Indeed Kurt Aland, who is coeditor of both of the most widely used critical Greek texts and who is certainly the leading textual scholar on the European continent, proposes that the text of P[75] and B represents a revision of a local text of Egypt which was enforced as the dominant text in that particular ecclesiastical province.[8] But if it is, in fact, possible that some such explanation may be given of the text of these ancient witnesses, it is clear that we must look for other reasons for preferring their evidence than age alone. For a revised text may be either good or bad and in any case is the result of the judgment of those who revised it. This illustrates one reason why most textual critics would not argue the superiority of a manuscript merely because it was older than others.

Another factor militating against an uncritical acceptance of the oldest manuscripts is that they show a capacity to unite behind readings which — even in the eyes of modern scholars — are likely to be wrong. John 5:2 is a case in point. Here the three oldest manuscripts extant are P[66] and P[75] (both about 200 A.D.) and B (4th cent.). All three unite to read "Bethsaida" in this verse instead of the familiar "Bethesda" found in our AV. But both of the most widely used critical editions of the Greek text, Nestle's text and the United Bible Societies text, reject "Bethsaida" in favor of the reading "Bethzatha," supported — among extant Greek texts — only by Aleph (4th century, somewhat later than B) and the ninth-century minuscule 33. But even this reading is most likely to be wrong as the prominent German scholar, Joachim Jeremias, has pointed out in his definitive monograph entitled, *The Rediscovery of Bethesda*. Jeremias confidently de-

---

[7] The recent Bible Societies text, edited by Kurt Aland, Matthew Black, Bruce M. Metzger and Allen Wikgren, does not often reject reading supported by both P[75] and B. Small wonder that it can thus be regarded as a near relative of these two manuscripts, which go back (see previous footnote) to a common ancestor. Cf. I. A. Moir's review of the Bible Societies text in *New Testament Studies*, XIV (1967), pp. 136-43.

[8] Aland in *The Bible in Modern Scholarship*, p. 336. Cf. also *Novum Testamentum*, IX (April, 1967), p. 91.

fends the reading "Bethesda" as original and adduces as evidence for this the Copper Scroll from Cave III at Qumran.[9] This scroll, which palaeography indicates to have been inscribed "between A.D. 35 and 65, that is, between the life and ministry of Jesus and John's writing of his Gospel,"[10] contains a Hebrew form of the name "Bethesda." Furthermore, as Jeremias points out, the variant "Bethzatha" (Aleph, 33) can now be explained as merely the Aramaic counterpart of the Hebrew form of "Bethesda" found on the Copper Scroll.[11] Thus the reading of the Majority text, which is not found in any extant Greek manuscript before the fifth century, has after all the superior claim to originality in John 5:2. This is a classic example of how the great mass of later manuscripts, without any strain on the imagination, may be thought of as going back to other manuscripts more ancient than any we currently possess.[12] The RSV may reasonably be charged with error in following the reading "Bethzatha," while the AV can continue to be followed here with considerable confidence.

Furthermore, the concurrence of P[66], P[75] and B in the spurious reading "Bethsaida" raises questions about their independence as witnesses to the original text. "Bethsaida" is not the type of variant reading which copyists normally produce by accident, but is most likely the result of some kind of correction of the text. It is quite possible, then, that all three manuscripts go back ultimately to a single parent manuscript in which this emendation was originally made. Thus their numerous agreements against the Majority text are suspect on the grounds that they may simply reproduce the readings of a single ancient copy —

---

[9] Joachim Jeremias, *The Rediscovery of Bethesda: John 5:2*, pp. 11-12.

[10] *Ibid.*, p. 36.

[11] *Ibid.*, p. 12. The Hebrew form on the Copper Scroll is a dual, fitting in precisely with the archaeological discovery that Bethesda was, in fact, a double pool. The Aramaic "Bethzatha" replaces the original dual with an emphatic plural termination.

[12] The point is that, if we concede the originality of "Bethesda," there is no valid reason why its presence in the majority of manuscripts may not be ascribed to direct transmission from the autograph of John's Gospel.

the extent of whose errors and revisions we do not know.[13]

II. The Majority Text Is a Revised, and Hence Secondary, Form of the Greek Text

It is still sometimes argued that the form of the Greek New Testament text which is found in the majority of Greek manuscripts derives from a revision of the text made sometime during the first four centuries of the Christian era (the third century has been a popular date for this).[14] This argument is frequently elaborated with the assertion that the revisers who created this text attempted to present a smooth, acceptable text that combined elements from other, earlier texts. Hence, so the argument runs, the very fact of revision, especially an eclectic revision of this kind, necessarily reduces the testimony of this majority of manuscripts to a secondary level. The "older manuscripts" are thus to be preferred because, even if they have suffered some revision, it was of a lesser and more discerningly critical nature.

We need not spend much time with this argument in view of the fact that contemporary critics are by no means agreed on the way in which the Majority text originated.

---

[13] Already scholars are willing to concede a common ancestor for P[75] and B (cf. footnote 6). We can postulate here that this common ancestor and P[66] meet even further back in the stream of transmission in a copy which read "Bethsaida" in John 5:2 (P[66] has an orthographical variation of this). In the same chapter (5:44) the word *God* is omitted by P[66], P[75], B, and Codex W alone among Greek manuscripts now known. The omission is rejected both by the Nestle text and the Bible Societies text and—if they do so correctly—we may suspect yet another faulty reading of the common ancestor. Once we concede that such variants are shared errors, we cannot insist that we have genuinely independent testimony in other places where these three manuscripts happen to agree.

[14] By Metzger the origination of the Majority text has been assigned to Lucian of Antioch (d. 312). He states, "As has been indicated in the previous pages, his [Lucian's] recension of the New Testament was adopted at Constantinople and from there it spread widely throughout Greek speaking lands." Bruce M. Metzger, "The Lucianic Recension of the Greek Bible," *Chapters in the History of New Testament Textual Criticism,* p. 27.

They are, indeed, generally agreed that its testimony to the original text is much inferior to that of the other and older Greek witnesses, but this inferiority is no longer traced by all critics with confidence to a definite, specific revision of the text. A leading American textual critic, Ernest C. Colwell, has stated for example, *"The Greek Vulgate* [i.e., the Majority text] *. . . had in its origin no such single focus as the Latin had in Jerome"* (italics in the original). [15] From Colwell's point of view, the Majority text — as well as the other major forms of the Greek text — are the result of a "process" rather than a single event in textual history. [16] Another scholar, Jacob Geerlings, who has done extensive work on certain "family" branches of the Majority text, has stated flatly concerning this text that, "Its origins as well as those of other so-called text-types probably go back to the autographs. It is now abundantly clear that the Eastern Church never officially adopted or recognized a received or authorized text and only by a long process of slow evolution did the Greek text of the New Testament undergo the various changes that we can dimly see in the few extant uncial codices identified with the Byzantine [i.e., Majority] text." [17] Thus the view popularized by Westcott and Hort before the turn of the century, that the Majority text issued from an authoritative, ecclesiastical revision of the Greek text, is widely abandoned as no longer tenable. Yet it was this view of the Majority text which was largely responsible for relegating it to a secondary status in the eyes of textual critics generally. Dean Burgon, the great proponent of the

---

[15] Ernest C. Colwell, "The Origin of Texttypes of New Testament Manuscripts," *Early Christian Origins; Studies in Honor of Harold R. Willoughby*, p. 137.

[16] *Ibid.,* pp. 136-37.

[17] Jacob Geerlings, *Family E and Its Allies in Mark,* Vol. XXXI of *Studies and Documents,* p. 1. It will be seen how Geerlings' statement contradicts Metzger's quoted above (f.n. 14). A more recent statement by Metzger, however, makes no mention of Lucian and seems to represent a "process" view of the Majority text. Cf. Bruce M. Metzger, "Bibliographic Aids for the Study of the Manuscripts of the New Testament," *Anglican Theological Review,* XLVIII, pp. 348-49.

Majority text who was a contemporary of Westcott and Hort, scoffed at their theory of official revision. But his protests were largely drowned out and ignored. Today, scholars like Geerlings and Colwell agree that such a revision did not occur.

It will be noted in this discussion that in place of the former idea of a specific revision as the source-point for the Majority text, some critics now wish to posit the idea of a "process" drawn out over a long period of time. It may be confidently predicted, however, that this explanation of the Majority text must likewise eventually collapse. The Majority text, it must be remembered, is relatively uniform in its general character with comparatively low amounts of variation between its major representatives. [18] No one has yet explained how a long, slow process spread out over many centuries as well as over a wide geographical area, and involving a multitude of copyists, who often knew nothing of the state of the text outside of their own monasteries or scriptoria, could achieve this widespread uniformity out of the diversity presented by the earlier

---

[18] The key words here are "relatively" and "comparatively." Naturally, individual members of the Majority text show varying amounts of conformity to it. Nevertheless, the nearness of its representatives to the general standard is not hard to demonstrate in most cases. For example, in a study of one hundred places of variation in John 11, the representatives of the Majority text used in the study showed a range of agreement from around seventy per cent to ninety-three per cent. Cf. Ernest C. Colwell and Ernest W. Tune, "The Quantitative Relationships between MS Text-types," *Biblical and Patristic Studies in Memory of Robert Pierce Casey,* eds. J. Neville Birdsall and Robert W. Thomson, pp. 28, 31. The uncial codex Omega's ninety-three per cent agreement with the Textus Receptus compares well with the ninety-two per cent agreement found between P^{75} and B. Omega's affinity with the TR is more nearly typical of the pattern one would find in the great mass of minuscule texts. High levels of agreement of this kind are (as in the case of P^{75} and B) the result of a shared ancestral base. It is the divergencies that are the result of a "process" and not the reverse.

A more general, summary statement of the matter is made by Epp, " . . . the Byzantine manuscripts together form, after all, a rather closely-knit group, and the variations in question within this entire large group are relatively minor in character." Eldon Jay Epp, "The Claremont Profile—Method for Grouping New Testament Minuscule Manuscripts," *Studies in the History and Text of the New Testament in Honor of Kenneth Willis Clark, Ph.D.,* eds. Boyd L. Daniels and M. Jack Suggs, Vol. XXIX of *Studies and Documents,* p. 33.

forms of text. Even an official edition of the New Testament — promoted with ecclesiastical sanction throughout the known world — would have had great difficulty achieving this result as the history of Jerome's Vulgate amply demonstrates.[19] But an unguided process achieving relative stability and uniformity in the diversified textual, historical, and cultural circumstances in which the New Testament was copied, imposes impossible strains on our imagination.

Herein lies the greatest weakness of contemporary textual criticism. Denying to the Majority text any claim to represent the actual form of the original text, it is nevertheless unable to explain its rise, its comparative uniformity, and its dominance in any satisfactory manner. All these factors can be rationally accounted for, however, if the Majority text represents simply the continuous transmission of the original text from the very first. All minority text forms are, on this view, merely divergent offshoots of the broad stream of transmission whose source is the autographs themselves. But this simple explanation of textual history is rejected by contemporary scholars for the following reason.

III. The Readings of the Majority Text Are Repeatedly Inferior to Those of the Earlier Manuscripts

Perhaps the greatest surprise to many Bible-believing Christians will be the discovery that textual critics seek to defend their preference for the older manuscripts by affirming that they are better because, in fact, they contain the better readings. The Majority text, they insist, repeatedly offers us variations with little or no claim to

---

[19] After describing the vicissitudes which afflicted the transmission of the Vulgate, Metzger concludes: "As a result, the more than 8,000 Vulgate manuscripts which are extant today exhibit the greatest amount of cross-contamination of textual types." *Text of the New Testament*, p. 76. Uniformity of text is always greatest at the source and diminishes—rather than increases—as the tradition expands and multiplies. This caveat is ignored by the "process" view of the Majority text.

being original. So that, in the last analysis, a manuscript is attested by its readings rather than the reverse.[20] In the minds of contemporary scholars, however, no circular argument is involved in this. Careful study of the context of a passage, plus a good acquaintance with scribal habits and with textual phenomena in general, permits the skilled critic — so they affirm — to pass a valid judgment on competing readings and in many cases to reach conclusions that may be regarded as nearly certain. Hence, it follows from this, that confidence in modern critical Greek texts depends ultimately on one's confidence in contemporary scholarly judgment.

It should be clear, however, that when the whole problem of textual criticism is reduced to a series of arguments about the relative merits of this reading over against that reading, we have reached an area where personal opinion — and even personal bias — can easily determine one's decision. This has recently been admitted by a leading textual critic who, himself, has in the past espoused this reading by reading methodology. Speaking of the two criteria primarily relied on by modern critics in deciding on a reading (namely, " 'Choose the reading which fits the context' " and " 'Choose the reading which explains the origin of the other reading' "), E. C. Colwell has confessed, "As a matter of fact these two standard criteria for the appraisal of the internal evidence of readings can easily cancel each other out and leave the scholar free to choose in terms of his own prejudgments."[21]

---

[20] So, for example, J. Neville Birdsall states: "And even if we were to arrive at a favorable view of the P[75]-B Text, we could do so only as Lagrange confessedly did, and perhaps Hort, not so explicitly: on internal criteria, not . . . on the basis of criteria drawn from the history of tradition." See his review of Carlo M. Martini's, *Il problema della recensionalita del codice B alla luce del papiro Bodmer XIV,* in *Journal of Theological Studies,* XVIII (1967), p. 465.

[21] E. C. Colwell, "External Evidence and New Testament Textual Criticism," *Studies in the History and Text of the New Testament in Honor of Kenneth Willis Clark, Ph.D.,* eds. Boyd L. Daniels and M. Jack Suggs, Vol. XXIX of *Studies and Documents,* p. 3. Contrast this statement with the same writer's discussion in his *What Is the Best New Testament?* pp. 75-77.

Indeed, it is Colwell who has most effectively pointed out that the generalizations which scholars have been making for so long about scribal habits are based upon a quite inadequate induction of the evidence. He calls for a fresh and comprehensive description of these.[22] But if this is needed then it is also clear that we must reconsider nearly all the judgments previously passed on individual readings on the basis of the alleged tendencies of scribes. Moreover, quite recently, another prominent textual critic has actually presented arguments that reverse the long standing judgment of textual critics against an appreciable number of readings found in the Majority text. G. D. Kilpatrick has argued that the "older manuscripts" not infrequently reveal various kinds of changes in the text, both accidental and deliberate, in places where the Majority text preserves the original reading.[23] What is important to note about Kilpatrick's work is how it is actually possible for a scholar who adopts the reading by reading method (in contrast to the use of manuscript authority) to find reasons for controverting long standing opinions on specific passages.[24] In short, the knowledge possessed by modern textual critics about scribes and manuscripts is so ambiguous that it can, without difficulty, be used to reach almost any conclusion.

Of course, it might be suggested that the text can be determined simply by careful study of the Biblical writers' style, argument, and theology. Logically such a method would have no real need for a reconstruction of the history of the transmission of the text. But few, if any, contemporary critics would espouse so extreme a view as

---

[22] *Ibid.*, pp. 9-11.

[23] G. D. Kilpatrick, "The Greek New Testament of Today and the *Textus Receptus*," *The New Testament in Historical and Contemporary Perspective: Essays in Memory of G. H. C. Macgregor,* eds. Hugh Anderson and William Barclay, pp. 189-206.

[24] To anyone schooled in the standard handbooks of textual criticism, it may come as a shock, for example, to find Kilpatrick defending so-called Byzantine "conflate" readings as original! *Ibid.*, pp. 190-93.

this.[25]   Its result could only be that the Bible would say to the scholar just what his training and perspective dispose him to think it says.

The present writer would like to suggest that the impasse to which we are driven when the arguments of modern criticism are carefully weighed and sifted is due almost wholly to a refusal to acknowledge the obvious. The manuscript tradition of an ancient book will, under any but the most exceptional conditions, multiply in a reasonably regular fashion with the result that the copies nearest the autograph will normally have the largest number of descendants.[26]   The further removed in the history of transmission a text becomes from its source the less time it has to leave behind a large family of offspring. Hence, in a large tradition where a pronounced unity is observed between, let us say, eighty per cent of the evidence, a very strong presumption is raised that this numerical preponderance is due to direct derivation from the very oldest sources. In the absence of any convincing contrary explanation, this presumption is raised to a very high level of probability indeed. Thus the Majority text, upon which the King James Version is based, has in reality the strongest claim possible to be regarded as an authentic representation of the original text. This claim is quite independent of any shifting consensus of scholarly judgment about its readings and is based on the objective reality of its dominance in the transmissional history of the New Testament text. This dominance has not and — we venture to suggest — cannot be otherwise explained.

---

[25] Cf. the statement of Harold Oliver, "In recent years the necessity of reconstructing the history of the text has become apparent." Harold H. Oliver, "Implications of *Redaktionsgeschicte* for the Textual Criticism of the New Testament," *Journal of the American Academy of Religion,* XXXVI (March, 1968), p. 44.

[26] This truism was long ago conceded (somewhat grudgingly) by Hort, "A theoretical presumption indeed remains that a majority of extant documents is more likely to represent a majority of ancestral documents at each stage of transmission than *vice versa.*" B. F. Westcott and F. J. A. Hort, *The New Testament in the Original Greek,* II, p. 45.

It is hoped, therefore, that the general Christian reader will exercise the utmost reserve in accepting corrections to his Authorized Version which are not supported by a large majority of manuscripts. He should go on using his King James Version with confidence. New Testament textual criticism, at least, has advanced no objectively verifiable reason why he should not.

THE INCOMPARABLE WILSON
THE MAN WHO MASTERED FORTY-FIVE
LANGUAGES AND DIALECTS

Henry W. Coray

It was the privilege of the compiler of this book to be one of the students at Princeton Theological Seminary of this great man who stood as a giant "ten feet tall" among the scholars of his day or any day. Readers who would question such a superlative statement should reserve judgment until they have finished learning about this genius among geniuses, who, among other things, spent years in research in 10,000 documents in many languages to prove that Dr. Driver of Oxford University was in error in his attempt to show that the book of Daniel was untrustworthy.

Professor Robert Dick Wilson, M.A., Ph.D., Princeton, who died in 1930, was a staunch defender of the doctrine of the verbal inspiration of Holy Scripture and claimed, with justice, to be an expert in all the questions involved in such a belief. Through long years of continuous study he mastered all the ancient languages and dialects needed to read the manuscripts of the Bible. In order to master the Babylonian language, not taught in any American University, he had to travel to Germany to study at the University of Heidelberg. To Babylonian he added Ethiopic, Phoenician, various Aramaic dialects, and so on, until he had mastered 45 ancient languages and dialects. In his book *Is the Higher Criticism Scholarly?* he writes, "I have seen the day when I set out on some Bible research with fear and trembling — wondering what I should discover — but now all that fear has passed." (See additional note, page 48.)

Robert Dick Wilson
(1856 — 1930)

The following biography was written by the Reverend Henry W. Coray, author of the biographies in *Valiant for the Truth*. He is pastor of the Orthodox Presbyterian Church, Glenside, Pennsylvania, and a graduate of Westminster Theological Seminary.

It has been said that "great tasks demand men of great preparation." A notable example would be Moses who invested two-thirds of his one-hundred-and-twenty-year career flexing the muscles of his mind and soul for the final third and arduous segment. A modern example would be Robert Dick Wilson.

Wilson took his undergraduate work at Princeton University, and was graduated in 1876. He went on to obtain an M.A. and a Ph.D., then put in two years at the University of Berlin in further postgraduate studies. He taught Old Testament courses at Western Theological Seminary in Pittsburgh, and returned to Princeton, where he won international fame as a scholar and defender of the historic Christian faith.

When liberalism took over the seminary at Princeton in 1929 he, with J. Gresham Machen, Oswald Allis, Cornelius Van Til, and others, withdrew to establish Westminster Seminary in Philadelphia.

So thoroughly versed was Dr. Wilson in Semitic languages that he was at home in over forty of them, incredible as it may seem. His book, *Scientific Investigation of the Old Testament,* is rated a classic in that important branch of theology. One of his pamphlets, *Is Higher Criticism Scholarly?* struck a devastating blow at the position of the destructive Biblical critics, and has been published in nine different languages. His greatest contri-

---

*This article reproduced beginning on page 49.

bution to Christian scholarship is on the book of Daniel. Two volumes contain a compilation of a dozen treatises on that prophecy, assembled from former articles printed in journals and papers. They represent scholarship at the very highest level.

"It is men such as Wilson," says Dr. Edward Young, "men who have not feared hard work, who have not avoided difficult problems, and who have been willing to join battle with the enemy that God has used to build His church."

Robert Dick Wilson's personal attitude toward the assaults of the destructive critics may be summarized in his own words:

"I have made it an invariable habit never to accept an objection to a statement in the Old Testament without subjecting it to a most thorough investigation, linguistically and factually. . . . If a man believes in the probability or certainty of miraculous elements wherein God is working, but is precluded from faith in the claims of the Bible to be a Divine revelation by alleged historical, scientific or philological evidence, I consider it my duty to do my best to show that this alleged evidence is irrelevant, inconclusive and false."

One of the stirring moments in the experience of his students occurred when, after a dissertation on the complete trustworthiness of Scripture, the renowned scholar said with tears: "Young men, there are many mysteries in this life I do not pretend to understand, many things hard to explain. But I can tell you this morning with the fullest assurance that

'Jesus loves me, this I know
For the Bible tells me so.' "

Let Dr. Wilson speak for himself. The following are selections from an address by Prof. Wilson on *What Is an Expert?*[1] —

"If a man is called an expert, the first thing to be done is to establish the fact that he is such. One expert may be worth more than a million other witnesses that are not

---

[1] *Bible League Quarterly*, 1955.

experts. Before a man has the right to speak about the history, the language, and the paleography of the Old Testament, the Christian church has the right to demand that such a man should establish his ability to do so.

"For forty-five years continuously, since I left college, I have devoted myself to the one great study of the Old Testament, in all its languages, in all its archaeology, in all its translations, and as far as possible in everything bearing upon its text and history. I tell you this so that you may see why I can and do speak as an expert. *I may add that the result of my forty-five years of study of the Bible has led me all the time to a firmer faith that in the Old Testament we have a true historical account of the history of the Israelite people;* and I have a right to commend this to some of those bright men and women who think that they can laugh at the old-time Christian and believer in the Word of God.

"You will have observed that the critics of the Bible who go to it in order to find fault have a most singular way of claiming to themselves all knowledge and all virtue and all love of truth. One of their favourite phrases is, 'All scholars agree.' When a man writes a book and seeks to gain a point by saying 'All scholars agree,' I wish to know who the scholars are and why they agree. Where do they get their evidence from to start with?

"I remember that some years ago I was investigating the word 'Baca,' which you have in the English Bible — 'Passing through the valley of Baca, make it a well.' I found in the Hebrew dictionary that there was a traveller named Burkhart, who said that 'Baca' meant mulberry trees. That was not very enlightening. I could not see how mulberries had anything to do with water. I looked up all the authority of the scholars in Germany and England since Burkhart's time and found they had all quoted Burkhart. Just one scholar at the back of it! When I was travelling in the Orient, I found that we had delicious water here and there. The water sprang up apparently out of the ground in the midst of the desert. I asked my brother who was a missionary where this water came from. He said, 'They bring this water from the mountains. It is an underground aqueduct. They cover it over to prevent it from evaporating.' Now the name of that underground aqueduct was *Baca.*

"My point is that you ought to be able to trace back this agreement among scholars to the original scholar who propounded the statement, and then find out whether what that scholar said is true. What was the foundation of his statement?

"I have claimed to be an expert. Have I the right to do so? Well, when I was in the Seminary I used to read my New Testament in nine different languages. I learned my Hebrew by heart, so that I could recite it without the intermission of a syllable; and the same with David, Isaiah and other parts of Scripture. As soon as I graduated from the Seminary, I became a teacher of Hebrew for a year and then I went to Germany. When I got to Heidelberg I made a decision. I decided — and I did it with prayer — to consecrate my life to the study of the Old Testament. I was twenty-five then; and I judged from the life of my ancestors that I should live to be seventy; so that I should have forty-five years to work. I divided the period into three parts. The first fifteen years I would devote to the study of the languages necessary. For the second fifteen I was going to devote myself to the study of the text of the Old Testament; and I reserved the last fifteen years for the work of writing the results of my previous studies and investigations, so as to give them to the world. And the Lord has enabled me to carry out that plan almost to a year.

"Most of our students used to go to Germany, and they heard professors give lectures which were the results of their own labours. The students took everything because the professor said it. I went there to study so that there would be no professor on earth that could lay down the law for me, or say anything without my being able to investigate the evidence on which he said it.

"Now I consider that what was necessary in order to investigate the evidence was, first of all, to know the language in which the evidence is given. So I went to Berlin, and devoted myself almost entirely to the study of the languages bearing upon the Bible; and determined that I would learn all the languages that throw light upon the Hebrew, all the cognate languages, and also all the languages into which the Bible had been translated down to 600 A.D., so that I could investigate the text myself.

"Having done this I claim to be an expert. I defy any man to make an attack upon the Old Testament on the ground of evidence that I cannot investigate. I can get at the facts if they are linguistic. If you know any language that I do not know, I will learn it. Now I am going to show you some of the results.

"After I had learned the necessary languages I set about the investigation of every consonant in the Hebrew Old Testament. There are about a million and a quarter of these; and it took me many years to achieve my task. I had to read the Old Testament through and look at every consonant in it; I had also to observe the variations of the text, as far as they were to be found in the manuscripts, or in the notes of the Massoretes (the Massoretes were a body of Jewish scholars who made it their business to hand down what they believed to be the true text of the Old Testament) or in the various versions, or in the parallel passages, or in the conjectural emendations of critics; and then I had to classify the results. I prize this form of textual research very highly; for *my plan has been to reduce the Old Testament criticism to an absolutely objective science; something which is based on evidence, and not on opinion.* I scarcely ever make a statement which rests merely on my own subjective belief.

"In order to be a textual expert of this kind it is necessary to be a master of paleography (the science which deals with ancient writings) and of philology; to have an exact knowledge of a dozen languages at least, so that every word may be thoroughly sifted. To ascertain the true text of the Old Testament is fundamental to everything concerning Bible history and Bible doctrine.

"The result of those thirty years' study which I have given to the text has been this: I can affirm that there is not a page of the Old Testament concerning which we need have any doubt. We can be absolutely certain that

44

substantially we have the text of the Old Testament that Christ and the Apostles had, and which was in existence from the beginning.

"I would like to give a few other examples of true Biblical criticism. I can remember when it was thought very unprofitable to read the long genealogies found in the first chapters of First Chronicles — nine chapters of proper names. But today, in the scientific criticism of the Old Testament, proper names are of the profoundest importance. The way in which they are written — indeed, all that is connected with them — has come to be one of the very foundations upon which scientific criticism of the Old Testament is built.

"Take the following case. There are twenty-nine ancient kings whose names are mentioned not only in the Bible but also on monuments of their own time; many of them under their own supervision. There are one hundred and ninety-five consonants in these twenty-nine proper names. Yet we find that in the documents of the Hebrew Old Testament there are only two or three out of the entire hundred and ninety-five about which there can be any question of their being written in exactly the same way as they were inscribed on their own monuments. Some of these go back for two thousand years, some for four thousand; and are so written that every letter is clear and correct. This is surely a wonder.

"Compare this accuracy with that of other writings. I have been blamed for not referring to the classical writings more frequently in my book on Daniel. Here is the reason — take the list made by the greatest scholar of his age, the librarian at Alexandria in 200 B.C. He compiled a catalogue of the kings of Egypt, thirty-eight in all; of the entire number only three or four of them are recognizable. He also made a list of the kings of Assyria; in only one case can we tell who is meant; and that one is not spelt correctly. Or take Ptolemy, who drew up a register of eighteen of the kings of Babylon. Not one of them is properly spelt; you could not make them out at all if you did not know from other sources to what he is referring. If any one talks against the Bible, ask him about the kings mentioned in it. There are twenty-nine kings of Egypt, Israel, Moab, Damascus, Tyre, Babylon, Assyria, and Persia, referred to, and ten different countries among these twenty-nine; all of which are included in the Bible accounts and those of the monuments. Every one of these is given his right name in the Bible, his right country, and placed in the correct chronological order. Think what that means!

"Here is yet another case in which the labours of the expert are needed. It is the contention of the critics that the presence of Aramaic (Aramaic was the language of Mesopotamia and adjacent lands) words in the Old Testament books is a clue to their date. I came to the conclusion that the critics said much about the Aramaisms that they could not substantiate. So I took a Hebrew dictionary and went through it from the first word to the last, and gathered up the results. Then I went to the Aramaic, and did the same. I compiled a list of all the relevant words and compared them with those in the Babylonian language.

"By carrying on the investigation in this scientific manner I found that, as a matter of fact, there is very little in the argument built on the presence of Aramaisms in the Old Testament. There are only five or six of these words in the whole of the book that could even be considered doubtful. The truth is that a century ago there was no Babylonian known; and when people found the Old Testament form of a noun or a verb that did not suit the Hebrew, they said it was Aramaic, and that the book which contained it was of a later date than it claimed to be. But since then God has given us a knowledge of Babylonian, with this result. Certain Aramaic nouns end in OOTH (rhyming with 'booth') and it was thought that this was peculiar to that language. But now we know that this is found in both Babylonian and Hebrew. The Babylonian records take us back before the time of Abraham; and from thence onward, until the Babylonian kingdom came to an end, we find this noun-ending recurring. Thus the foundation of the old argument fell to pieces.

"In closing, I desire to call attention to the fact that

while the study of the religious systems of the ancient peoples has shown that there was amongst them a groping after God, *nowhere* is it to be seen that they reached any clear apprehension of the One True God, the Creator, Preserver, Judge, Saviour and Sanctifier of His people. Their religions were of an outward kind; the Old Testament religion is essentially one of the mind and heart; a religion of love, joy, faith, hope, and salvation through the grace of God. How can we account for this?

"The prophets of Israel declared that their teaching came from God. The modern critical school is antagonistic to this claim. They say that the prophets gave utterance to the ideas of their own time, and that they were limited by their environment. But if this is so how does it come about that neither from the oracles of Thebes and Memphis, nor from Delphi and Rome, nor from Babylon, nor from the deserts of Media, but from the sheep-folds and humble homes of Israel, yea, from the captive by the river of an alien land, came forth those great messages of hope and salvation? One of the mighty phrases of Scripture is that of 'God with us'; this is the key which unlocks the mysterious chambers of the Old Testament, and opens to us their rich and enduring treasure."

The late scholarly Principal J. Willoughby, a former President of the Sovereign Grace Union, wrote: "In recent times many scholars have attempted to discredit the written Word, especially of the Old Testament. Many other scholars of repute, however, have found that the evidences on which the destructive critics base their conclusions are utterly worthless. The late Professor Dick Wilson was a scholar of massive learning. At the age of twenty-five he could read the New Testament in nine different languages. He could repeat from memory a Hebrew translation of the entire New Testament without missing a single syllable. He could do the same thing with large portions of the Old Testament also. He says: 'For forty-five years continuously since I left college I have devoted myself to the one great study of the Old Testament in all its languages, in all its archaeology, in all its translations, and, as far as possible, everything bearing upon its text and history.' He was acquainted with about forty-five languages and dialects. He probably knew more about the Old Testament and everything connected with it than did all the destructive critics put together.

"Professor Wilson, having long and thoroughly examined the evidence on which the destructive critics base their conclusions, found that it was utterly worthless. Concerning the evidence for the orthodox position he writes: 'The evidence in our possession has convinced me that "at sundry times and in divers manners God spoke unto our fathers through the prophets," and that the Old Testament in Hebrew, "being immediately inspired by God," has "by His singular care and providence been kept pure in all ages." ' "

(Since Dr. Wilson dealt primarily with the Old Testament, it may be asked, "What bearing does Dr. Wilson's studies have upon the Received Text in connection with the New Testament in particular?" The answer is obvious. Dr. Wilson held the highest regard for the Masoretic Text; namely, the Old Testament canon of 39 books which, through the centuries, was transcribed with meticulous accuracy by the Masoretes. These scholars were chosen with the greatest care by the Jewish nation to keep pure and intact the sacred Scriptures given to them by God in the beginning. And it is the Masoretic text which forms part of the Textus Receptus or the Received Text.)

IS THE HIGHER CRITICISM SCHOLARLY?

Clearly attested facts showing that the destructive "assured results of modern scholarship" are indefensible

Robert Dick Wilson

Philip E. Howard Sr., late editor of the *Sunday School Times*, personally interviewed Dr. Wilson in his home in Princeton. The following are some of the things he learned.

When Dr. Wilson was a little chap only four years old, he could read. He began to go to school at five, and at eight he had read, among other books, Rawlinson's *Ancient Monarchies.*

In college young Wilson specialized in language, psychology, and mathematics. In such Bible courses as he then studied, he says that he received "a very low grade of 90, which pulled down my average." To him language was the gateway into alluring fields. He prepared himself for college in French, German, and Greek, learned Hebrew by himself, and received a hundred dollar prize in Hebrew when he entered the seminary.

How did he do it? He tells us he used his spare time. When he went out for a walk he would take a grammar with him and when he sat down to rest he would take out the book, study it a little and learn what he could. He made up his mind that he wanted to read the great classics in the originals. In order to answer a single sentence of a noted destructive critic of the Bible, Professor Wilson read all the extant ancient literature of the period under discussion in numerous languages and collated no less than one hundred thousand citations from that literature in order to get at the basic facts, which when found showed that the critic was wrong. One reason why Dr. Howard was so stirred by his many personal talks with this stalwart scholar was Dr. Wilson's habit of presenting proof for each statement he made.

It is made very evident by a study of any of Dr. Wilson's keen critiques of the destructive critics' work that much of the material so often called by the critics "the assured results of modern scholarship" is nothing more than the quicksand footsteps of inexcusable ignorance. "Criticism," says Dr. Wilson, "is not a matter of brains, but a matter of knowledge."

Is the Higher Criticism Scholarly?

The history of the preparation of the world for the Gospel as set forth in the Old Testament is simple and clear and in the light of the New Testament eminently reasonable. In fact, it has been considered so reasonable, so harmonious with what was to have been expected, that Christ and the apostles seem never to have doubted its veracity, and the Christian Church which they founded has up to our times accepted it as fully consonant with the facts.

Within the last two centuries, however, largely as a result of the Deistical movement in England and of the application to sacred history of the so-called critical method, there has arisen a widespread doubt of the truthfulness of the Old Testament records. To such doubt many have refused to listen, and blessed are all those who have no doubts.

Countering With Defensive and Offensive Proof

But there are many whose faith in the veracity of the Scriptures has been shaken; and the best, and in some cases the only, way to re-establish their faith is to show them that the charges which are brought against the Bible are untrue and unwarranted.

The attempt to show this may be made along two lines. We may take the purely defensive line and endeavor to show that the general and particular attacks upon the truthfulness of the Old Testament narratives are unsupported by facts. Or, we may take the offensive and show that the Old Testament narratives are in harmony with all that is really known of the history of the world in the times described in the Old Testament records, and that these records themselves contain the ineffaceable evidence that the time and place of their origin agree with the facts recorded. The best method, perhaps, will be to make an offensive-defensive, showing not merely that the attacks are futile, but that the events recorded and the persons and things described are true to history, that is, that they harmonize in general with what we learn from the contemporaneous documents of other nations.

This is true of the very earliest narratives of the Old Testament. Even when we look at the two great events occurring before the time of Abraham — the Creation and the Flood — we find that these events are the same that are emphasized among the Babylonians, from the midst of whom Abraham went out. However we may account for the difference between the Babylonian and Hebrew accounts of the Creation and of the Deluge, there is sufficient resemblance between them to point to a common origin antedating the time of Abraham's departure from Ur of the Chaldees.[1]

The Old Testament Derived from Written Sources Based on Contemporary Documents

From this time downward there is no good reason for doubting that the Biblical narrative is derived from *written* sources based on *contemporaneous* documents. First, Abraham came out of that part of Babylonia in which writing had been in use for hundreds of years; and he lived during the time of Hammurabi, from whose reign we have scores of letters, contracts, and other records, of which by far the most important is the so-called code of laws which bears his name.[2] Second, writing had been in existence in Egypt already for two thousand years or more, so that we can well believe that the family of Abraham, traveling from Babylonia to Egypt and at last settling in Palestine in between these two great literary peoples, had also formed the habit of conducting business and keeping records in writing.[3] Abraham would naturally use the cunei form system of writing, since this is known to have existed in Western Asia long before the time of Hammurabi, and the

---

[1] King, The Seven Tablets of Creation; and Jensen, Assyrisch-Bablonischen Mythen and Epen.

[2] King, The Letters and Inscriptions of Hammurabi; and Harper, The Code of Hammurabi.

[3] See especially Schorr, Urkunden des altbabylonischen Zivilund Prozess-Rechts.

Amarna letters show clearly that Hebrew was sometimes written in that script.[4]

But not only do we know that there was a script in which to write; we know, also, that the Hebrew language was used in Palestine before the time of Moses. This is clear not merely from more than a hundred common words embedded in the Amarna letters but from the fact that the names of the places mentioned in them are largely Hebrew. [5] In the geographical lists of the Egyptian king, Thothmes III, and of other kings of Egypt, we find more than thirty good Hebrew words naming the cities of Palestine and Syria that they conquered.[6] From these facts we conclude that books may have been written in Hebrew at that early period. Further, we see that the sons of Abraham, Isaac, and Jacob may have been called by Hebrew names, as the Biblical record assures us. [7]

Agelong Correspondence in the Chronology of the Bible and Profane History

Having found that writing and the Hebrew language were in existence long before the time of Moses, we turn next to the documents of the Old Testament which purport to give a history, more or less connected, of the period from Abraham (circa 2000 *B.C.*) to Darius II (circa 400 *B.C.*), in order to find out, if possible, whether the general scheme of *chronology* and *geography* presented to us in the Hebrew records corresponds with what we can learn from other documents of the same period.

Here we find that the nations mentioned in the Scriptures as having flourished at one time or another are exactly the same as those that profane history reveals to us. Thus, in the period from Abraham to David we find in both Biblical and profane sources that Egypt is recognized

---

[4] Winckler, Tel-el-Amarna Letters; and Knudtzon, Die El-Amarna-Tafeln.

[5] Knudtzon, loc. cit., p.1545f.

[6] Max Muller, *Die Palastinaliste* Thutmoses III.

[7] Was Abraham a Myth? in "Bible Student and Teacher" for 1905.

as already in 2000 *B. C.* a great and predominant power, and that she continued to the time of Solomon to be looked upon as the great enemy of the Israelites. In the same period, we see Elam and Babylon occupying the first place in the far East, and the Hittites, Amorites, Canaanites, Sidonians, Moabites, Edomites, and Damascenes in the intervening section, the "debatable ground" between Egypt and Babylon.

In the next period, from 1000 to 625 *B. C.*, Assyria has become the chief power among the nations in the neighborhood of Palestine, with Babylon of only secondary importance. Egypt has lost the first rank and is at times subject to Cush or dominated by Assyria. Media appears on the scene, but as a subject of Assyria. Between the Euphrates and Egypt, the Hittites are prominent in the earlier part, and next to them Hamath, Damascus, Tyre, Ammon, Moab, and Edom. Further, the distinction between Samaria and Judah is clearly recognized in the monuments.

In the last period, from 625 to 400 *B. C.*, Babylon has become the leading power until its hegemony is taken over by Persia under Cyrus. Egypt as a world power disappears from history with the conquests by Nebuchadnezzar and Cambyses. The Hittites, Damascus, Hamath, Israel, Judah, and all the tribes and cities between Babylon and Egypt have ceased to exist as independent powers.

A Foundation for Reliance

Now, into this framework of world history, the history of Israel fits exactly. The Bible records in succession the relations of Israel with Babylon, Elam, Egypt, Hittites, Assyria, and Persia; and the smaller nations, or powers, appear in their proper relation to these successively great powers. *These are facts that cannot be denied and they afford a foundation for reliance upon the statements of the Biblical documents.*

Correct Order and Character of the Kings

This foundation is strengthened when we observe that the kings of these various countries whose names are mentioned in the Old Testament are all listed in the order and in the synchronism required by the documents of the kings themselves. Thus, Chedorlaomer, possibly, and certainly Hammurabi (the Amraphel of Genesis 14) and Arioch lived at about 2000 *B.C.;* Shishak, Zerah, So, Tirhakeh, Necho, and Hophra, kings of Cush and Egypt; Tiglath-Pileser, Shalmaneser, Sargon, Sennacherib, and Esarhaddon, kings of Assyria; Merocach-Baladan, Nebuchadnezzar, Evil-Merodach, and Belshazzar, kings of Babylon; and Cyrus, Darius, Xerxes, and Artaxerxes, kings of Persia; all appear in the Scriptures in their correct order as attested by their own records, or by other contemporaneous evidence. The same is true, also, of the kings of Damascus, Tyre, and Moab.

Again, we find that the Assyrian documents that mention the kings of Israel and Judah name them in the same order in which they appear in the chronicles of Israel and Judah. We find, also, that the statements made with regard to the kings of all these countries correspond as closely as different documents ever correspond in reference to their relative power, importance, characteristics, and deeds. Especially noteworthy are the close resemblances in this respect between the accounts of Shishak, Tiglath-Pileser, Sennacherib, Nebuchadnezzar, and Cyrus; *but the whole fabric of the historic structure of the Old Testament harmonizes beautifully in general outline and often in detail with the background of the general history of the world as revealed in the documents from the nations surrounding Israel.*

A Biblical Phenomenon Unequaled in the History of Literature

Moreover, an extraordinary confirmation of the careful transmission of the Hebrew documents from original sources lies in the exact manner in which the names of the kings are spelled. The twenty-four names of kings of Egypt, Assyria, Babylon, et al., contain 120 consonantal letters, of which all are found in the same order in the inscriptions of the kings themselves or in those of their contemporaries. That the Hebrew writers should have transliterated these names with such accurateness and con-formity to philological principles is a wonderful proof of their thorough care and scholarship and of their access to the original sources.

That the names should have been transmitted to us through so many copyings and so many centuries in so complete a state of preservation is a phenomenon un-equaled in the history of literature. The scribe of Assurbanipal in transcribing the name of Psammetichus, the contemporary king of Egypt, makes the mistake of writing a *t* for the *p* at the beginning and an *l* for the *t* in the middle.[8]

Abulfeda, the author of the Arab ante-Islamic history, gives the names of the kings of Persia of the Achawmenid line as "Kei-Kobad, Kei-kawus, Kei-Chosrew, Kei-Lohrasp, Kei-Bushtasf, Kei-Ardeshir-Bahman and Chomani his daughter, and Dara the First, and Dara the Second who was killed by Alaskander," and writes the name of Nebuchadnezzar as *Bactnosar.*

In the list of names of the companions of Alexander given by the Pseudo-Callisthenes, nearly every name is changed so as to be unrecognizable, [9] and the same is true of most of the names of the kings of Egypt as we have them preserved in the lists of Manetho, Herodotus, and Diodorus Siculus, and of the kings of Assyria and Babylonia as given in Africanus, Castor, and the Canon of Ptolemy. [10]

The Correctness of Hebrew Authors a Basis for Faith

This almost universal inaccuracy and unreliability of the Greek and Arab historians with reference to the kings of Egypt, Assyria, and Babylon *is in glaring contrast with the*

---

[8] Annals of Assurbanipal, Col. II, 114; and Streck's *Assurbanipal,* p. 715.

[9] President Woolsey, the *Journal of the American Oriental Society,* Vol. III, pp. 359-440.

[10] Cory, *Ancient Fragments;* and Muller, *Fragmenta Historicorum Graecorum;* and article on "Darius the Mede," by R. D. Wilson, in *Princeton Theological Review,* April, 1922.

exactness and trustworthiness of the Hebrew Bible. It can be accounted for, humanly speaking, only on the grounds that the authors of the Hebrew records were contemporaries of the kings they mention, or had access to original documents; and secondly, that the Hebrew writers were good enough scholars to transliterate with exactness; and thirdly, that the copyists of the Hebrew originals transcribed with conscientious care the text that was before them.

Having given such care to the names of heathen kings, it is to be presumed that they would give no less attention to what these kings said and did; and so we have, in this incontestable evidence from the order, times, and spelling of the names of the kings, an indestructible basis upon which to rest our faith in the reliability of the history recorded in the books of the Old Testament Scriptures. Doubt about some of the minor details can never invalidate this strong foundation of facts upon which to erect the enduring structure of the history of Israel.

Since we have secured a framework for our history, let us look next at the doorways of language which let us inside the structure. These doorways are the passages through which converse with the outer world was carried on by the people of Israel. On their thresholds will be seen the footprints of the nations who introduced their ideas and their products to the household who dwelt within.

Intruding Foreign Words as Date-Setters

In order that the force of the evidence that I am about to produce may be fully appreciated, let me here say that the time at which any document of length, and often even of small compass, was written can generally be determined by the character of its vocabulary, and especially by the foreign words which are embedded in it.

Take, for example, the various Aramaic documents. The inscriptions from Northern Syria written in Assyrian times bear evident marks of Assyrian, Phoenician, and even Hebrew words.[11] The Egyptian papyri from Persian times

---

[11] Lidzbarski, *Nordsemitische Epigraphik;* and Cooke, *North Semitic Inscriptions.*

have numerous words of Egyptian, Babylonian, and Persian origin, as have also the Aramaic parts of Ezra and Daniel. [12]

The Nabatean Aramaic written probably by Arabs is strongly marked, especially in its proper names, by Arab words.[13] The Palmyrene, Syriac, and Rabbinical Aramaic, from the time of the Graeco-Roman domination, have hundreds of terms introduced from Greek and Latin. [14] Bar Hebraeus and other writings after the Mohammedan conquest have numerous Arabic expressions, and the modern Syriac of Ouroumiah has many words of Persian, Kurdish, and Turkish origin. [15]

The Ever-Changing Influx of New Words in Hebrew Scriptures

Now, if the Biblical history is true, we shall expect to find Babylonian words in the early chapters of Genesis and Egyptian in the later; and so on down, an everchanging influx of new words from the languages of the ever-changing dominating powers.

As a matter of fact, this is exactly what we find. The accounts of the Creation and the Flood are marked by Babylonian words and ideas. The record of Joseph is tinged with an Egyptian coloring. The language of Solomon's time has Indian, Assyrian, and probably Hittite words. From his time to the end of the Old Testament, Assyrian and Babylonian terms are often found, as in Jeremiah, Nahum, Isaiah, Kings, and other books. Persian words come in first with the conquest of Babylon by Cyrus and are frequent in Daniel, Ezra, Nehemiah, Chronicles, and Esther, and in the case of proper names, one at least occurs in both Haggai and Zechariah.

---

[12] Sayce-Cowley, *Papyri; Sachau, Papyrus;* and Lidzbarski, *Ephemeris* for 1911.

[13] Euting, *Sinditische Inschriften* and the *Corpus Inscriptionum Semiticarum,* Vol. II.

[14] Lidzbarski and Cooke as cited in Note 11; Brockelmann, *Lexicon Syriacum;* and Dalman, *Aramdisch-neuhebraisches Worterbuch.*

[15] Brockelmann, *Lexicon Syriacum;* and MacLean, *Dictionary of Vernacular Syriac.*

No Greek words are to be found in the Hebrew of the Old Testament, except *Javan* and possibly one or two other terms. That Aramaic words may have been in Hebrew documents at any time from Moses to Ezra is shown by the fact that two or more words and phrases found elsewhere only in Aramaic occur already in the Tel-el-Amarna letters, and one in a letter to the king of Egypt from Abd-Hiba of Jerusalem. [16]

It may be known to the reader that one verse in Jeremiah and about half of the books of Ezra and Daniel are written in Aramaic. This is what we might have expected at a time when, as the Egyptian papyri [17] and the Babylonian indorsements [18] show, the Aramaic language had become the common language of Western Asia and in particular of the Jews, at least in all matters of business and commerce.

That the Hebrew parts of Daniel and Ezra should have a large number of Aramaic words would therefore be expected, and, they also would naturally be found in Chronicles and Nehemiah and other documents coming from the latter part of the sixth century (when Aramaic was the *lingua franca* of the Persian empire) and in other works down to the latest composition of the Old Testament.

In later Hebrew this process of absorbing foreign words may be illustrated by numerous examples. Thus the tract Yoma, written about *A.D.* 200, has about twenty Greek words in it, and Pesahim, about fourteen; while hundreds of them are found in Dalman's *Dictionary of New Hebrew.* Many terms of Latin origin also appear in the Hebrew literature of Roman times.

No Different from Our Own Language Today

We thus see that the Hebrew, just like the Aramaic, has embedded in it traces of the nations that influenced its

---

[16] Winckler and Knudtzon as cited in Note 4.

[17] Sayce-Cowley, *Papyri;* and Sachau, *Papyrus.*

[18] Article by A. T. Clay in *The W. R. Harper Memorial* Volume.

history from 200 *B.C.* to *A.D.* 1500, or indeed to the present time. The reader will compare this with the marks which have been left upon American nomenclature by the different nations that have influenced its history.

The native Indian appears in the names: *Massachusetts, Connecticut, Allegheny, Ohio, Mexico, Yucatan,* and countless other terms. The Spanish appears in *Florida, San Anselmo, Los Angeles, Vera Cruz, New Granada,* and numerous appellations of mountains, rivers, and cities; the French, in *Montreal, Detroit, Vincennes, Duquesne, Louisiana, St. Louis,* and *New Orleans;* the Dutch in *Hackensack, Schenectady, Schuyler;* the German, in *Germantown* and *Snyder.* Some of these languages have also contributed various words of common use, such as, *moccasin, succotash, potato, maize, tomato, tomahawk, prairie, sauerkraut, broncho,* and *corral.*

These languages all have left their mark, but the predominating language and nation were the English, as is shown not merely in our literature and laws, but also in such names as *New Hampshire, Boston, New York, Albany, New Jersey, Pennsylvania, Pittsburgh,* and the names of most of our cities, counties, and statesmen. But that the English received their laws largely from the Romans and the Normans is evident in any law book or court room; that they received their religion from the Hebrews through the Greek and Latin churches is evident from the words we use every day such as *amen, hallelujah, priest, baptism, cathedral, bishop, chant, cross, resurrection, glory,* and countless others.

Critics Undervalue the Totality of the Evidence

Thus, the vicissitudes of the life of the English people for the last fifteen hundred years can be traced in the foreign words that have been taken over into its literature during that period. It is the same with the Hebrew people for the last four thousand years, and in the first part of sixteen hundred years, it is no less evident than since that time.

In the study of the Hebrew literature in the light of the

foreign elements embedded in it, we find that the truthfulness of the history is incidentally but convincingly confirmed. In each state of the literature, the foreign words in the documents are found to belong to the language of the peoples that (according to the Scriptures and the records of the nations surrounding Israel) influenced and affected the Israelites at that time. *The critics of the Old Testament have never given sufficient weight to the totality of this evidence.*

No one will dispute that the presence of Babylonian terms in the first chapter of Genesis points to a time when Babylonian influence was predominant, but the same influence is manifest in the second chapter and also in Daniel. This influence can easily be accounted for in all three instances on the supposition that the contents of Genesis 1 and 2 were brought by Abraham from Babylon and that the book of Daniel was written at Babylon in the sixth century *B.C.*

While it might be accounted for in Genesis 1, if it were composed at Babylon during or after the exile, how can it have influenced Genesis 2; if, as the critics assert, it were written somewhere between 800 and 750 *B.C.*? How, also, can we account for the Babylonian influence in Daniel if, as the same critics assure us, it were written in Palestine in 164 *B.C.*?

Why Are Persian Words Missing in Critic-Belated Bible Books?

The same problem exists with the Persian words. They are found especially in Chronicles, Ezra, Nehemiah, Esther, and Daniel, all ostensibly from the Persian period of world domination. According to analogy, this Persian domination accounts for their presence in these books.

But how about their *absence* from Jonah, Joel, Job, the Psalms, the Song of Songs, the so-called Priest-Code of the Pentateuch, and other writings which the critics place in the Persian period? Why especially should the Priest-Code have no Persian and probably no Aramaic words, if it were written between 500 and 300 *B.C.*, in the very age and, as some affirm, by the very author of the book of Ezra?

And why should the only demonstrably Babylonian words in this part of the Pentateuch be found in the accounts of the Creation and the Flood, which may so well have come with Abraham from Ur of the Chaldees? And how could the Egyptian word for "kind" *(min)* have come to be used by the man who is supposed to have written this latest part of the Pentateuch in Babylon in the fifth century B.C.?

These and other similar questions that ought to be asked we may leave to the critics of the Old Testament to attempt to answer. *They dare not deny the facts without laying themselves open to the charge of ignorance.* They dare not ignore them without submitting to the charge of willful suppression of the facts in evidence.

But someone will say: "How about the Greek words in Daniel?" No one claims that there are any Greek words in the Hebrew of Daniel. In the Aramaic parts of Daniel there are three words, all names of musical instruments, which are alleged, *not proved,* to be Greek. It is more likely than not, I think, that they are of Greek origin, though no one of them is exactly transliterated. However, assuming that they are Greek, and waiving the question as to whether this part of the book was originally written in Hebrew or Babylonian, and afterwards translated into Aramaic, there is good reason for supposing that Greek musical instruments, retaining their original names though in a somewhat perverted form, may have been used at the court of Nebuchadnezzar.

How Greek Words May Have Crept into Daniel

It is known for a certainty that from the earliest times the kings and peoples of Babylon and Nineveh delighted in music. Now, the Greeks, according to all their traditions and habits, both in war and worship, had practiced music at all periods of their history and far excelled all ancient peoples in their attainments in the art of music.

We all know how readily musical instruments and their native names travel from land to land. We might cite the ukulele, the guitar, the organ, and the trumpet. The Greeks themselves imported many foreign musical instruments which retained their foreign names. From at least 1000 *B. C.* there was an active commerce between the Greeks and the Semites, Cyprus and Cilicia were subdued by the Assyrian kings and Sennacherib about 700 *B. C.* conquered a Greek fleet and carried many prisoners to Nineveh. Assurbanipal received the homage of Gyges, king of Lydia, the neighbor and overlord of many Greek cities in Asia Minor.

Greeks had been settled in Egypt since long before the time of Assurbanipal and Nebuchadnezzar and served as mercenaries in the armies of the Egyptian kings who were subdued by the great kings of Nineveh and Babylon, and also in the army of Nebuchadnezzar himself. Thousands, perhaps, tens of thousands, of captive Greek soldiers would, according to custom of those days, be settled in the cities of the Euphrates and Tigris valleys. And these valleys were filled with people who spoke Aramaic. The Greeks would mingle with them and, as in the case of the Jews at Babylon, the natives would ask of them a song; and they would sing their strange songs to the accompaniment of their native instruments.

This is one way in which the instruments and their names could get into Aramaic long before the time when the Aramaic of Daniel was written. Another was through the slaves, both men and girls, who would certainly be brought from all lands to minister to the pleasure of the luxurious court of the Chaldean king.

Why Daniel May Have Used Persian Words

That Daniel may have used the so-called Persian words in a document dating from the latter part of the sixth century *B. C.* is manifest when we remember that the children of Israel from the kingdom of Samaria had been captive among the Medes for two hundred years before the time of the conquest of Babylon by Cyrus, and that the Jews had been carried to the banks of the Chebar and other localities where Aramaic was spoken nearly two generations before Daniel died.

The Medes spoke a dialect of the Persian and had ruled over large numbers of Aramaean tribes on the upper Tigris ever since 600 *B.C.* when they had overthrown Nineveh. Such Medo-Persian terms as are found in Daniel, being mostly official titles like *governor* and names of persons, are the ones which would most readily be adopted by the subject nations, including the Aramaeans and Jews. That the words *satrap* and *Xerxes* were taken directly from the Medo-Persian and not from the Greek is shown by the fact that the Hebrew and Aramaic spelling of these names in Daniel is exactly the equivalent of that in the original language and not such as it must have been if these words had been taken over indirectly through the Greek historians.

Before leaving this subject of language, attention must be called to two matters that the critics have made of supreme importance in their attempts to settle the dates of the documents of the Old Testament. The first matter is that of the value, as evidence of date of the occurrence, of Aramaic words in a Hebrew document; and the second is the value, as evidence of date, of Hebrew words that occur but once, or at most a few times, in the Old Testament and that reoccur in the Hebrew of the Talmud.

Hebraisms in Aramaic, Not Aramaisms in Hebrew

As to the first of these, the so-called Aramaisms, the number has been grossly exaggerated. Many of the words and roots formerly called Aramaisms have been found in Babylonian records as early as Abraham. As to the remainder, many of them occur in the Old Testament *but once.* In view of the fact that there are about 1500 words used but once in the Old Testament, it is impossible to select some of these and call them Aramaisms, simply because they are used in Aramaic also.

Hundreds of words in both Aramaic and Hebrew, and also in Babylonian and Arabic, have the same meaning irrespective of the number of times or the documents in which they occur. According to the laws of consonantal change existing among the Semitic languages, not more than five or six Aramaic roots can be shown to have been adopted by the Hebrew from the Aramaic. These roots can be shown to have been adopted by the Hebrew from the

Aramaic. These roots are found in what the critics class as early documents as well as in the later. Besides, a large proportion of the words designated as Aramaisms do not occur in any Aramaic dialect except those that were spoken by Jews.

In all such cases the probability is that instead of the word being an Aramaism in Hebrew, *it is a Hebraism in Aramaic.* For the Hebrew documents in all such cases antedate the Aramaic by hundreds of years and it is evident that the earlier cannot have been derived from the later. Again, the critics find words which they call Aramaisms not merely in the books which they assert to be late, but in those that, according to their own dating, are the earliest. In this case, *without any evidence except their own theory of how it ought to be,* they charge that the original text has been changed and the Aramaic word inserted. *Such procedure is contrary to all the laws of evidence, fairness, and common sense.* For there is *no reason* why the early documents of the Hebrews should not have contained linguistic marks of Aramaic influence. According to Genesis 31, Laban spoke Aramaic. David conquered Damascus and other cities where Aramaic was spoken and the Israelites have certainly been in continuous contact with Aramaean tribes from that time to the present. Sporadic cases of the use of Aramaic words would, therefore, prove nothing as to the date of a Hebrew document.

A Theory That Would Make All Documents Late

In the second place, critics who are attempting to prove the late date of a certain document are accustomed to cite the words in that document which occur nowhere else, except possibly in another work claimed as being late and in the Hebrew of the Talmud. Such evidence is worthy of being collected in order to show the peculiarities of an author, *but it does not necessarily have anything to do with proving the date.* For there are three thousand words in the Old Testament that occur five times only or under, and fifteen hundred that occur but once. Besides, such words occurring elsewhere in the Talmud are found in every book of the Old Testament and in almost every chapter. *If such words were proof of the lateness of a document, all documents would be late; a conclusion so absurd as to be held by nobody.*

Hebrew Literary Forms Duplicated in Babylon and Egypt

From the language of the Old Testament we naturally turn next to the literature, in order to see if the literary forms of the documents are such as we would expect to find in existence when the documents claim to have been written. Our only evidence here must be derived from comparative literature and history. [19] Turning then to the vast body of the literature of the Babylonians and Egyptians, we find that in one or both of them is to be found every type of literary form that is met with in the literature of the Old Testament except perhaps the discourses of the prophets. As no serious dispute of the date or authorship of the works of the prophets is made on the ground of mere literary form, the general statement will stand unimpeached; for poetry, history, laws, and biographies are all amply duplicated in form and style in the many productions of the great nations that surrounded Israel.

The Same Is True of Legal Forms

With regard to the laws it may be said that, not merely in the form in which the individual laws are stated, but also in the manner in which they are collected together in a kind of code, there was a pattern for the Israelites already existing at least from the time of Hammurabi, a contemporary of Abraham. This code of Hammurabi, it is true, deals almost entirely with civil and criminal laws such as we find in parts of Deuteronomy. But the plan of the tabernacle in Exodus 25-29 may be likened to the plans of the Babylonian temples which were placed in their foundation stones.

Laws similar to those concerning leprosy and other diseases have also come down from the old Sumerians. It is

---

[19] See further on this subject in article by R. D. Wilson on "Scientific Biblical Criticism," in the *Princeton Theological Review* for 1919.

almost certain that the elaborate ceremonies of the Egyptian and Babylonian temples must have been regulated by written laws, though thus far we have discovered no complete code treating of such matters.

That Moses with his education in all the wisdom of the Egyptians at 1500 B.C. might have produced the laws of the Pentateuch under the divine guidance seems beyond dispute. Lycurgus, Mohammed, Charlemagne, Peter the Great, and Napoleon have performed similar feats without any special divine help. It does not follow that systems of law and constitutions were not written or inaugurated because they were never carried out nor permanently established. Theodoric and Alfred the Great and even Charlemagne organized governments which scarcely survived their demise. The critics are in the habit of stressing the fact that so little mention of the law is made in the period before Hezekiah or even Josiah and assert that the law of the Priest-Code was not fully established before Ezra.

An Argument from Silence Which Proves Nothing

This is an argument from silence which proves nothing absolutely. There is a history of the United States called *Scribner's* by William Cullen Bryant and others. It has 53 pages, double column, of index. The word *Presbyterian* does not occur in this index; the word *Christian* only in the phrase, *Christian Commission;* the word *church,* only twice. *And yet, this is a history of a republic founded by Christians, observing the Sabbath, devoted to foreign missions, and full of Christian churches and activities.* In thirty-five hundred pages quarto, there is no mention of Thanksgiving Day, nor of the days of fasting and prayer during the Civil War, nor of the Bible except in the relation of the Bible Society to slavery! Nor does it prove that the law did not exist, that it was not completely observed, or that things forbidden in it were done. Does the crime wave that has been sweeping the world since the close of the war prove that the Gospel does not exist? In one week of December, 1920, the front page of one of our great New York dailies had scarcely space for anything except reports of murders, burglaries, and other crimes. Are the Ten Commandments unknown in New York City?

But the critics assert that a long period of development was necessary before such a system of laws could have been formulated, accepted, and enforced. I agree readily to this but I claim that all the development necessary for the formulation may have taken place before the time of Moses and that its hearty acceptance by the people and its enforcement depended upon moral rather than intellectual conditions. As far as intellectual requirements are concerned, there is nothing in the law that might not have been written either in Babylon or Egypt a thousand years before Moses. Then, as now, it was spiritual power and moral inclination that was wanted rather than intellectual perception in order to do the right and abhor the wrong. In each successive generation of Israelitish men, each individual of the nation had to be converted and to submit his soul and conduct to the teachings of the Divine law. The ancient Jewish church had its ups and downs, its times of strenuous faith and of declension and decay, just as the Christian church has had.

Ample Time for the Revision of Laws

It is claimed by the critics that signs of progress, or change, are to be observed in some of the laws as given in Exodus 20-24, Leviticus, and Deuteronomy. This may be admitted. It is, however, a sufficient answer to this claim that in the forty years from the arrival at Sinai to the final address of Moses at Shittim, there was plenty of time for revision and adaption of these laws to suit all probable variety of circumstances awaiting the people of God.

Consider the changes in forty years in the fish laws of Pennsylvania, or in the tariff or railroad legislation of the United States! Besides, many of these apparently variant legislations with regard to the same thing are, as Mr. Wiener has so clearly shown in his "*Studies in Biblical Law,*" really laws affecting different relations of the same thing. Some, also, like the Income Tax Laws upon our yearly declaration sheet, are general laws for the whole people; while others, like the detailed statement of the

Income Tax Law that is meant to guide the tax officials, are meant for the priests and Levites who officiated at the sanctuary.

That there are repetitions of the laws affecting the Sabbath, festivals, idolatry, and so forth, does not argue against unity of authorship. The central facts of a new system are frequently emphasized by such repetition, as is manifest in almost every chapter of the Koran, and in almost every epistle of the apostle Paul. Why they thus repeat is not always clear to us; but it is to be supposed that it was clear to the *authors* of the repetitions. That is a question of motives and not of text or evidence. What the peace treaty says is evident; why the treaty-makers said thus and so is not always apparent, and cannot be produced in evidence.

Were the Redactors Slipshod Editors?

That there should be *apparent* contradictions among so many laws was inevitable. Some of these are doubtless due to errors of transmission, especially if, as seems probable, the original was written in cuneiform and afterwards transferred to an alphabetic system of writing. Some of them appear contradictory, but really relate to different persons or circumstances. Certainly, if they were as contradictory and irreconcilable as the critics suppose, we have a right to express our astonishment that such contradictions were not removed by one or another of those numerous and canny redactors, editors, and *diaskeuasts* ("revisers"), of unknown but blessed memory, whom the critics allege and assume to have labored for centuries upon the elaboration of these laws.

Surely, these alleged contradictions cannot have escaped their notice. Surely, they cannot have seemed incongruous to the priest of the second temple and to the Scribes and Pharisees who put them into execution. Surely, if real contradictions exist in the laws, it is more likely that they were not in the ancient documents and that they arose in the process of transmission through the vicissitudes of many centuries, than that they should have been inserted in the time of Jeremiah or of Ezra, that ready scribe in the Law of Moses.

Will Objectors Please Answer a Few Questions?

Before leaving the matter of the law, it may be well to propose for the consideration of the objectors to the Biblical account of the origin of the laws of Moses a few questions that, it seems to me, require an answer before we can accept their theory of its origin, unsupported as it is by any direct evidence.

First, if Exodus 20-24 and Deuteronomy were written in the period of the kingdoms of Israel and Judah, how can we account for the fact that the king is referred to but once (Deuteronomy 16) in a passage difficult to read and explain and claiming to be anticipatory? And why should this passage make no reference to the house of David, and place its emphasis on a warning against a return to Egypt?

Second, why should the law never mention Zion, or Jerusalem, as the place where men ought to worship, if these laws were written hundreds of years *after* the temple had been built?

Third, why should the temple itself receive no consideration, but be set aside for a "mythical" tabernacle whose plan to the minutest particular has been elaborated with so much care? And why, if this plan were devised at Babylon in the fifth century *B. C.,* should it in its form and divisions show more resemblance to an Egyptian than to a Babylonian house of God?

Fourth, if the laws of the Priest-Code were made at Babylon, how does it come about that the main emphasis in these laws is upon the shedding of blood and that the principal offerings are bloody offerings; whereas, in the Babylonian religion it is doubtful if any reference is ever made to the importance of the blood, and no word corresponding to the Hebrew word for "altar" *(mizbeach)* has ever yet been found in the Babylonian language?

How is it, also, that almost the entire vocabulary bearing upon the ceremonial observances is different in Babylonian from what it is in Hebrew? The Hebrew names for the various articles of clothing worn by the priests, for the stones of the breastplate, for the sacrifices, for the altar and the many spoons and other implements used in its service, for the festivals, for the ark and the multifarious articles used in its construction, for sins and removal of sins, and for nearly all the gracious acts of God in redemption, differ almost altogether from the Babylonian. How account for all this, if the ceremonies of the second temple were first conceived by the rivers of Babylon under the shadow of the tower of Bel?

Fifth, if the ceremonial law were written between 500 and 300 *B.C.,* at a time when the Persian power was supreme, how account for the entire absence of Persian words and customs from the priestly document? Why should Ezra and his contemporaries have used so many Persian words in their other compositions and have utterly eschewed them in the lengthiest of their works? Not one Persian word, forsooth! How careful they must have been in this endeavor to camouflage their attempt to foist their work on Moses! They should have spent more of their time and energy on the removal of alleged incongruities in the subject matter.

Sixth, if the Israelitish religion is a natural development like that of the nations surrounding them, how does it happen that the Phoenicians who spoke substantially the same language have an almost entirely different nomenclature for their ceremonial acts, for sacrifices, and the material of sacrifice; and that the Phoenicians and Carthaginians and their colonies remained polytheistic to the last?

Seventh, if the ceremonial law were written after the exile, when all the Jews, from Elephantine in Egypt on the west to Babylon on the east, were speaking and writing Aramaic, *how did it come to pass that the law was written in a Hebrew so different from anything found in any Aramaic dialect that almost every word used in it had to be translated in order to make it understood by the Aramaic-speaking Jews?*

Are we to suppose that the exiled Hebrews invented their religious vocabulary arbitrarily after their language had ceased to be spoken by any great body of living men? Are we to suppose that they invented or borrowed the names of the stones of the breastplate, and then forgot so completely their Aramaic equivalents that scarcely any two of the four Aramaic Targums, or versions, should afterward be able to agree as to the meaning in Aramaic of more than two or three of them at most?

Why, also, should the articles of dress, the names of the sacrifices, the materials of the tabernacle, the verbs to denote the ceremonial acts, and in fact the general coloring and the particular shades of the coloring of the whole fabric, be so different?

Eighth, how is the fact to be explained that the Aramaic of the Targum and Talmud has taken over so many roots and vocables from the Hebrew of the Old Testament? For a comparison of the Old Testament Hebrew with the Aramaic of the Targums and of both these with the Syriac shows that about six hundred roots and words found in the two former do not appear in Syriac, nor in any other Aramaic dialect not written by Jews.

The critics are in the habit of charging that such words are Aramaisms in Hebrew; but it is manifest that, while it is possible for the Jews who wrote Aramaic two hundred years after Christ to have taken over Hebrew words from the Old Testament into their translations and commentaries, it would have been impossible for Hebrew authors living from two hundred to five hundred years before Christ to have taken over into their vocabulary Aramaic words not in use till *A.D.* 200 or later. All of the introductions to the Old Testament need to be revised along this line.

To the Text and to the Testimony

That a word occurs in the Old Testament but once and then reappears five hundred or a thousand years later in an Aramaic document written by Jews is to be expected. To say that such a word may have been in the spoken Aramaic before ever the Hebrew document was written, but that it did not appear in writing till *A.D.* 200, may be met by affirming that it may have existed in the spoken Hebrew for a thousand years before it was written.

When we once attempt to argue on the basis of what is *not contained* in documents, one man's conjecture is just about as good as another's. I am willing to leave all such cases to the written testimony found in the documents we possess, *and I demand that the assailants of the Scriptures confine themselves in like manner to that which has been written.* To the text and to the testimony! By these let us stand or fall.

Why Do the Critics Reject Chronicles?

Leaving the consideration of the Law of Moses, I pass on next to the regulations which David is said to have formulated for the guidance of the priests in the service of the sanctuary and especially for the musical accompaniments of worship. It will be necessary in the course of this discussion to examine the reasons why the critics reject the historical character of the Books of Chronicles which refer so often to the music of the first temple.[20] Since the Chronicler refers only to regulations made by David for the divisions of the priests and of singers, and the like, it is to be presumed that regulations with regard to other matters connected with the service were already in use.

No man surely would deny that a temple was actually built by David and Solomon on Mount Zion at Jerusalem. The whole history of both Israel and Judah turns upon that fact. The analogy of all other ancient nations and the whole literature of the Israelites proves beyond question that such a temple must have been constructed.

Now, when this temple was first built, it would be necessary only to take over the priests and the ritual already in existence and vary them only in so far as was required to meet the new conditions of an enlarged and more dignified place of worship. The old priesthood of the temple at Shiloh and the old laws of the tabernacle with reference to sacrifices and festivals would be found sufficient; but to make the service more efficient and suitable to the great glory of the magnificent house that had been erected for the God of Israel, certain new regulations as to the time and manner of the services were instituted by David. Whatever is not referred to as having originated with him must be presumed to have been already in

---

[20] For a further discussion of Chronicles, see article referred to in Note 19.

existence. Since David and Solomon built the temple, it is common sense to suppose that they organized the priests into regular orders for the orderly service of the sanctuary. These priests had already had their clothing prescribed by Moses after the analogy of the Egyptian and all other orders of priesthood the world over.

David also had prescribed the kinds and times of offerings and the purpose for which they were offered. The Israelites also, like the Egyptians and Babylonians, had for their festive occasions such regulations as are attributed to David for the observance of these festivals, so as to avoid confusion and to preserve decency in the house of God.

An Inconsistent Theory Made to Fit

Is it to be supposed that on these festive occasions no music was to be employed and no hymns of praise to God to be sung? Even the most savage tribes have music at their festivals, and we know that the ancient Egyptians had numerous hymns to Amon and other gods, and that the Assyrians and Babylonians and even the Sumerians delighted in singing psalms of praise and penitence as a part of their ritual of worship. These hymns in all cases were accompanied by instrumental music. Some of the Babylonian and Egyptian hymns were current in writing for hundreds or even thousands of years before the time of Solomon and some musical instruments had existed for the same length of time.

Are we to suppose that the Hebrews alone among the nations of antiquity had no vocal and instrumental music in their temple services? The critics maintain that poetry is the earliest form of expression of a people's thoughts and history. Many of them assert that the song of Deborah antedates all other literary productions in the Bible. Most of them will admit that David composed the lament over Saul and Jonathan.

But they draw the line at his Psalms of praise and penitence. Why? Because it suits their theory that the Psalms were prepared for use in the second temple. The critics hold at the same time that certain poems, like the songs of Deborah and Miriam and the blessings of Jacob

73

and Moses, antedate by centuries the historical narratives in which they are found, but that the Psalms were all, or nearly all, composed *after* the captivity.

What grounds have they for holding such seemingly inconsistent theories? *Absolutely none that is based on any evidence,* unless their wish to have it so, in order to bolster up their conception of the history of Israel's religion, be called evidence. We all know into what condition the German conception that the "will to power" is the same as the power itself has brought the world today.

Let us remember that it is the critic's conception, that the will to have the text of the Old Testament what they want to have it, is considered by them to be the same as having the text as they *will it. Willing* the power has destroyed what power there really was; *willing* the text has destroyed the text itself.

Psalm Writers Would Not Have Absurdly Attributed Their Work to Pre-Captivity Authors

Of course, it is obvious that music is mentioned in the Books of Kings but it is made prominent in Chronicles, and the headings of many of the Psalms attribute them to David and in three cases to Moses and Solomon. It is hardly to be supposed that the writer would have made his work absurd by making statements that his contemporaries would have known to be untrue.

Whether the headings are all trustworthy or not, it is absurd to suppose that the writers of them would have attributed so many of the Psalms to pre-captivity authors, when their contemporaries must have known that the whole body of Psalms had arisen after the fall of the first temple, had such been actually the case. The most natural supposition would be that David either made or collected a sufficient number of Psalms to meet the requirements of the temple worship.

Common sense and universal analogy compel us to believe, also, that an orderly worship conducted by priests in accordance with prescribed regulations and a service of song commensurate with the dignity and decency becoming the house of God must have existed among the

Hebrews, certainly from the time that the first temple was constructed and probably from the time that the tabernacle was erected and the annual festivals established.

Historians of royal courts and of diplomacy and war, like the author of the Books of Kings, may not mention such things; but we may be sure that they existed. The temple itself proves this. Universal experience proves it. The weeping stone at the foundation of the temple, where the Jews of today congregate to bewail the long departed glories of Mount Zion and the glorious house of Israel's God, testifies that the traditions about the sweet Psalmist of Israel were not all figments of the imagination nor mythical creations of later times.

Besides, why should the critics treat the Books of Chronicles as if their statements, additional to those in Kings, were not to be credited? They assert that the genealogical list in I Chronicles 3:17-24 would bring down the date of the composition of Chronicles to about 300 B. C. and that we cannot rely upon the statements of a work written so long after the events recorded.

But, at the same time, they all agree that the text of this passage has not been correctly transmitted and that its interpretation admits of the sixth generation after Zerubbabel as the period of its composition. As the word *son* in all such genealogies means "successor," whether it be a real son or an adopted son or an official successor, it is fair, judging by the analogy of other similar lists, to suppose that from fifteen to twenty years would be amply sufficient for each generation of priests, or kings. Since Zerubbabel lived about 520 B. C., such a calculation would bring the date of Chronicles to about 400 B. C.

The "Jaddua" of Chronicles and of Josephus Not Necessarily the Same

That the mention of Jaddua as high priest renders this date impossible cannot be maintained for the following reasons. First, it is supposed that the Jaddua mentioned in Nehemiah 12:11, 22 is the same as the Jaddua mentioned by Josephus as having been high priest when Alexander came up to Jerusalem in 336 *B. C. But the critics them-*

selves assert that this account of Alexander's visit is utterly unreliable. Why then should they consider the name and the time of the high priesthood of Jaddua to be the only valid date of the account given by Josephus and that they alone are reliable enough to overthrow the accepted date of Chronicles?

Second, there may have been two high priests of the name of Jaddua, just as, between 300 and 100 *B.C.,* there were two or three of the name of Simon and six of the name of Onias. Third, the same Jaddua may have been high priest at 400 *B.C.* and also in 336 *B.C.* Josephus says he was very old, and men in such positions not infrequently reach ninety or more years of age. I, myself, had a great-grandfather and a great-uncle who lived to be over a hundred, and a great-grandmother who was ninety-nine, one great-uncle ninety-four, another ninety-two. Besides, my mother died at eighty, and half a dozen uncles and aunts between eighty and ninety years of age. Everyone of these was old enough and active enough to have been high priest for sixty-five years, and several of them for eighty years, had they lived in the times of the Chronicles, and been eligible to the office!

Ewald Utterly Refuted in the Argument Regarding the Title "King of Persia"

Second, the critics affirm that Ezra, Nehemiah, and Chronicles were put together in their present form by the same redactor and that this redactor must have lived in the Greek period, because he calls the kings of Persia by the title "king of Persia." The great German critic, Ewald, said it was "unnecessary and contrary to contemporary usage" to call the kings of Persia by the title "king of Persia" during the time that the kings of Persia actually ruled; and that consequently the presence of this title in a document shows that the document must have been written after the Persian empire had ceased to exist.

The present writer has shown by a complete induction of all the titles of the kings of Egypt, Babylon, Assyria, Greece, and all the other nations of that part of the world including the Hebrews themselves, from 4000 *B.C.* down to Augustus, *that it was the custom in all times, languages, and kingdoms to use titles similar to this.*[21] Further, he has shown that the title "king of Persia" was given by Nabunaid, king of Babylon, to Cyrus in 546 *B.C.*, seven years before the first use of it in the Bible, and that it is used by Xenophon in 365 *B.C.* probably forty years after it is used for the last time in the Bible. Moreover, he has shown that, between 546 and 365 *B.C.*, it was used thirty-eight different times by eighteen different authors, in nineteen different documents, in six different languages, and in five or six different countries; and that it is used in letters and dates in Scripture just as it is used in the extra-Biblical documents. Lastly, he has shown that it was unusual for the Greek authors after the *Persian period* to employ the title.[22]

Inexcusable Ignorance of Evidence on the Part of Notable Critics Exposed

Thus, with regard to this title, by a mass of incontestable evidence, the writers of Chronicles and Ezra and also of Daniel are shown to be in harmony with the contemporaneous usage of documents written in the Persian period and to be out of harmony with the common usage in Greek times.

The Bible is right. Professor Ewald of Gottingen, the greatest German Old Testament scholar of his time, and Professors Driver and Gray of Oxford, the writers of many books and of many articles in the *Encyclopedia Britannica, Hastings,* and the *Expository Times,* are proved to be wrong. They all might have read that part of the evidence which is found in Herodotus, Thucydides, Aeschylus, Xenophon, and other Greek authors. Drs. Driver and Gray also ought to have read for themselves or to have had Professor Sayce or Dr. King or Dr. Budge gather for them the evidence on the subject to be found in the Babylonian,

---

[21] R. D. Wilson, "The Titles of Kings in Ancient Times," the *Princeton Theological Review,* 1905-6.

[22] R. D. Wilson, the *Festchrift Edouard Sachau,* Berlin, 1911.

Persian, Susian, and Egyptian writings. Unless one has sufficiently mastered the languages in which the texts containing the evidence on such subjects, as the titles of the kings of Persia, are written, he cannot be called an expert witness and should be ruled out of court.

Having read carefully and repeatedly what these critics have to say on this title, I have failed to find any hint indicating that they have ever appealed for their information to any original sources outside of Greek, Hebrew, and Aramaic; and as to these, they pay no attention to the great Greek writers mentioned above. If they are so careless and unreliable where their assertions can be investigated, what ground have they for expecting us to rely upon them where their assertions cannot be tested? If the statements of the Biblical writers are found to be confirmed when they can be tested by outside evidence, is it not right to presume that they are correct when no evidence for or against their statements is within our knowledge?

Variations in Numbers Will Be Better Understood When Israel's Numerical Signs Are Discovered

The other objections to the trustworthiness of the records of Chronicles are almost purely subjective in character, utterly devoid of any objective evidence in their favor; or they are based upon interpretations which are impossible to prove. Are we driven to conclude, for example, that a "thousand of thousands" means exactly "one million," neither more nor less? May it not mean "many" or "countless thousands," just as a "generation of generations" means "many generations?" And are the critics who find the account that the Chronicler gives of the conspiracy against Athaliah inconsistent with that given in Kings quite sure that the captain and the guard of Kings cannot have been priests and Levites? Besides, how can we expect to explain satisfactorily all apparent incongruities in documents that are thousands of years old?

As to the variations in numbers in the different sources, they are probably due to different readings of the original signs. But we do not know what signs the Hebrews used;

and so we cannot at present discuss intelligently the reasons for the variations, and never shall until the system of numerical signs used by the Israelites has been discovered. Everybody knows how difficult it is to copy numerical signs correctly. There is nothing usually in the context to help us to determine just how many men were in an army or how many were killed in a given battle. *The important thing is who won the fight.*

I once inquired what was the population of a certain southern city. One told me 40,000; another, 120,000. When I asked for an explanation of the discrepancy, I was told that there were 40,000 whites and 80,000 Negroes. Both estimates were true; but if they had been written down in two different documents, what charges of inconsistency might have been made by future scientific historians!

The Chronicler Need Not Have Copied from Kings

In their criticism of Chronicles, the critics proceed on the presumption that, in the portions that are parallel to Kings, the author has merely copied from Kings, and that he has no further sources of reliable information. The author of Chronicles himself states that he had a number of such sources. Can the critics give any good reason to show that he did not have these sources?

Since the Chronicles of the kings of Israel were not destroyed by Sargon when Samaria was overthrown, and Hosea, Amos, and the so-called Jehovist and Elohistic parts of the Pentateuch, Deuteronomy, and other works of the Hebrews were not destroyed at the time of the destruction of Jerusalem by Nebuchadnezzar, why should we suppose that the records of the kings of Israel and Judah were not in existence when the writers of Kings and Chronicles composed their works?

And why, since so many hundreds of works of the ancient Greeks, such as those mentioned by Pliny, [23] have utterly disappeared, are we to suppose that the Jews of Ezra's time did not also possess many works that have

---

[23] *Natural History,* Book 1.

been obliterated? The Aramaic recension of the Behistun Inscription of Darius Hystaspis and the Aramaic work of Ahikar were buried at Elephantine for twenty-three hundred years, but have now been unearthed and show that the Aramaic-speaking Jews of the sixth and fifth centuries *B.C.* had produced at least *some* literary documents in addition to the Aramaic portions of Ezra and Daniel. [24]

How many more of such works may have been possessed by them both in Hebrew and Aramaic we cannot say, but the probability is that they were numerous. We cannot see sufficient reason for doubting the claim of the Chronicler to have had access to sources extending from the time of David down to his own time. He says that he did have such sources. How can the critics know that he did not?

An Unjustifiable Assault

One of the most unjustifiable of the assaults upon the Old Testament Scriptures lies in the assumption that the larger part of the great poetical and legal productions and some of the finest prophecies were produced during the period of her political and linguistic decay, which followed the year 500 *B.C.*

The only time after the end of the captivity at which we might naturally have expected a recrudescence of such literary activity was the period from 200 *B.C.* to the time of Pompey. And here in fact are to be placed the apocryphal and pseudepigraphical works of Ecclesiasticus, Wisdom, Maccabees, Jubilees, parts of Enoch, and many other works of greater or less value. The only one of these that has been preserved in Hebrew is Ecclesiasticus; and its Hebrew has no word that is certainly Greek, and not one of Persian origin that is not found in the Old Testament. [26]

Many traces of Persian influence are visible in Chroni-

---

[24] Sachau, *Papyrus.*

[25] R. H. Charles, *Apocrypha and Pseudipigrapha of the Old Testament.*

[26] Strack's and Smend's editions.

cles, Esther, Ezra, and Nehemiah.[27] When, however, we come to the Hebrew of the Psalms (of which so many are placed by the critics in this period), of Ecclesiastes, and of the Hebrew part of Daniel, we find that the language differs markedly from Ecclesiasticus both in vocabulary and forms. The use of the conjunction "and" with the perfect, which is said to be a mark of the lateness of Ecclesiastes, is not found in Ecclesiasticus. Ecclesiastes is devoid of any words that are certainly Babylonian, Persian, or Aramaic. The so-called Maccabean Psalms have no Persian or Greek words and few, if any, that are certainly Babylonian; and only a few that are even alleged to have Aramaic vocables or forms.

The period between 500 and 164 *B.C.* was one in which the Israelites were subservient to the government of Persia and the Greeks. The only reliable information from this time about a revival of national feeling and semi-independence among the Jews is that to be found in Ezra and Nehemiah and a few hints in Ecclesiasticus and Tobit. And the only literary works in Hebrew that were certainly written during this period of decay are the books of Esther, Ezra, Nehemiah and Chronicles. As we would expect, they are all characterized by Persian, Babylonian, and Aramaic words, and Ezra is nearly half composed in Aramaic.

Prophecies That Contain No Persian or Greek Word

But how about Jonah, Joel, Isaiah 24-27, the Priest-Code, the Song of Songs, and the multitude of Psalms, which the critics arbitrarily place in this period? There is not in them one certainly Persian word, nor a single Greek word. Not a Babylonian word, not already found in the earlier literature, appears in any one of them, and scarcely a word that the critics even can allege to be an Aramaism. In language, style, and thought, no greater contrast can be found in the whole literature of the Old Testament than there is between the books that purport to have been

---

[27] Driver, *Introduction to the Literature of the Old Testament,* in loc.

written and those which the critics allege to have been written in this period.

It is to be hoped that the reader appreciates the value and the bearing of these facts. The Higher Criticism, as Dr. Driver affirms in the preface to his *Introduction to the Literature of the Old Testament,* is based upon a "comparative study of the writings." No one will object to this method of investigation. *Only, let us abide by the results. Let us not bring in our subjective views and make them outweigh the obvious facts.*

Nothing in 1800 Years of History to Invalidate the Old Testament

Last of all, we must cast a glance at the history of the religion of Israel. It must be admitted that, before we can attempt such a history, we must determine two great facts: first, the dates of the documents on which the history is based; and second, the attitude we are going to take with regard to miracle and prophecy.

As to the first of these facts, I have already given a number of the reasons for holding that *there is no sufficient ground for believing that the Pentateuch did not originate with Moses,* or that David did not write many of the Psalms; and that there is every reason in language and history for supposing that all but a few of the books were written before 500 *B.C.* I have not attempted to fix the exact dates of composition or final redaction of the books composed before that time, preferring rather to show that there is nothing in the history of the world from 2000 to 164 *B.C.* that militates against the possibility nor even against the probability of the trustworthiness of the history of Israel as recorded in the Old Testament.

Nor, in spite of some apparent inconsistencies and of many passages difficult to explain satisfactorily, owing to our ignorance of all the facts, is there anything in the history of Israel as recorded in the Old Testament that makes it appear incredible or unveracious. No one knows enough to affirm with confidence that any one of the prophetic books was not written by the man whose name is bears. No one knows enough to assert that the kings and others mentioned did not do and say what is ascribed to them. If, then, we can accept the documents of the Old Testament as substantially correct, we come to the further question of whether the presentment of the Israelitish religion, as we find it described in the Old Testament, is true.

But there is no use of discussing this subject until at least the possibility of God's making known his will to man is admitted. Whoever admits this possibility is in a fair way to become a Christian. So long as one denies this, he cannot possibly become a Christian nor even a Theist. For those who believe in the resurrection of Jesus and what it implies as to the person and work of the Son of God and of His apostles under the guidance of the Holy Ghost, the question of the history of the religion of Israel assumes an entirely different character and purpose. It becomes part of the plan of God for the world's redemption. They who accept the statements of the New Testament writers and of the Lord as true will accept what they say about the Old Testament as true until it is proved to be false. And when the Old Testament is shown not to agree with what Christ and the apostles say, it will be presumed that the text has not been rightly transmitted or correctly interpreted.

The Plan, Purpose, and People of the History of Redemption Offer a Reasonable Basis for Belief

The attitude of one who believes that God spoke to man through the prophets to whom he gave a message for his people is also fundamentally different from that of one who disbelieves this hundred-times repeated statement of the Old Testament.

A *believer* in *Theism* can accept the statements of the old Testament books, especially in the light of the New, as being what they appear to be. If any statements of the Old Testament are proved to be false, he lays the blame to a corruption of the text or to a wrong interpretation of the evidence. For he is convinced that the Bible contains the revelation of the Divine plan for the redemption of humanity from sin to holiness and everlasting life.

All that he wants or needs to have established, is that this plan has been handed down to us in a sufficiently reliable form to insure the purpose of the Divine Author. *The reasonable Christian can rejoice and believe that the Bible has thus been handed down.* The plan is there in the documents of the Old Testament and of the New, as clear as day. The purpose is there. *The Jewish people existed and exists, according to the Scripture, as an ever-present evidence that the plan and purpose were of God.*

The Christian church in like manner exists as an evidence that the Gospel of salvation was really meant for the whole world. This Gospel has met and satisfied the need and the hope of human nature for pardon and communion with God, and it is meeting them today. Millions exult in their present faith and die at peace and in hope of a blessed and an everlasting life. The Bible and the church are the foundation of this faith and peace and hope. The history of Israel is continued in the history of the Christian church. *He who attacks one attacks both.* United they stand; divided they fall. Unitedly they present a reasonable foundation for the belief that God has never left Himself without a witness that He loves mankind and will have all men believe and come to a knowledge of the truth.

Looked at in the light of the whole world's history from the beginning until now, the history of the religion of the Old Testament as given in the books themselves, unrevised and fairly interpreted, is rational and worthy of trust. In this faith we live; in this faith let us die.

A Parallel Monstrosity to the Denial of Old Testament History Imagined

Nothwithstanding this evident plan and purpose of a Divine redemption which runs all through the Scriptures, there are today many professedly Christian writers who treat the Israelitish religion as if it were a purely natural development. They diligently pick out every instance of a superstitious observance or of a departure from the law or of a disobedience to the Divine commands, as if these represented the true religion of ancient Israel.

They cut up the books and doctor the documents and change the text and wrest the meaning to suit the perverted view of their own fancy. *They seem to think that they know better what the Scriptures ought to have been than the prophets and apostles and even the Lord himself!* They tell us when revelations must have been made, and how and where they must have been given, and what their contents could have been, *as if they knew more about such matters than God Himself.*

Imagine a man's writing the history of the last eighteen hundred years and denying that the New Testament had been in existence during all that time, denying that the Christian church with all its saving doctrines and benevolent institutions and beneficent social system derived from the New Testament had been active and, in a sense, triumphant for at least fifteen hundred years, *simply because* he could select thousands of examples of superstitious customs and hellish deeds and impious words and avowed agnostic and heaven-defying atheists, that have disgraced the pages of history during this time!

Grovel for Beetles or Pluck Violets?

Let us not grovel for the beetles and the earth worms of almost forgotten faiths which may perchance be discovered beneath the stones and sod of the Old Testament, while the violets and the lilies-of-the-valley of a sweet and lowly faith are in bloom on every page, and every oracle revealed within the Word of God is jubilant with songs of everlasting joy. The true religion of Israel came down from God arranged in the beautiful garments of righteousness and life. We cannot substitute for this heaven-made apparel a robe of human manufacture, however fine it be.

THE MAGNIFICENT BURGON

Edward F. Hills

Doughty Champion and Defender of the Byzantine (true) Text. Extracts
from Preface of the book *The Last Twelve Verses of Mark*, by J. W. Burgon.[1]

John William Burgon was born August 21, 1813. He
matriculated at Oxford in 1841, taking several high honors
there, and his B.A. in 1845. He took his M.A. there in
1848.

Burgon's days at Oxford were in the period when the
tractarian controversy was flaming. The assault upon the
Scriptures as the inerrant Word of God aroused him to
study in the textual field. He was a deep and laborious
student, and a very fierce competitor. He left no stone
unturned, examining the original manuscripts on every
occasion, and he himself discovered many manuscripts in
his search for the truth in textual matters.

Burgon wrote a brilliant monograph on Mark 16:9-16 in
1871.

Most of Burgon's adult life was spent at Oxford, as
Fellow of Oriel College and then as vicar of St. Mary's (the
University Church) and Gresham Professor of Divinity.
During his last twelve years he was Dean of Chichester. His

---

[1] J. W. Burgon, *The Last Twelve Verses of Mark*, 1959, Preface.

father was an English merchant with business interests in Turkey, and his mother a native of Smyrna of Austrian and Greek extraction. It was from this foreign blood, no doubt, that Burgon derived his warm and enthusiastic nature, not typically English, which expressed itself in a lively literary style. In theology he was a High-church Anglican, strenuously upholding the doctrine of baptismal regeneration but opposing the ritualism into which even in his day the High-church movement had begun to decline.[2] Throughout his life he remained unmarried, but, like many other celibates, he is said to have been unusually fond of children. As for his learning, even his adversaries acknowledged that it was very great.

The thing about Burgon, however, which lifts him out of his nineteenth century English setting and endears him to the hearts of earnest Christians of other lands and other ages is his steadfast defense of the Scriptures as the infallible Word of God. He strove with all his power to arrest the modernistic currents which during his lifetime had begun to flow within the Church of England, continuing his efforts with unabated zeal up to the very day of his death. With this purpose in mind he labored mightily in the field of New Testament textual criticism. In 1860, while temporary chaplain of the English congregation at Rome, he made a personal examination of Codex B, and in 1862 he inspected the treasures of St. Catherine's Convent on Mt. Sinai. Later he made several tours of European libraries, examining and collating New Testament manuscripts wherever he went.

It is on the strength of these labors that K. W. Clark[3] ranks him with Tregelles and Scrivener as one of the "great contemporaries" of Tischendorf. And Rendel Harris (1908) had high praise for Burgon's great Index of New Testament quotations in the Church Fathers, which was deposited in the British Museum at the time of his death but has never been published. "It is possible," Harris said,

---

[2] He was no advocate of reunion with Rome, and he did not hesitate to describe the Church of Rome as apostate.

[3] Parvis and Wikgren, *New Testament Manuscript Studies,* 1950, p. 9.

"to object to many of his references and to find fault with some of the texts which he used, but I only wish that I possessed a transcript of those precious volumes."[4]

Burgon was amassing all these materials for a definitive work in which he would defend the Traditional Text. This was Burgon's name for that type of text which is found in the vast majority of the extant Greek New Testament manuscripts, which was adopted by Protestants at the time of the Reformation and used by them universally for more than three hundred years, and which forms the basis of the King James Version and other early Protestant translations.

Unfortunately, however, Burgon did not live to complete his project. The fragments of it, which he left at his death, were pieced together by his friend E. Miller and published in 1896 in two volumes entitled *The Traditional Text of the Holy Gospels* and *The Causes of the Corruption of the Traditional Text.* That Burgon died before he could finish his *opus magnum* is a matter of deep regret, but enough of it survives in Miller's volumes to convey to us Burgon's fundamental ideas, together with the arguments by which he supported them.

And these same basic concepts had been expressed in two earlier books which had won him fame as a textual critic, namely, *The Last Twelve Verses of Mark* (1871), a defense of this portion of the New Testament text, and *The Revision Revised* (1883), a reprint of three articles in the *Quarterly Review* against the Revised Version of 1881, together with a reply to a pamphlet by Bishop Ellicott against these three articles. Such, then, were the publications in which Burgon laid down the principles of consistently Christian New Testament textual criticism and elaborated them with considerable fullness. Of all the great textual critics of the nineteenth century Burgon alone was consistently Christian in his vindication of the Divine inspiration and providential preservation of the text of Holy Scripture.

---

4 J. Rendel Harris, *Side Lights on New Testament Research,* 1908, p. 22.

Dean Burgon the Champion of the Traditional (Byzantine) Text

According to Kenyon,[5] there are about 4,489 Greek New Testament manuscripts known to be extant. Of these 170 are papyrus fragments, dating from the second century to the seventh; 212 are uncial (capital letter) manuscripts, dating from the fourth century to the tenth; 2,429 are minuscule (small letter) manuscripts dating from the ninth century to the sixteenth; and 1,678 are lectionaries (lesson books for public reading containing extracts from the New Testament).

The vast majority of these extant Greek New Testament manuscripts agree together very closely, *so closely,* indeed that they may fairly be said to contain the same New Testament text. This Majority Text is usually called the Byzantine Text by modern textual critics. This is because all modern critics acknowledge that this was the Greek New Testament text in general use throughout the greater part of the Byzantine Period (312–1453).

For many centuries before the Protestant Reformation this Byzantine text was the text of the entire Greek Church, and for more than three centuries after the Reformation it was the text of the entire Protestant Church. Even today it is the text which most Protestants know best, since the King James Version and other early Protestant translations were made from it.

Burgon was an ardent defender of this Byzantine text found in the vast majority of the Greek New Testament manuscripts. He gave to this text the name Traditional Text,[6] thus indicating his conviction that this was the true text which by a perpetual tradition had been handed down generation after generation without fail in the Church of

---

[5] *Our Bible and the Ancient Manuscripts* (New York, 1940), pp. 105-106.

[6] He used the word *Traditional* in its proper sense, signifying "handed down." In this sense the Scriptures are the "Divine Tradition" as opposed to "the traditions of men."

Christ from the days of the apostles onwards. Burgon believed this because he believed that it was through the church that Christ had fulfilled His promise always to preserve for His people a true New Testament text.

The Byzantine text, he maintained, is the true text because it is that form of the Greek New Testament which is known to have been used in the Church of Christ in unbroken succession for many centuries, first in the Greek Church and then in the Protestant Church. And all orthodox Christians, all Christians who show due regard for the Divine inspiration and providential preservation of Scripture, must agree with Burgon in this matter. For in what other way can it be that Christ has fulfilled His promise always to preserve in His Church the true New Testament text?

"No sooner," writes Dean Burgon, "was the work of Evangelists and Apostles recognized as the necessary counterpart and complement of God's ancient Scriptures and became the 'New Testament,' than a reception was found to be awaiting it in the world closely resembling that which He experienced Who is the subject of its pages. Calumny and misrepresentation, persecution and murderous hate, assailed Him continually. And the Written Word in like manner, in the earliest age of all, was shamefully handled by mankind. Not only was it confused through human infirmity and misapprehension, but it became also the object of restless malice and unsparing assaults."[7]

"Before our Lord ascended up to heaven," continues Dean Burgon, "He told His disciples that He would send them the Holy Ghost, who should supply His place and abide with His Church for ever. He added a promise that it should be the office of that inspiring Spirit not only to bring to their remembrance all things whatsoever He had told them, but also to guide His Church 'into all Truth' or 'the whole Truth' (John 16:13).

"Accordingly, the earliest great achievement of those days was accomplished in giving to the Church the

---

[7] *Traditional Text*, p. 10.

Scriptures of the New Testament, in which, authorized teaching was enshrined in written form. . . . There exists no reason for supposing that the Divine Agent, who in the first instance thus gave to mankind the Scriptures of Truth, straightway abdicated His office; took no further care of His work; abandoned those precious writings to their fate. That a perpetual miracle was wrought for their preservation — that copyists were protected against all risk of error, or evil men prevented from adulterating shamefully copies of the Deposit — no one, it is presumed, is so weak as to suppose. But it is quite a different thing to claim that all down the ages the sacred writings must needs have been God's peculiar care; that the Church under Him has watched over them with intelligence and skill; has recognized which copies exhibit a fabricated, which an honestly transcribed text; has generally sanctioned the one, and generally disallowed the other."

In connection with Westcott and Hort's theory Dean Burgon writes: "We oppose facts to their speculation. They exalt B and Aleph and D[8] because in their own opinions those copies are the best. They weave ingenious webs and invent subtle theories, because their paradox of a few against the many requires ingenuity and subtlety for its support. Dr. Hort revelled in finespun theories and technical terms, such as 'Intrinsic Probability,' 'Transcriptional Probability,' 'Internal evidence of Readings,' 'Internal evidence of Documents,' which of course connote a certain amount of evidence, but are weak pillars of a heavy structure. Even conjectural emendation and inconsistent decrees are not rejected. They are infected with the theorizing which spoils some of the best German work, and with the idealism which is the bane of many academic minds especially at Oxford and Cambridge.

"In contrast with this sojourn in cloudland, we are essentially of the earth though not earthy. We are nothing if we are not grounded in facts: Our appeal is to facts, our test lies in facts, so far as we can we build testimonies upon testimonies and pile facts on facts. We imitate the

---

8 B=Codex Vaticanus, Aleph=Codex Sinaiticus, D=Codex Bezae.

procedure of the courts of justice in decisions resulting from the converging product of all evidence, when it has been cross-examined and sifted."

Burgon continues: "I proceed to offer for the reader's consideration seven tests of Truth concerning each of which I shall have something to say in the way of explanation by-and-by. In the end I shall ask the reader to allow that where these seven tests are found to conspire we may confidently assume that the evidence is worthy of all acceptance, and is to be implicitly followed. A reading should be attested then by the seven following: 1. Antiquity or Primitiveness; 2. Consent of Witnesses, or Number; 3. Variety of Evidence, or Catholicity; 4. Respectability of Witnesses, or Weight; 5. Continuity, or Unbroken Tradition; 6. Evidence of the Entire Passage, or Context; 7. Internal Considerations, or Reasonableness.

"In the balances of these seven Tests of Truth the speculations of the Westcott and Hort school, which have bewitched millions are 'Tekel,' weighed in the balances and found wanting.

"I am utterly disinclined to believe," continues Dean Burgon, "so grossly improbable does it seem — that at the end of 1800 years 995 copies out of every thousand, suppose, will prove untrustworthy; and that the one, two, three, four or five which remain, whose contents were till yesterday as good as unknown, will be found to have retained the secret of what the Holy Spirit originally inspired.

"I am utterly unable to believe, in short, that God's promise has so entirely failed, that at the end of 1800 years, much of the text of the Gospel had in point of fact to be picked by a German critic out of a wastepaper basket in the convent of St. Catherine; and that the entire text had to be remodelled after the pattern set by a couple of copies which had remained in neglect during fifteen centuries, and had probably owed their survival to that neglect; whilst hundreds of others had been thumbed to pieces, and had bequeathed their witness to copies made from them. . . .

"Happily, Western Christendom has been content to

employ one and the same text for upwards of three hundred years. If the objection be made, as it probably will be, 'Do you then mean to rest upon the five manuscripts used by Erasmus?' I reply that the copies employed were selected because they were known to represent the accuracy of the Sacred Word; that the descent of the text was evidently guarded with jealous care, just as the human genealogy of our Lord was preserved; that it rests mainly upon much the widest testimony; and that where any part of it conflicts with the fullest evidence attainable, there I believe it calls for correction."

Since all the non-Byzantine New Testament manuscripts have been condemned by some noted modern critic or other, no scholar ought to be offended at Burgon's treatment of this minority group. He also condemned these non-Byzantine texts in strongest terms, deeming them depraved — far inferior, that is, to the Byzantine (true) text found in the vast majority of the Greek New Testament manuscripts. "By far the most depraved text is that exhibited by CODEX D."[9] And concerning B and ALEPH his remarks are similar. "As for the origin of these two curiosities, it can perforce only be divined from their contents. That they exhibit fabricated texts is demonstrable. No amount of honest copying — persevered in for any number of centuries — could by possibility have resulted in two such documents. Separated from one another in actual date by 50, perhaps by 100 years, they must needs have branched off from a common corrupt ancestor, and straightway become exposed to fresh depraving influences."[10]

Burgon regarded the good state of preservation of B and ALEPH in spite of their exceptional age as a proof not of their goodness but of their badness. If they had been good manuscripts, they would have been read to pieces long ago. "We suspect that these two manuscripts are indebted for their preservation, *solely to their ascertained evil character;*

---

[9] *Revision Revised*, p. 12.
[10] *Ibid.*, p. 318.

which has occasioned that the one eventually found its way, four centuries ago, to a forgotten shelf in the Vatican Library; while the other, after exercising the ingenuity of several generations of critical Correctors, eventually (viz. in A.D. 1844) got deposited in the wastepaper basket of the Convent at the foot of Mount Sinai. Had B and ALEPH been copies of average purity, they must long since have shared the inevitable fate of books which are freely used and highly prized; namely, they would have fallen into decadence and disappeared from sight."[11]

Thus the fact that B and ALEPH are so old is a point against them, not something in their favor. It shows that the Church rejected them and did not read them. Otherwise they would have worn out and disappeared through much reading. Burgon has been accused of sophistry in arguing this way, but certainly his suggestion cannot be rejected by naturalistic critics as impossible. For one of their "own poets" favored the idea that the scribes "usually destroyed their exemplars when they had copied the sacred books."[12]

If Lake could believe this, why may not orthodox Christians believe that many ancient Byzantine manuscripts have been worn out with much reading and copying? And conversely, why may we not believe that B, ALEPH and the other ancient non-Byzantine manuscripts have survived unto the present day simply because they were rejected by the Church and not used?

How False Readings Originated

Burgon attributed the false readings present in B, ALEPH, D, and the other non-Byzantine manuscripts to two principal causes. The first of these was the deliberate falsification of the New Testament Scriptures by heretics during the second and third centuries. The second was the doubtless well meant but nevertheless disastrous efforts of

---

[11] *Ibid.,* p. 319.

[12] See Kirsopp Lake, *Harvard Theological Review,* Vol. 21 (1928), pp. 347-349.

certain learned Christians during this same early period to improve the New Testament text through the use of "conjectural emendation." In support of these contentions Burgon brought forth a number of quotations from the writings of the Church Fathers.

The early Christians of Alexandria were probably much influenced by the heretics who flourished there and who are known to have corrupted the New Testament text, by Basilides, for example, and Valentinus and their disciples. Moreover, the only Alexandrian Christian of whose New Testament textual criticism we have specimens is Origen, and his decisions in this field seem fanciful rather than sound.

Burgon refers us to an outstanding example of Origen's New Testament textual criticism. In his comment on Matthew 19:17-21 (Jesus' reply to the rich young man) [13], Origen reasons that Jesus could not have concluded His list of God's commandments with the comprehensive requirement, "Thou shalt love thy neighbor as thyself." For the reply of the young man was, "All these things have I kept from my youth up," and Jesus evidently accepted this statement as true. But if the young man had loved his neighbor as himself, he would have been perfect, for Paul says that the whole law is summed up in this saying, "Thou shalt love thy neighbor as thyself." But Jesus answered, "If thou wilt be perfect. . . ," implying that the young man was not yet perfect. Therefore, Origen argued, the commandment, "Thou shalt love thy neighbor as thyself," could not have been spoken by Jesus on this occasion and was not part of the original text of Matthew. This clause, he believed, was added by some tasteless scribe.

Thus it is clear that this renowned Father was not content to abide by the text which he had received but freely indulged in the boldest sort of conjectural emendation. In the very passage in which he speaks most fully concerning his critical work on the Old Testament text he gives us this specimen of his handling of the New. It is

[13] Berlin, *Origenes Werke*, Vol. 10, pp. 385-388.

likely, moreover, that there were other Christian scholars at Alexandria who were even less restrained in their speculations than Origen. These well-meaning but misguided critics evidently deleted many readings from the original New Testament text, thus producing the abbreviated text found in B and ALEPH and in other manuscripts of their type.

Burgon's View of the History of the New Testament Text

In his *Revision Revised* Burgon gives his reconstruction of the history of the New Testament text in the vivid style that was habitual to him. "Vanquished by THE WORD Incarnate, Satan next directed his subtle malice against the Word written. Hence, as I think — hence the extraordinary fate which befell certain early transcripts of the Gospel. First, heretical assailants of Christianity — then, orthodox defenders of the Truth — lastly and above all, self constituted Critics . . . such were the corrupting influences which were actively at work throughout the first hundred years after the death of St. John the Divine.

"Profane literature has never known anything approaching to it — can show nothing at all like it. Satan's arts were defeated indeed through the Church's faithfulness, because — (the good Providence of God has so willed it) — the perpetual multiplication in every quarter, of copies required for Ecclesiastical use — not to say the solicitude of faithful men in diverse regions of ancient Christendom to retain for themselves unadulterated specimens of the inspired Text — proved a sufficient safeguard against the grosser forms of corruption. But this was not all.

"The Church, remember, hath been from the beginning the 'Witness and Keeper of Holy Writ.' Did not her Divine Author pour out upon her in largest measure, 'the SPIRIT of truth'; and pledge Himself that it should be that Spirit's special function to guide her children "into all the truth'? . . . That by a perpetual miracle, sacred manuscripts would be protected all down the ages against depraving influences of whatever sort — was not to have been expected; certainly, was never promised. But the Church, in her collective capacity, hath nevertheless — as a matter of fact — been perpetually purging herself of those shamefully depraved copies which once everywhere abounded within her pale: retaining only such an amount of discrepancy in her Text as might serve to remind her children that they carry their 'treasure in earthen vessels' — as well as to stimulate them to perpetual watchfulness and solicitude for the purity and integrity of the Deposit. Never, however, up to the present hour, hath there been any complete eradication of all traces of the attempted mischief — any absolute getting rid of every depraved copy extant. These are found to have lingered on anciently in many quarters. A few such copies linger on to the present day. The wounds were healed, but the scars remained — nay, the scars are discernible still.

"What, in the meantime, is to be thought of those blind guides — those deluded ones — who would now, if they could, persuade us to go back to those same codices of which the Church hath already purged herself?"[14]

Burgon's reconstruction of the history of the New Testament text is not only vividly expressed but eminently biblical and therefore true. For if the true New Testament text came from God, whence came the erroneous variant readings ultimately save from the evil one; and how could the true text have been preserved save through the providence of God working through His Church?

No doubt most Christians, not being High-church Anglicans, will place less emphasis than Dean Burgon did on the organized Church, and more emphasis on the providence of God working through the Church, especially the Greek Church, but this possible defect in Burgon's presentation does not in any essential way affect the eternal validity of his views concerning the New Testament text. They are eternally valid because they are consistently Christian. In elaborating these views Burgon, unlike most other textual critics, was always careful to remember that the New Testament is not an ordinary book but a special

---

14 *The Revision Revised,* pp. 334-335.

book, a book which was written under the infallible inspiration of the Holy Spirit, a book whose text Christ has promised to preserve in His Church down through the ages.

The Canon and Text of the New Testament

The essential soundness of Burgon's views is most readily seen when we compare the history of the New Testament canon with the history of the New Testament text, and, therefore, it is to this task that we must now address ourselves.

Why did the Christian Church receive the twenty-seven New Testament books and these only as her canonical New Testament Scripture? Harnack[15] and other noted students of the New Testament canon have asked this question repeatedly and have endeavored to answer it in their own fashion. But, as Greijdanus[16] and Grosheide[17] point out, this question can be satisfactorily answered only on the basis of Christian faith. And when we look with the eye of faith upon the history of the New Testament canon, then we see in that history a mighty conflict between God and Satan, between the Holy Spirit on the one hand and the spirit of darkness on the other.

First, God gave to His Church the twenty-seven New Testament books through the inspiration of the Holy Spirit, and then through the Spirit also He began to lead the Church into a recognition of these books as her canonical New Testament Scripture. During the second century, however, Satan endeavored to confuse the Church by raising up deceitful men who wrote pseudonymous works, falsely claiming to be apostolic. These satanic devices hindered and delayed the Church's recognition of the true New Testament canon but could not prevent it. Soon after the beginning of the fifth century the opposition of the devil was completely overcome. Under the

---

15 *The Origin of the New Testament* (New York, 1925), pp. 2-3.

16 *Schriftgeloof en Canoniek* (Kampen, 1927), pp. 76-77.

17 *Algemeene Canoniek van het Nieuwe Testament* (Amsterdam, 1935), pp. 206-207.

leading of the Holy Spirit the Church was guided to receive only the twenty-seven New Testament books as canonical and to reject all others.

Dean Burgon believed that the history of the New Testament text was similar to the history of the New Testament canon; and all orthodox Christians will do well to agree with him in this, for a study of the New Testament manuscripts bears him out. In other words, during the early Christian centuries Satan directed his assault not only upon the New Testament canon but also upon the New Testament text.

No sooner had the New Testament books been given to the Church through the inspiration of the Holy Spirit than the spirit of darkness began his endeavors to corrupt their texts and render them useless, but in these efforts also the evil one failed to attain his objective. In regard to the New Testament text as well as in regard to the New Testament canon God bestowed upon His Church sufficient grace to enable her to overcome all the wiles of the devil. Just as God guided the Church to reject, after a period of doubt and conflict, all non-canonical writings and to receive only the true canonical New Testament books, so God guided the Church during this same period of doubt and conflict, to reject false readings and to receive into common usage the true New Testament text.

For an orthodox Christian Burgon's view is the only reasonable one. If we believe that God gave the Church guidance in regard to the New Testament books, then surely it is logical to believe that God gave the Church similar guidance in regard to the text which these books contained. Surely it is very inconsistent to believe that God guided the Church in regard to the New Testament canon but gave the Church no guidance in regard to the New Testament text. But this seems to be just what many modern Christians do believe. They believe that all during the medieval period and throughout the Reformation and post-Reformation era the true New Testament text was lost and that it was not regained until the middle of the nineteenth century, when Tischendorf discovered it in the Sinaitic manuscript Aleph and Westcott and Hort found it in the Vatican manuscript B. Such inconsistency, however, is bound to lead to a skepticism which deprives the New Testament text of all authority. If we must believe that the true New Testament text was lost for fifteen hundred years, how can we be certain that it has now been found? What guarantee have we that either B or Aleph contain the true text? How can we be sure that Harris (1908), Conybeare (1910), Lake (1941), and other radical critics are not correct in their suspicions that the true New Testament text has been lost beyond possibility of recovery?

Burgon's Rejection of Contemporary New Testament Textual Criticism

Burgon, therefore, was right in utterly rejecting the claims of Tischendorf (1815-74), Tregelles (1813-75), Westcott (1825-1901), Hort (1828-92), and other contemporary scholars, who insisted that as a result of their labors the true New Testament text had at last been discovered after having been lost for well-nigh fifteen centuries. "And thus it would appear," he remarks ironically, "that the Truth of Scripture has run a very narrow risk of being lost forever to mankind. Dr. Hort contends that it more than half lay *'perdu'* on a forgotten shelf in the Vatican Library; — Dr. Tischendorf that it had been deposited in a wastepaper basket in the convent of St. Catherine at the foot of Mount Sinai; — from which he rescued it on the 4th of February, 1859; — neither, we venture to think, a very likely circumstance. We incline to believe that the Author of Scripture hath not by any means shown Himself so unmindful of the safety of the Deposit, as these distinguished gentlemen imagine."[18]

According to Burgon, the fundamental mistake of contemporary New Testament textual critics was that they ignored the unique character of the New Testament text. They would not recognize that they were dealing with a Book that was different from all other books, in short,

---

[18] *The Revision Revised,* p. 343.

with a divinely inspired and providentially preserved book. "That which distinguishes Sacred Science from every other Science which can be named is that it is Divine, and has to do with a Book which is inspired, and not regarded upon a level with the Books of the East, which are held by their votaries to be sacred. It is chiefly from inattention to this circumstance that misconception prevails in that department of Sacred Science known as 'Textual Criticism.'

"Aware that the New Testament is like no other book in its origin, its contents, its history, many critics of the present day nevertheless permit themselves to reason concerning its Text, as if they entertained no suspicion that the words and sentences of which it is composed were destined to experience an extraordinary fate also. They make no allowances for the fact that influences of an entirely different kind from any with which profane literature is acquainted have made themselves felt in this department, and therefore that even those principles of Textual Criticism which in the case of profane authors are regarded as fundamental are often out of place here."[19]

We see here the fundamental difference between Burgon's approach to the problem of the New Testament text and that adopted by his contemporaries, especially Westcott and Hort. In matters of textual criticism, at least, these latter scholars followed a Naturalistic method. They took particular pride in handling the text of the New Testament just as they would the text of any other ancient book. "For ourselves," Hort declared, "we dare not introduce considerations which could not reasonably be applied to other ancient texts, supposing them to have documentary attestation of equal amount, variety, and antiquity."[20]

Burgon, on the other hand, followed a consistently Christian method of New Testament textual criticism. He believed that the New Testament had been divinely inspired and providentially preserved, and when he came

---

19 *Traditional Text,* p. 9.

20 *The New Testament in the Original Greek* (London, 1881), Vol. 2, p. 277.

to the study of the New Testament text, he did not for one instant lay this faith aside. On the contrary, he regarded the Divine inspiration and providential preservation of the New Testament as two fundamental facts which must be taken into account in the interpretation of the details of New Testament textual criticism, two basic verities which make the textual criticism of the New Testament different from the textual criticism of any other book.

As we have seen, Burgon believed that it was through the usage of the Church that Christ fulfilled His promise always to preserve the New Testament text in its purity. By His Holy Spirit Christ guided His Church to reject false readings and to receive into common usage the true New Testament text. This Divine guidance, moreover, centered in the Greek Church, because it was this Church especially that actually used the Greek New Testament text. Such was Burgon's view of the history of the New Testament text. There are, however, many orthodox Christians who cannot see their way clear to agree with Burgon. It is necessary, therefore, to devote some space to a consideration of their theories. How do they think that Christ fulfilled His promise always to preserve a pure New Testament text? A realization of the inadequacy of these alternative views will dispose us more than ever to follow Burgon.

The Alleged Agreement of All the New Testament Manuscripts in Matters of Doctrine. Is This a Fulfillment of Christ's Promise?

In dealing with the problems of the New Testament text most conservatives place great stress on the amount of agreement alleged to exist among the extant New Testament manuscripts. These manuscripts, it is said, agree so closely with one another in matters of doctrine that it does not make much difference which manuscript you follow. The same essential teaching is preserved in them all. This reputed agreement of all the extant New Testament manuscripts in doctrinal matters is ascribed to Divine providence and regarded as the fulfillment of the promise of Christ always to preserve in His Church a trustworthy New Testament text.

Dean Burgon in the Light of Recent Research

It may be that certain orthodox Christians who have read the foregoing pages will reason thus within themselves. "Burgon's views seem very reasonable and much more in accord with the fundamentals of our Christian faith than the theories of Westcott and Hort and other naturalistic textual critics. It is certainly much more reasonable to believe with Burgon that the true New Testament text has been preserved in the vast majority of the New Testament manuscripts than to suppose with Westcott and Hort that the true text is hardly to be found in any place save in Codex B, now securely locked up in the library of the pope — and in the small minority of the manuscripts which exhibit the same kind of text.

"Who but those with Roman Catholic sympathies could ever be pleased with the notion that God preserved the true New Testament text in secret for almost one thousand years and then finally handed it over to the Roman pontiff for safekeeping? Surely every orthodox Protestant will prefer to think with Burgon that God preserved the true text of the Greek New Testament in the usage of the Greek-speaking Church down through the centuries and then at length delivered it up intact to the Protestant reformers. Burgon's views, in short, seem eminently reasonable and in accord with our orthodox Christian faith. We feel inclined to adopt them, but how about the facts? Are Burgon's views in agreement with the facts?"

The answer to this question is an unqualified "Yes!" The evidence now available is amply sufficient to support the orthodox view that regards the Byzantine text as the authentic New Testament text and is even greater now than it was in Burgon's day. There is now greater reason than ever to believe that the Byzantine text, which is found in the vast majority of the Greek New Testament manuscripts and which was used well-nigh universally throughout the Greek Church for many centuries, is a faithful reproduction of the original New Testament and is the divinely appointed standard by which all New Testament manuscripts and all divergent readings must be judged. No non-Byzantine reading may be regarded as possibly or probably true which in any way detracts from the divine fullness of the doctrine contained in the Byzantine text, for it is in the Byzantine text that Christ has fulfilled His promise always to preserve in His Church the true New Testament text.

Thus the evidence which has accumulated since Burgon's day is amply sufficient to justify the view held by him and by all consistently orthodox Christians; namely, that it was through the usage of the Church that Christ has fulfilled His promise always to preserve the true New Testament text, and that therefore the Byzantine text found in the vast majority of the Greek New Testament manuscripts is that true text. To reject this view is to act unreasonably. It is to fly in face of the facts.

Those, moreover, who reject this orthodox view of the New Testament text have rejected not merely the facts but also the promise of Christ always to preserve the true New Testament text and the doctrines of the Divine inspiration and providential preservation of Scripture implied in this promise. Has Christ kept this promise or has He not? If we believe this promise, then we must do as Burgon and other orthodox Christians have done. Like Burgon, we must allow this promise to guide us in our dealings with the New Testament text. We must interpret all the data of New Testament textual criticism in the light of this promise.

It is just here, however, that many Christians are fatally inconsistent. They say that they believe in the promise which Christ has given always to preserve the true New Testament text, but in practice they ignore this promise and treat the text of the New Testament exactly like the text of an ordinary book concerning which no such promise has been made. Thus they are guilty of a basic unfaithfulness. In their efforts to be pleasing to naturalistic critics they themselves have lapsed into unbelief. They have undermined their own faith and deprived themselves of all ground for confidence in the infallibility of the Bible. For if the New Testament is just an ordinary book, then the trustworthiness of its text is, at best, only a *probability,* never a *certainty.*

Dean Burgon has a message for these waverers and for all who desire to attain unto a firmer faith. In his controversy with the revisionists of 1881 Burgon stood forth as the uncompromising champion of the King James (Authorized) Version. "As a companion in the study and for private edification: as a book of reference for critical purposes, especially in respect of difficult and controverted passages: — we hold that a revised edition of the Authorized Version of our English Bible (if executed with consummate ability and learning) would at any time be a work of inestimable value. The method of such a performance, whether by marginal Notes or in some other way, we forbear to determine. But certainly only as a handmaid is it to be desired. As something *intended to supersede* our present English Bible, we are thoroughly convinced that the project of rival Translation is not to be entertained for a moment. For ourselves we deprecate it entirely."[21]

Burgon's main purpose, however, was to defend the Byzantine (Traditional) text of the Greek New Testament upon which the King James Version is based. He was removed from earth, it is true, before he could complete his grand design; but even before his death he had in great measure accomplished his purpose. Christians who desire to study the problems of the New Testament text should make every effort to procure Dean Burgon's works for their own possession. From him they will learn what it is to take first the standpoint of faith and then to deal faithfully and conscientiously with all the pertinent facts.

---

[21] E. C. Colwell and D. W. Riddle, *Prolegomena to the Study of the Lectionary Text of the Gospels* (Chicago, 1933). J. R. Branton, *The Common Text of the Gospel Lectionary* (Chicago, 1934). M. W. Redus, *The Text of the Major Festivals of the Menologion* (Chicago, 1936). B. M. Metzger, *The Saturday and Sunday Lesson from Luke in the Greek Gospel Lectionary* (Chicago, 1944).

THE PRINCIPLE

AND TENDENCY OF THE REVISION EXAMINED

George Sayles Bishop

These extracts are- taken from a book by Dr. Bishop, *The Doctrines of Grace* published by Bible Truth Depot, Swengel, Pa., n.d. This is part of a discourse preached June 7, 1885, soon after the Revised Version of the Bible first appeared. The committee of the Revised Version was dominated and practically controlled by Westcott and Hort, which makes the message of Dr. Bishop most pertinent and timely for this generation of Christians who are seeking to stand true to the Scriptures, come what may.

I have set before myself a simple straight-forward task — to translate into the language of the common people and in lines of clear, logical light the principles involved in the new version of the Bible and just in what direction it tends. This thing is needed. Nothing at the present time is more needed nor so needed, for I am convinced that the principle at the root of the revision movement has not been fairly understood, not even by many of the revisers themselves, who, charmed by the siren-like voices addressed to their scholarly feeling, have yielded themselves to give way, in unconscious unanimous movement, along with the wave on which the ship of inspiration floats with easy and accelerating motion, toward rebound and crash upon the rocks.

That a few changes might be made in both Testaments, for the better, no man pretends to deny; but that all the learned twaddle about "intrinsic and transcriptional probability," "conflation," "neutral texts," "the unique position of B" (the Vatican manuscript), and behind it the "primitive archetype," i.e., text to be conjectured, not now in existence; and finally the flat and bold and bad assertion that "we are obliged to come to the individual mind at last" — that all this so-called science shutting right up to one "group" of manuscripts, at the head of which are two — both of them, Aleph and B, as the drift of the proof goes to show, of a common, perhaps questionable, Egyptian, origin — one of them discovered in 1859, and first published in October, 1862, *little more than twenty years ago* — the other the Vatican Codex, supposed to be earlier, first — and behind that forsooth, to supply its defects, conjecture, cloudland, where divine words float on the air, — that all this theory is false and moonshine and, when applied to God's Word, worse than that; I firmly believe.

Because I am a minister of Christ, just as responsible to God as any man or minister on earth; because my business is to preach and to defend this Book, I cannot and will not keep silence. "If the foundations be destroyed, what can the righteous do?"

A sword in the hands of a child is mightier than a straw in the hands of a giant, and no amount of earnestness can be condemned when pleading, on straight lines, the cause of God. I quote Dr. Thornwell, "To employ soft words and honeyed phrases in discussing questions of everlasting importance; to deal with errors that strike at the foundations of all human hope as if they were harmless and venial mistakes; to bless where God disapproves, and to make apologies where He calls us to stand up like men and assert, though it may be the aptest method of securing popular applause in a sophistical age, is cruelty to man and treachery to Heaven. Those who on such subjects attach more importance to the rules of courtesy than they do to the measures of truth do not defend the citadel, but betray it into the hands of its enemies. Love for Christ, and for the souls for whom He died, will be the exact measure of our zeal in exposing the dangers by which men's souls are ensnared."

That the Revised Version of the New Testament is based

upon a new, uncalled for, and unsound Greek text — that mainly of Drs. Westcott and Hort, which was printed simultaneously with the revision and never before had seen light and which is the most unreliable text perhaps ever printed — one English critic says, "the foulest and most vicious in existence."

In 1845 Dr. Tregelles, armed with a letter from Cardinal Wiseman, went to Rome with the design of seeing the manuscript, Codex Vaticanus. After much trouble Dr. Tregelles did see it. "Two prelates were detailed to watch him, and they would not let him open the volume without previously searching his pockets and taking away from him ink and paper. Any prolonged study of a certain passage was the signal for snatching the book hurriedly away. He made some notes upon his cuffs and fingernails."

In 1867 Tischendorf, by permission of Cardinal Antonelli, undertook to study this same Vatican Codex. He had nearly finished three Gospels when his efforts to transcribe them were discovered by a Prussian Jesuit spy. The book was immediately taken away. It was restored again, months later, by the intervention of Vercellone for a few hours. In all Tischendorf had the manuscript before him forty-two hours and only three hours at any one time, and all but a few of those hours were spent on the Gospels; and yet, he says, "I succeeded in preparing the whole New Testament for a new and reliable edition, so as to obtain every desired result." Every desired result in forty-two hours — all but two or three of them spent on the Gospels alone! Every desired result in three hours' hurried glancing through 146 pages of old and stained and mutilated manuscript written on very thin vellum, in faded ink, with its letters throughout large portions touched and re-touched, bearing marks of a very peculiar treatment of the Epistles of St. Paul, and confessed to have received some corrections from the first and the filling up of certain blank spaces from the beginning!

Codex B, the Vaticanus manuscript, must be the purest because of *omissions!* We have cut things down to the bone. To criticize is to cut. Whatever manuscript adds anything, the Vatican *does not*. Retrenchment, not contribution, is her forte. The manuscript which *omits* most, which has least of God's Word, is the best because the least clogged with extraneous matter! See Westcott and Hort, Introduction, page 235. Let me quote: "The nearer the document stands to the autograph the more numerous must be the omissions laid to its charge."

Omissions are what may be expected from Rome — Rome has had every opportunity to make the omissions — to tear off, for instance Hebrews 9 to 13 — and all the omissions are straight in her line.

The principle laid down is nonsense. Take Israel in the captivity. The ark was gone — Aaron's rod was gone — the pot of manna was gone — the tabernacle curtains were gone. These things had been left in the path of *bad progress!* — first the curtains, then the pot of manna, then Aaron's rod, then the ark — relics of their apostasy all the way down! History is against Drs. Westcott and Hort. The further back you go, if you go rightly, the *more you get* of any single document or ordinance given and settled of God.

Grant the principle, "the more numerous the omissions the purer, until you get back to the Vatican manuscript." By that time you have cut out four and a half whole books. But you have three or four more conjectural manuscripts back of the Vatican — three or four links. Cut out three or four books at each link, and what will you have left when you get back to Peter and Paul!

Against all this we oppose, and firmly and steadily, the principle of the old translators. "External, prima-facie evidence is after all the best guide." Call in all your manuscripts, all your data — uncials, cursives, versions, fathers — and that reading carries which brings the highest evidence, from numbers, from weight, from congruity with the rest of the Scriptures, and from the open and manifest mind of the Spirit of God.

We take the ground that *on the original parchment* every word, line, point, and jot and tittle was put there by God. Every sacred writing, every word as it went down on the primeval autograph was God-breathed. You breathe your breath on a glass; it congeals. So God breathed originally, Divinely, out of Himself and through Moses, through St. Paul, as through a bending and elastic tube upon the sacred page.

And every scrap or relic of that original writing found anywhere in the world (and God in spite of men will take care of it all) will shine wherever you find it by native irradiation, by light convincing, overwhelming and complete in glory all Divine. We do not say every "conjectural emendation" will so shine — in the transmission of God's Word is no room for "conjectural emendation" — but every *honest writing* will so shine. We take the ground, the Sun needs no critic. When he shines, he shines the Sun — and so each word of God. We take the open ground that a single stray leaf of God's Word found by the wayside by a pure savage — let it be the eighth chapter of John for instance — that this single stray leaf will so speak to that savage, if he can read it, that if he never heard or saw one syllable of the Bible before, that single leaf will shine all over to him, cry out "God!" and condemn him. That is our doctrine, and *that,* the New Departure, led in by Drs. Westcott and Hort, and their principle in the Revision, weakens not only, but kills and destroys.

The Revised Version weakens and removes the Deity of Christ in many places — one I mention in particular. I Timothy 3:16, "Great is the mystery of *godliness,* God was manifest in the flesh." The Revised Version leaves out *Theos,* God, and renders it "Great is the mystery of *godliness, He who* was manifest in the flesh" — i.e., the manifested One was only *one phase* — the highest — of godliness, the precise rendering for which all the unitarians have been contending the last 1800 years. Codex "A" of the British Museum makes it, according to all testimony of 300 years, *Theos.* Dr. Scrivener, the foremost English critic, says it is *Theos.* He says his senses report it *Theos.* I quote him. "I have examined it twenty times within as many years and seeing (as every man must do for himself) with my own eyes, I have always felt convinced that Codex 'A' reads *Theos.*" That conviction of Dr. Scrivener is my conviction and on the very same grounds — a conviction so deep that I will never yield it, nor admit as a test of my faith a Book pretending to be a Revelation from God which leaves that word out. The Holy Ghost has written it — let no man dare touch it — "Great is the mystery of godliness, *God* was manifest in the flesh."

"Oh, but it is only one word!" Yes, but one word of Scripture of which it is said "Thou hast magnified Thy Word above all Thy Name!" "Only one word!" But that word "God." Better the whole living church of God should perish than that that one word should perish. "If any man take away from the words of the book of this prophecy God shall take away his part." Let criticism pause. The principle at stake is solemn.

The point at issue in the whole controversy with "modern criticism" is, whether the Bible can be placed upon the same plane with other, merely human, literature and treated accordingly; or whether, as a Divine Revelation, it addresses us with a command and sanction? The power of the Book is shaken from the moment we deny its *a priori* binding claim on our belief and obedience. The Book is a royal document, or series of documents issued by the King of kings, and binding upon every subject. The Book, then, is to be received with reverence by one who falls upon his bended knees beneath the only shaft of light which, from unknown eternity, brings to the soul the certainties of God — of His dealings in grace with men, and of a judgment. The Old Testament is — in some sense — more awful than the New — as it begins with a creation out of nothing — as it thunders from Sinai, and as it prefigures and predicts the momentous facts of Calvary and the Apocalypse. But it has been represented that the Bible has twisted itself up like a worm from the dust by an Evolution in which the human element is most conspicuous.

Grant that a human element is in the Old Testament, who can determine how far that element extends? No one. Grant that something has been found out about the Bible, within the last fifty years, that makes it less reliable — less inerrant, in plain English, less free from mistakes than it was — in some ways, a book that is under *suspicion,* and the result is that the mind is unsettled. Grant this, and then grant that the story of the Fall itself, on which St. Paul grounds all his theology, is but a myth — or as Westcott and Bishop Temple — not to speak of pronounced heresiarchs — put it, an *allegory* covering a long succession of evolutions which had done their work, in forming man such as he is, before the narrative begins — Grant these things and what becomes of the awful impress of responsibility laid on the conscience by the Sacred Volume? What becomes of the tremendous parallel between the First and Second Adam on which is built the covenant of grace?

There is no reason, and there can be none, why God, who has made man in His own image and capable of communion with Himself, should not speak to man and, having taught him letters, *write* to man, in other words, to put His communication in permanent form. The man who denies the supernatural is one who contradicts his own limitations. Either *he* is the universe, or there is something outside of him. Either *he* is his own god or there is a God above him. The inspiration of the Old Testament including that of the whole Bible, is a matter, first of all, of pure Divine testimony, which leaves us nothing but to receive it. God says, "I am speaking." That ends it. The instant order of the Book to every reader is "Believe or die!" The Book brings with it its authentication. Who would think of standing up under the broad blaze of the noonday sun to deny the existence of the sun? His shining is his authentication.

The Jews cherished the highest awe and veneration for their sacred writings which they regarded as the "Oracles of God." They maintained that God had more care of the letters and syllables of the Law than of the stars of heaven, and that upon each tittle of it, mountains of doctrine hung. For this reason every individual letter was numbered by them and account kept of how often it occurred. In the transcription of an authorized synagogue manuscript, rules were enforced of the minutest character. The copyist must write with a particular ink, on a particular parchment. He must write in so many columns, of such a size, and containing just so many lines and words. No word to be written without previously looking at the original. The copy, when completed, must be examined and compared within thirty days; if four errors were found on one parchment, the examination went no farther — the whole was rejected. When worn out, the rolls were officially and solemnly burned lest the Scripture might fall into profane hands or into fragments.

The Old Testament, precisely as we have it, was endorsed by Jesus Christ, the Son of God. When He appeared on the earth, 1500 years after Moses, the first of the prophets, and 400 years after Malachi, the last of them, He bore open testimony to the sacred canon as held by the Jews of His time. Nor did He — among all the evils which He charged upon His countrymen — ever intimate that they had, in any degree, corrupted the canon, either by addition, diminution, or alteration of any kind. By referring to the "Scriptures," which He declared "cannot be broken," the Lord Jesus Christ has given His full attestation to all and every one of the books of the Old Testament as the unadulterated Word of God.

Our Blessed Lord puts "what is written" equal to His own declaration. He saw the Old Testament inspired from one end to the other, divine from one end to the other. Ah! how He valued the sacred text! Our modern critics, with arrogance which rises to daring impiety, deny to Christ the insight which they claim for themselves. The point right here is this, Did Jesus fundamentally misconceive the character of the Old Testament? Did He take for a created and immediate revelation what was of a slow and ordinary growth? Or was He *dishonest,* and did He make about Abraham, for example, statements and representations which belong only to a geographical myth — a personality which never existed?

The authority of Jesus Christ, God speaking — not from heaven only, but with human lips — has given a sanction to every book and sentence in the Jewish canon, and blasphemy is written on the forehead of any theory which alleges imperfection, error, contradiction, or sin in any book in the sacred collection. The Old Testament was our Lord's only study book. On it His spiritual life was nurtured. In all His life it was His only reference. Through His apostles He reaffirmed it. Five hundred and four (504) times is the Old Testament quoted in the New. The whole Jewish nation, down to this day, acknowledge, *without one dissenting voice,* the genuineness of the Old Testament. The Book reflects upon them and condemns them; it also goes to build up Christianity, a system which they hate, and yet, impressed with an unalterable conviction of their divine origin, they have, at the expense of everything dear to man, clung to the Old Testament Scriptures.

All churches, everywhere and always, and with one accord, declare the Bible in both Testaments to be the foundation of their creed. All the fathers, Melito, Origen, Cyril, Athanasius, in their lists include the whole thirty-nine books. The Council of Laodicea, held in the year 363, names and confirms them. A while ago an effort was made to discredit Jonah as fable, but it was found that the Deity of Christ went down with Jonah, that the linchpin between the Testaments fell out with Jonah, and the mass of evidence in favor of the book became so overwhelming that its doughty opponents beat a hasty and cowardly retreat into apology, retraction, and silence.

The Old Testament is inspired from end to end. What do we mean by this? We mean infallibility and perfection. We mean that the books are of absolute authority, demanding an unlimited submission. We mean that Genesis is as literally the Word of God as are the Gospels — Joshua as is the Acts — Proverbs as are the Epistles — the Song of Solomon as is the Revelation. We mean that the *writings* were inspired. Nothing is said in the Bible about the inspiration of the *writers.* It is of small importance to us who wrote Ruth. It is of *every* importance that Ruth was *written by God.* How did God write? On Sinai, He wrote, we are told, with His finger. We are told this in seven different places. God used men with different degrees of style. He made Amos write like a herdsman and David like a poet. He made the difference, provided for it, and employed it because He would have variety and adapt Himself to all classes and ages.

He wrote *through* the men. How did He do this? I do

114

not know. The fact, I know, for I am told it. The secret is His own. I read that "holy men of old spake as they were moved" — then they did not choose their own language. I do not know how the electric fluid writes letters on a strip of paper. I do not know how my soul dictates to and controls my body so that the moving of my fingertips is the action of my soul. I do not know how, in regeneration, God does all and I do all. He produces all and I act all, for what He produces is my act.

"But there are discrepancies — contradictions." No! Scores of times I have corrected myself, but never God's Word. Patience and a larger knowledge will solve every knot. Dr. Hodge, of Princeton, says: "Not one single instance of a discrepancy in Scripture has ever been proved." Would all the united wisdom of men have led them to relate the history of the creation of the universe in a single chapter, and that of the erection of the tabernacle in thirteen? The description of the great edifice of the world, would it not seem to require more words than that of a small tent?

To discredit the statement repeated in almost every chapter of Exodus and Leviticus — "And the Lord said to Moses." "As the Lord commanded Moses." To charge Christ with falsehood, who says, "Moses said," "Moses taught you," "David says" — quoting as He does not from the 7th and the 18th only, but from the 41st, the 110th, the 118th, and other Psalms. The result is to disintegrate the Bible and throw it into heaps of confusion mingled with rubbish — to shake faith to the very foundations and scatter Revelation to the winds. It is to elevate Robertson Smith, Wellhausen, Baur, Astruc, Cheyne, and other heretics, who seem to have taken God into their own hands, to a level with the Saviour of men and His prophets, whom they criticize freely. This is not exegesis, it is conspiracy. It is not contribution to religious knowledge, it is *crime!*

Think of the amazing, the stupendous difference between Christ quoting from a human compilation, or from the living Oracles of God! "I came not to destroy," He says, "but to fulfil" — to fulfil what? A haphazard collection of Ezra's time — made up of fragmentary documents of men, some of whom had an inspiration little above that of Browning and Tennyson! Had we the Old Testament alone it would be sufficient to save us. I myself was converted on that very part of Isaiah which the critics say he did not write. Men have been converted by the millions and are now in heaven who never knew anything but the Old Testament. They found God in it, and so may you and so may I. The Old Testament throws a light upon Christ and upon the whole Christian system without which the New Testament could not be understood. Atonement looms in Abel's altar and runs on to the Great Substitute to be stricken for His people, upon whom the Lord hath laid the iniquity of us all. "The life of the flesh is in the blood," says Leviticus, "and I have given it to you upon the altar to make an atonement for the soul — for it is the blood that maketh an atonement for the soul." Blood drips from each page of the Old Testament. Each letter stars crimson. What is all this, if not Christ? The Old Testament is the dictionary and key to the New. If *with* the Old Testament and without Christ we were helpless, equally — *without* the Old Testament and with Christ — we should be helpless. I beseech you, therefore, Brethren, beware of what is called "the modern school."

"In the beginning, God created the heavens and the earth!" Here are the Pillars of Hercules through which we pass from Time with all its changes into Eternity — a shoreless, changeless sea. Here are the frontiers of human exploration, beyond which rolls and surges the illimitable Ocean of Deity, self-existent, blessed forever and independent of all creatures.

The first utterance of the Bible fixes it that matter is not eternal. That there was a point when the universe was not and when God, by simple fiat, brought it into being. So that, as the apostle says, He called the existent out of the non-existent — the visible from that which had no visibility. In other words, God made the world out of nothing — an awful nothing — the idea of which we cannot comprehend. A lonely and a solitary Worker, out of emptiness, He created fullness — out of what was not, all things — getting from Himself the substance as well as the shaping — the fact as well as the how.

"In the beginning, God created the heavens and the earth." *He* had to tell us that, for He *only* was there. He had to *tell* us that, but — being told, we, at once, believe it, for everything outside the Self-existent must have a beginning. Matter must have had a beginning, for — push its molecules back as far as you will, either matter was the egg out of which God was hatched or God hatched matter. Can there be any question as to which of these is true? "In the beginning, God created the heavens and the earth." If this first sentence is unauthentic, the whole Bible is untrue and for six thousand years men have been duped and deluded who have loved and cherished its teachings. The credibility of the Bible, then, depends upon the truth of the First Chapter of Genesis. If that chapter contains "a few small scientific lies," then the Book is a compilation of deceptions from cover to cover. Thus we are either Christians or skeptics! It has been claimed that no essential injury is done to Christian faith by concessions made to modern criticism — that if one believes in redemption, it is of small account what he believes of creation. But men who speak so rashly, overlook the fact that creation is the basis of redemption — that there must be man and man *fallen* before there can be man *saved* — and that the belief in creation depends entirely upon the acknowledgment of Genesis, as a historical document.

The difficulty with Higher Criticism is that it disbelieves in advance and the reason of this too frequently is that it is working with a brain whose crooked and vapid conclusions are guided by a heart averse to God — at enmity with God and working every way to get rid of Him.

THE BIBLE AND MODERN CRITICISM

Sir Robert Anderson

The following extracts are taken from the book by the same title, by Sir Robert Anderson.

. . . the extreme reverence with which the Jews regarded their Scriptures affords a powerful guarantee against any deliberate corruption of the text. It may be taken as certain that any errors which have crept in are errors accidentally made in copying the manuscripts. And when estimating the number and, what is of more importance, the character of such errors, the Jewish reverence for the text claims very special consideration. For it insured such care in copying as to make any blunder of a really serious kind improbable in the extreme.

We know, for example, that in the days of the Masoretes, to whom we practically owe our text of the Old Testament, not only the words, but the very letters, contained in the sacred books were counted. And we know also that even when words were believed to have been erroneously inserted or omitted, the scribes never dared to make a correction save by a marginal note. And there is no reason to doubt that these practices were based on the habits and traditions of earlier days.

Hostile critics have sometimes sought to score a point by appealing to the Samaritan Pentateuch and the Septuagint version. But not even a hostile critic would deny that if the Masoretic text were revised in the light of those authorities, the result would be prejudicial to accuracy; and, further, that even if the revision were drastic and reckless, it would not affect a single question of morals or a single point of Christian truth or doctrine. And this being so, the whole question, so far as the Old Testament is concerned, is one of purely academic interest.

And a kindred remark applies equally in regard to the New Testament. A fact which is all the more striking and important because the materials for hostile criticism here are vastly greater than in the case of the Old Testament. All our leading commentators have grappled with the question. As it has been well said, "All of them face that formidable phantom of textual criticism, with its 120,000 various readings in the New Testament alone, and will enable us to march up to it, and discover that it is empty air; that still we may say with the boldest and acutest of English critics, Bentley, 'choose (out of the whole MSS) as awkwardly as you will, choose the worst by design out of the whole lump of readings, and not one article of faith or moral precept is either perverted or lost in them. Put them into the hands of a knave or a fool, and even with the most sinistrous and absurd choice, he shall not extinguish the light of any one chapter, or so disguise Christianity but that every feature of it will still be the same.' "

These words have since received most striking confirmation. In the Revised Version of the New Testament, textual criticism has done its worst. It is inconceivable that it will ever again be allowed to run riot as in the work of the Revisers of 1881. When that version appeared, Bishop Wordsworth of Lincoln raised the question "whether the Church of England — which in her Synod, so far as this Province is concerned, sanctioned a Revision of her Authorized Version *under the express condition,* which she most wisely imposed, that no changes *should be made in it except what were absolutely necessary* — could consistently accept a version in which 36,000 changes have been made; *not a fiftieth of which can be shown to be needed, or even desirable.*"

But what concerns us here is not the changes in the translation, but the far more serious matter of the changes in the *text*. The question at issue between the majority of the Revisers, who followed Doctors Hort and Westcott, and the very able and weighty minority led by Dr. Scrivener, the most capable and eminent "textual critic" of the whole company, was one with which every lawyer is familiar, but of which the Revisers may have had no experience, and with which they were not competent to deal.

We have a far greater number of MSS of the New Testament than of the heathen classics; but, strange to say, with four exceptions, none of these are older than the sixth century of. our era. But we possess "versions" (or translations) which are older than any known MSS; and the writings of the early Fathers abound in quotations from the New Testament. We are thus enabled indirectly to reach MSS much older than the oldest that have survived. And as the Fathers were scattered over the Christendom of their time, their acquaintance with the text was derived, of course, from very many independent sources. And when their quotations agree with one another, and also with the "versions," as well as with our later MSS, many of which must have been copied from MSS more ancient than any which have survived, this agreement will satisfy any one who is versed in the rudiments of the science of evidence.

But while the lawyer understands the value of indirect evidence, the layman is always inclined to disparage it in favor of the direct. Witnesses of credit and repute testify that they saw the accused commit the crime with which he is charged. What more can any one want? The average juryman is ready at once to convict; and he cannot imagine why the judge should allow further time to be spent upon the case. But the judge knows well that evidence of this kind is apt to err, and needs to be tested with the utmost care. Now the old MSS are the witnesses of credit and repute, and the Revisers played the part of the average juryman; and there being unfortunately no one to check them, they convicted the Authorized Version of inaccuracy in numberless instances. But, in the opinion of the greatest critical authority among the Revisers, whose protests were unavailing to prevent this deplorable mutilation of the sacred text, the system on which these changes were made "is entirely destitute of historical foundation."

If the Revisers had kept to the terms of their commission, and been content with the correction of "manifest errors," a very few sessions would have sufficed to produce a text which might have commanded universal acceptance. But it is certain that errors were not *manifest* when many of the greatest of contemporary critics and scholars could not regard them as errors at all — men like the minority upon their own company, men like the eminent prelate I have quoted, and the learned editor of *The Speaker's Commentary*. And as several of the Revisers themselves have explained in detail the principles on which the revision of the text was conducted, and those principles are found to be unsound when judged by the science of evidence, our confidence in the result of their labors is destroyed.

The "argument" of the present volume demands a reference to this question, but a fuller discussion of it would be out of place. I will therefore dismiss it by citing a single illustrative instance of reckless and erroneous alteration of the text. And instances of the kind abound, especially in the Gospels.

The instance I select is "the Herald Angels' song," and I choose it not only as being thoroughly typical of the methods of the Revisers, but also because of its importance and the interest attaching to it. "Glory to God in the highest, and on earth peace, good will toward men": for these words, which hold such a place in the memory and heart of every English-speaking Christian, the miserable substitute offered us is, "Glory to God in the highest, and on earth peace among men in whom He is well pleased." This one piece of mutilation might suffice to discredit the work of the Revisers.

Two questions are here involved, the altered text, and

the translation of that text. The English of the Revisers, says one of the most eminent of their own number, "can be arrived at only through some process which would make any phrase bear almost any meaning the translator might like to put upon it." " 'Men in whom He is well pleased,' " says the editor of *The Speaker's Commentary,* "seems to me impossible as a translation of their text. I do not know whether those Greek words have *any* meaning, but if they have they must designate men of a certain quality or character." Then, as regards the text, the whole difference is the addition of the letter *s* to the word *eudokia;* and the manuscript authority for this addition is the reading of four ancient Greek MSS, *every other known copy of the Gospels being against it.*

Now this is precisely the sort of question in respect of which any one who has practical acquaintance with the science of evidence would appeal to Patristic authority, and that appeal would dispose of the whole matter; for the testimony of the Greek Fathers in favor of the familiar reading is overwhelming.

"On earth peace, good will toward men" — the Christian may still rejoice in these hallowed and most precious words. And he may assume with confidence that here, as in so many other instances, the Revisers' changes in the text are new errors, and not the correction of old errors. And yet the fact remains — indeed it is universally acknowledged — that even a revision conducted so unwisely and on a system so opposed to all the principles and rules of evidence, has not destroyed a single truth of Christianity or left a single point of Christian doctrine or practice in jeopardy.

IN DEFENSE OF THE TEXTUS RECEPTUS —
THE BASIS OF THE KING JAMES VERSION

Selections by David Otis Fuller

Excerpts taken from two books, *The Traditional Text of the Holy Gospels* and *Causes of Corruption in the Traditional Text*, by the late John William Burgon, B.D., Dean of Chichester. Published by George Bell and Sons, Cambridge, England, 1896. (Dean Burgon has proved to be one of the greatest orthodox scholars of the last century or indeed of any century. He ranks on an equality with Tregelles, Tischendorf, Westcott and Hort, Griesbach, Lachmann and many others, if not surpassing them in some instances.)

Burgon speaks of the "pericope de adultera" (meaning the first 11 verses of John 8).

"But my experience as one who has given a considerable amount of attention to such subjects tells me that the narrative before us carries on its front the impress of divine origin. I venture to think it vindicates for itself a high, unearthly meaning. . . . the more I study it, the more I am pressed with its divinity.

"I contend that on all intelligent principles of sound criticism the passage before us must be maintained to be genuine scripture and that without a particle of doubt." Burgon requests the student to go to the British museum and ask for the 73 copies of John's Gospel, turn to the close of chapter 7 and in 61 copies you will find these verses 8:1-11. [Burgon took up the defense of these verses because of the many liberal critics who would eliminate them from the Gospel altogether, saying they were not of the original text.]

"Tischendorf's last two editions of the four gospels in the Greek text differ from one another in no less than 3,572 particulars. He reverses in every page in 1872 what in 1859 he offered as the result of his deliberate judgment."

Continuing on this theme of John 8:1-11 Burgon says: "Hort's theory involves too much violation of principles generally received and is too devoid of anything like proof ever to win universal acceptance — It stands in sharp antagonism to the judgment passed by the church all down the ages and in many respects does not accord with the teaching of the most celebrated critics of the century who preceded him.

"I request that apart from proof of some sort it shall not be taken for granted that a copy of the New Testament written in the fourth or fifth century will exhibit a more trustworthy text than one written in the 11th or 12th century."

Page 11 — "There exists no reason for supposing that the divine agent who in the first instance thus gave to mankind the scriptures of truth and straightway abdicated his office, took no further care of his work, abandoned these precious writings to their fate."

Page 16 — "There can be no science of textual criticism, I repeat — and therefore no security for the inspired Word — so long as the subjective judgment, which may easily degenerate into individual caprice, is allowed ever to determine which readings shall be rejected, which retained."

"Strange as it may appear, it is undeniably true, that the whole of the controversy may be reduced to the following narrow issue: Does the truth of the text of Scripture dwell with the vast multitude of copies, uncial and cursive, concerning which nothing is more remarkable than the marvelous agreement which subsists between them? Or is it rather to be supposed that the truth abides exclusively with a very little handful of manuscripts, which at once differ from the great bulk of the witnesses, and — strange to say — also amongst themselves."

Page 20 — "Every fresh discovery of the beauty and preciousness of the Deposit in its essential structure does but serve to deepen the conviction that a marvelous provision must needs have been made in God's eternal counsels for the effectual conservation of the inspired text."

Page 22 — "The practice of reading Scripture aloud before the congregation — a practice which is observed to have prevailed from the apostolic age — has resulted in the increased security of the Deposit. The ear once thoroughly familiarized with the words of Scripture is observed to resent the slightest departure from the established type."

Prebendary Scrivener, another great scholar, is quoted by Burgon as follows: "It is no less true to fact than paradoxical in sound that the worst corruptions to which the New Testament has ever been subjected originated within one hundred years after it was composed — that Irenaeus and the African fathers and the whole western with a portion of the Syriac church used far inferior manuscripts to those employed by Stunica or Erasmus or Stevens thirteen centuries later when molding the Textus Receptus." "Therefore, [Burgon] antiquity alone affords no security that the manuscript in our hands is not infected with the corruption which sprang up largely in the first and second centuries."

"That witnesses are to be weighed — not counted — is a maxim of which we hear constantly. It may be said to embody much fundamental fallacy. It assumes that the witnesses we possess are capable of being weighed and that every critic is competent to weigh them, neither of which proposition is true. Number is the most ordinary ingredient of weight. If ten witnesses are called into court and nine give the same account while one contradicts the other nine, which will be accepted? The nine, of course. 63 uncials — 737 cursive — 413 lectionaries are known to survive of the gospels alone. By what process of reasoning can it be thought credible that the few witnesses shall prove the trustworthy guide and the many witnesses the deceivers.

"It is doubtless inconvenient to find some 1490 witnesses contravening some 10 or, if you will, 20 favorites, but truth is imperative and knows nothing of the inconvenience or convenience of critics.

"When, therefore, the great bulk of the witnesses — in proportion suppose of 100 or even 50 to 1 — yield unfaltering testimony to a certain reading; and the remaining little handful of authorities while advocating a different reading are yet observed to be unable to agree among themselves as to what that different reading shall precisely be, then that other reading concerning which all that discrepancy of detail is observed to exist may be regarded as certainly false.

"It is pretended that what is found in either B (Codex Vaticanus) or in Aleph (Codex Sinaiticus) or in D (Bezae) although unsupported by any other manuscript may reasonably be claimed to exhibit the truth of the scripture in defiance of the combined evidence of all other documents to the contrary.

"Let a reading be advocated by B and Aleph in conjunction, and it is assumed as a matter of course that such evidence must needs outweigh the combined evidence of all other manuscripts which can be named. I insist that readings so supported are clearly untrustworthy and may be discussed as certainly unauthentic."

Page 74 — "I have cited upon the last twelve verses of Mark no less than twelve authorities before the end of the third century, that is down to a date which is nearly half a century before Codex B and Aleph appeared. The general mass of quotations found in the books of the early fathers witnesses to what I say. So that there is absolutely no reason to place these two manuscripts upon a pedestal by themselves on the score of supreme antiquity. They are eclipsed in this respect by many other authorities older than they are."

Page 75 — "I insist and am prepared to prove that the

text of these two Codexes (B and Aleph) is very nearly the foulest in existence.

"On the other side (favoring the last twelve verses of Mark) I have referred to six witnesses of the second century, six of the third, fifteen of the fourth, nine of the fifth, eight of the sixth, and six of the seventh, all the other uncials and all the other cursives including the universal and immemorial liturgical use.

"Here as you must see B and Aleph in faltering tones and with an insignificant following are met by an array of authorities which is triumphantly superior, not only in antiquity, but in number, variety, and continuity.

"In point of hard and unmistakable fact there is a continual conflict going on all through the gospels between B and Aleph and a few adherents of theirs on the one side and the bulk of the authorities on the other. The nature and weight of these two Codexes may be inferred from it. They will be found to have been proved over and over again to be bad witnesses, who were left to survive in their handsome dresses while attention was hardly ever accorded to any services of theirs.

"Fifteen centuries, in which the art of copying the Bible was brought to perfection, and printing invented, have by unceasing rejection of their claims sealed forever the condemnation of their character and so detracted from their weight."

Page 78 — "Codex B is discovered not to contain in the gospels alone 237 words, 452 clauses, 748 whole sentences, which the later copies are observed to exhibit in the same places and in the same words. By what possible hypothesis will such a correspondence of the copies be accounted for if these words, clauses, and sentences are indeed, as is pretended, nothing else but spurious accretions to the text?"

Page 79 — "Such recensions never occurred. There is not a trace of them in history. It is a mere dream of Dr. Hort. They must be 'phantom recensions,' as Dr. Scrivener terms them."

Page 84 — "Let me next remind you of a remarkable instance of this inconsistency which I have already described in my book on 'The Revision Revised.' The five Old Uncials (Aleph, A, B, C, D) falsify the Lord's Prayer as given by St. Luke in no less than forty-five words.

"But so little do they agree among themselves that they throw themselves into six different combinations in their departures from the traditional text; and yet they are never able to agree among themselves as to one single variant reading: while only once are more than two of them observed to stand together, and their grand point of union is no less than an omission of the article. I should weary you, my dear student, if I were to take you through all the evidence which I could amass upon this disagreement with one another."

Page 88 — "B and Aleph are covered all over with blots — Aleph even more than B. How could they ever have gained the characters which have been given them, is passing strange. But even great scholars are human [he refers to Westcott and Hort, Tregelles and Tischendorf] and have their prejudices and other weaknesses, and their disciples follow them everywhere submissively as sheep — If men of ordinary acquirements in scholarship would only emancipate themselves and judge with their own eyes, they would soon see the truth of what I say."

Page 89 — "My leading principle is to build solely upon facts — upon real, not fancied facts — not upon a few favorite facts, but upon all that are connected with the question under consideration."

Page 90 — Dr. Miller, speaking of Dr. Hort: "It is to his arguments sifted logically, to the judgment exercised by him upon texts and readings, upon manuscripts and versions and fathers, and to his collisions with the record of history, that a higher duty than appreciation of a theologian however learned and pious compels us to demur."

Page 93 — "Above all, did he [Dr. Hort] fancy, and do his followers imagine, that the Holy Ghost who inspired the New Testament could have let the true text of it drop into obscurity during fifteen centuries of its life (which Dr. Hort implies) and that a deep and wide and full investigation (which by their premises they will not admit) must issue in the proof that under His care the Word of God has been preserved all through the ages in due integrity? This admission alone when stripped of its disguise, is plainly fatal to Dr. Hort's theory.

"Again, in order to prop up his contention, Dr. Hort is obliged to conjure up the shadows of two or three 'phantom revisions' of which no recorded evidence exists. But Dr. Hort, as soon as he found that he could not maintain his ground with history as it was, instead of taking back his theory and altering it to square with facts, tampered with historical facts in order to make them agree with his theory."

Page 116 — "As far as the fathers who died before 400 A.D. are concerned, the question may now be put and answered. Do they witness to the traditional text as existing from the first or do they not? The results of the evidence, both as regards the quantity and the quality of the testimony, enable us to reply not only that the traditional text was in existence, but that it was predominant during the period under review."

Page 117 — "Besides establishing the antiquity of the traditional text, the quotations in the early fathers reveal the streams of corruption which prevailed in the first ages, till they were washed away by the vast current of the transmission of the text of the gospels."

Page 121 — "The original predominance of the traditional text is shown in the list given of the earliest fathers. Their record proves that in their writings, and so in the church generally, corruption had made itself felt in the earliest times, but that the pure waters generally prevailed.

"Not the slightest confirmation is given to Dr. Hort's notion that a revision or recension was definitely accomplished at Antioch in the middle of the fourth century. There was a gradual improvement as the traditional text gradually established itself against the forward and persistent intrusion of corruption."

Page 125 — "Dr. Hort was perfectly logical when he suggested or rather asserted dogmatically that such a drastic revision as was necessary for turning the Curetonian into the Peshitto was made in the third century at Edessa or Nisibis. The difficulty lay in his manufacturing history to suit his purpose instead of following it. The Curetonian must have been an adulteration of the Peshitto or it must have been partly an independent translation helped from other sources: from the character of the text it could not have given rise to it."

Page 130 — "It is well known that the Peshitto is mainly in agreement with the traditional text. What therefore proves one, virtually proves the order. If, as Dr. Hort admits, the traditional text prevailed at Antioch from the middle of the fourth century, is it not more probable that it should have been the continuance of the text from the earliest times, than that a change should have been made without a record in history, and that in a part of the world which has been always alien to change?"

Page 159 — "Codex B was early enthroned on something like speculation, and has been maintained upon the throne by what has strangely amounted to a positive superstition.

"It was perhaps to be expected that human infirmity should have influenced Tischendorf in his treatment of the treasure-trove (Codex Aleph) by him: though his character for judgment could not but be seriously injured by the fact that in his eighth edition he altered the mature conclusions of his seventh edition in no less than 3572 instances, chiefly on account of the readings in his beloved Sinaitic guide."

Page 160 — "The fact is that B and Aleph were the products of the school of philosophy and teaching which found its vent in Semi-Arian or Homoean opinions. It is a circumstance that cannot fail to give rise to suspicion that the Vatican and Sinaitic manuscripts (B and Aleph) had their origin under a predominant influence of such evil fame."

Page 219 — "With the blindness proverbially ascribed to parental love, Tischendorf follows Aleph, though the carelessness that reigns over that manuscript is visible to all who examine it."

Page 238 — "We oppose facts to their [Westcott and Hort] speculation. They weave ingenious webs, and invent subtle theories, because their paradox of a few against the many requires ingenuity and subtlety for its support.

"We are nothing if we are not grounded in facts: our appeal is to facts, our test lies in facts, so far as we can build testimonies upon testimonies and facts upon facts.

"Our opponents are gradually getting out of date. Thousands of manuscripts have been added to the known stores since Tischendorf formed his system and Hort began to theorize."

Page 240 — Luke 24:42 ". . . a piece of a broiled fish, *and of an honeycomb.*" Four last words not found in six copies of the gospel. Westcott and Hort reject them. Revisers of 1881 persuaded by Westcott and Hort to exclude them also.

Page 246 — "Upon us, the only effect produced by the sight of half a dozen Evangelia — whether written in the uncial or in the cursive character we deem a matter of small account, — opposing themselves to the whole body of the copies, uncial and cursive alike, is simply to make us suspicious of these six Evangelia. We must answer those distinguished critics who have ruled that Codexes B and Aleph, D, and L, can hardly if ever err."

Page 259 — "The eternal Godhead of Christ was the mark at which, in the earliest age of all, Satan persistently aimed his most envenomed shafts. Matthew 19:16-17. This place was eagerly fastened on by the enemies of the gospel — the most illustrious of the fathers sought to vindicate this divine utterance — certain of the orthodox with the best intentions, doubtless, but with misguided zeal in order to counteract the precious teaching which the enemies of Christianity elicited from this place of scripture deliberately falsified the inspired record. They turned our Lord's reply 'Why callest thou me good?' in the first gospel into this 'Why askest thou me concerning good?'

"The four uncial Codexes (B, Aleph, D, L) omit the epithet 'good' in 'good master,' but good (agathe) is found in the nearly 30 sources named including a number of the fathers so that at the end of 1700 years six witnesses of the second century, three of the third, fourteen of the fourth, four of the fifth, two of the sixth, come back from all parts of Christendom to denounce the liberty taken by the ancients and to witness to the genuineness of the traditional text."

Page 272 — "The Church in her corporate capacity has been careful all down the ages that the genuine reading shall be rehearsed in every assembly of the faithful — and behold, at this hour it is attested by every copy in the world except that little handful of fabricated documents which it has been the craze of the last fifty years to cry up as the only authentic witnesses to the truth of scripture; namely, Codexes B, Aleph, D, L, and Origen.

"Dr. Scrivener has pronounced that [B and Aleph] subsequent investigations have brought to light so close a relation as to render it impossible to regard them as independent witnesses; while every page of the gospel bears emphatic witness to the fact that Codexes B, Aleph, D, and L are, as has been said, the depositories of a hopelessly depraved text."

Page 279 — "Mark 1:17 the beginning of the gospel of Jesus Christ, *the Son of God.* It has of late become the fashion to call in question the clause 'Huios Tou Theou.' Westcott and Hort shut up the words in brackets. Tischendorf ejects them from the text. The revisers brand them with suspicion. Surely, if there be a clause in the gospel which carries on its front the evidence of its genuineness, it is this. Irenaeus (A.D. 170) unquestionably read Huios Tou Theou in this place. He devotes a chapter of his great work to the proof that Jesus is the Christ, very God as well as very man."

In summary, you might say that if the honest student will continue to read more of the works of John W. Burgon, he will find him to be one of the greatest scholars and linguists that the church of Jesus Christ has produced. His book *The Last Twelve Verses of the Gospel of Mark* is a masterpiece. Another one, *The Revision Revised.* The former is in print — the latter is out of print and has been for many years. Whatever the reader of these extracts can secure of the writings of Burgon, by all means, do so. He was a genius and we believe raised up of God at that particular time to stand against the critics who were seeking to bring into disrepute the traditional text which God in His marvelous providence has kept intact through the ages. The whole question may be summarized in this statement: If you and I believe that the original writings of the Scriptures were verbally inspired by God, then of necessity they must have been providentially preserved through the ages. That being the case, the next question is, which of the versions is the closest to the original writings? Without hesitation, we say that the King James Version is nearer to the original autographs than any other version in the English language.

CODEX VATICANUS AND ITS ALLIES

Herman C. Hoskier
Introduction by David Otis Fuller

The following extracts were taken from a book entitled *Codex B and Its Allies — A Study and an Indictment*, by Herman C. Hoskier. This distinguished scholar marshalled a vast amount of convincing documentary evidence in a volume of nearly 500 pages demonstrating the unreliability of the group of manuscripts headed by the Codex Vaticanus and Codex Sinaiticus, which were held in such high esteem by Professors Westcott and Hort, and other nineteenth century textual critics and revisers.

It is high time that the bubble of Codex B should be pricked. It had not occurred to me to write what follows until recently. I had thought that time would cure the extraordinary Hortian heresy, but when I found that after a silence of twenty years my suggestion that Hort's theories were disallowed today only provoked a denial from a scholar and a critic who has himself disavowed a considerable part of the readings favored by Hort, it seemed time to write a consecutive account of the crooked path pursued by the manuscript B, which — from ignorance I know — most people still confuse with purity and "neutrality."

I proceed to "name" the aforesaid scholar, since he has challenged me. Dr. A. Souter began a review of my "Genesis of the Versions" by saying that — "It is the business of a critic first to destroy his enemy's position before he seeks to build up his own."

He ended by expressing gratitude for my collations of manuscripts as such, but added some very strong advice to hold my tongue as regarded commenting on the evidence so painfully accumulated, which he and others would use — but which I must not use or discuss. He said: "We cannot afford to do without his valuable cooperation in New Testament textual criticism, but would suggest that he confine his energies to the collection and accurate presentation of material, and leave theorizing to others, at least meantime."

I refuse to be bound by such advice. I demand a fair hearing on a subject very near to my heart, and with which by close attention for many years I have tried to make myself sufficiently acquainted to be able and qualified to discuss it with those few who have pursued a parallel course of study.

I present therefore an indictment against the manuscript B (Vaticanus) and against Westcott and Hort, subdivided into hundreds of separate counts. I do not believe that the jurymen who will ultimately render a verdict have ever had the matter presented to them formally, legally, and in proper detail.

Dr. Souter has said that "it is the business of a critic first to destroy his enemy's position," but I beg to observe that the enemy, under deepest cover of night, has already abandoned several important positions. And there is such a thing as a flanking movement which compels retirement or surrender without striking a more direct blow in front. Thirty years and more have been allowed for them to retire in good order. If the finale is to be a rout it is not owing to lack of patience on the part of the other side. But it will be owing to apathy, to unfaithfulness, to pride, to incomplete examination of documentary evidence, and to an overweening haste to establish the "true" text without due regard to scientific foundations.

My thesis is then that it was B (Vaticanus) and Aleph (Sinaiticus) and their forerunners with Origen who revised the "Antioch" text.[1] And that, although there is an older base than either of these groups, the "Antioch" text is purer in many respects, if not "better," and is nearer the original base than much of that in vogue in Egypt.

The text of Westcott and Hort is practically the text of Aleph and B. The Old Syriac sometimes supports the true text of the Aleph and B family, where Aleph singly or B singly deserts the family to side with a later variation; is it not therefore possible, and indeed likely, that in some instances Aleph and B may both have deserted the reading which they ought to have followed, and that *they* and not the Old Syriac are inconsistent? That Aleph and B occasionally (over 3,000 real differences between Aleph and B are recorded in the Gospels alone!) are inconsistent with themselves appears certain in several places. Carefully as B is written, now and again it presents an ungrammatical reading, which proves on examination to be the fragment of a rival variant.

I suppose that it will readily be conceded that C. H. Turner is without question the most brilliant writer on Textual Criticism today. It is always a pleasure to read him, and to be carried along in his racy and well-balanced style, which shows large mastery of the historical side of the problem as far as we have gathered it today. But there are certain weak points in his argument.

On pages 183 and 184 he says: "Hort was the last and perhaps the ablest of a long line of editors of the Greek Testament, commencing in the eighteenth century, who very tentatively at first, but quite ruthlessly in the end, threw over the later in favor of the earlier Greek manuscripts: and that issue will never have to be tried again. In Hort's hands this preference for the earlier manuscripts was pushed to its most extreme form."

This sentence seems to me to lack a grasp of what the testimony of the later documents is (as evidenced by the

---

[1] Westcott and Hort accounted for the prevalence of the Traditional Text by assuming that there must have been a revision, probably at Antioch, which resulted in the rejection of the form of the text represented by B. Hoskier suggests that B and Aleph were revisions of the text underlying the Majority Text.

contents of those which we know) and what the testimony may be of those which are yet unexamined, of which of course there are hundreds and hundreds.

Dr. Hoskier quotes the following from Dr. Salmon in his book *Some Thoughts on the Textual Criticism of the New Testament.* "Yet, great as has been my veneration for Hort and my admiration of the good work that he has done, I have never been able to feel that his work was final, and I have disliked the servility with which his history of the text has been accepted, and even his nomenclature adopted, as if now the last word had been said on the subject of New Testament criticism" (p. 33).

"That which gained Hort so many adherents had some adverse influence with myself — I mean his extreme cleverness as an advocate; for I have felt as if there were no reading so improbable that he could not give good reasons for thinking it to be the only genuine" (pp. 33, 34).

"On this account I am not deterred by the general adoption of Westcott and Hort's decisions from expressing my opinion that their work has too readily been accepted as final, and that students have been too willing to accept as their motto 'Rest and be thankful.' There is no such enemy to progress as the belief that perfection has been already attained" (p. 38).

"In Hort's exposition the student is not taken with him along the path that he himself had followed; he must start with the acceptance of the final result. Consequently one of the first things at which I took umbrage in Westcott and Hort's exposition was the question begging nomenclature" (p. 43).

"I strongly feel that Hort would have done better if he had left the old nomenclature undisturbed, and distinguished his neutral text from that which he calls 'Alexandrian' by the names 'early Alexandrian' and 'later Alexandrian.' Names will not alter facts, though they may enable us to shut our eyes to them" (p. 52).

"Naturally Hort regarded those manuscripts as most trustworthy which give the readings recognized by Origen; and these no doubt were the readings which in the third century were most preferred at Alexandria. Thus Hort's method inevitably led to the exclusive adoption of the Alexandrian text" (p. 53).

"To sum up in conclusion, I have but to express my belief that what Westcott and Hort have restored is the text which had the highest authority in Alexandria in the third century, and may have reached that city in the preceding one. It would need but to strike out the double brackets from the so-called non-Western interpolations, and to remove altogether the few passages which W & H reluctantly admitted into their pages with marks of doubt when we should have a pure Alexandrian text. Their success is due to the fact that W & H investigated the subject as a merely literary problem; and the careful preservation at Alexandria of a text which had reached that city was but a literary problem" (p. 155).

"That Westcott and Hort should employ the Alexandrian 'use' as their chief guide to the recovery of the original text may be quite right; but that they should refuse a place on their page to anything that has not that authority is an extreme which makes me glad that the Revised New Testament, which so closely follows their authority, has not superseded the Authorized version in our Churches. For, if it had, the result might be that things would be accounted unfit to be read in the churches of the nineteenth century which were read at Rome in the second century, during the lifetime of men who had been members of the apostolic company who had visited their city" (pp. 157, 158).

After these quotations from Dr. Salmon, Hoskier continues — I charge Westcott and Hort with having utterly failed to produce any semblance of a "neutral" text. I charge them with the offense of repeated additions to the narrative on most insufficient evidence.

I charge the Oxford edition of 1910 with continual errors in accepting Westcott and Hort's text for many verses together where the absence of footnotes shows that the editors consider their text as settled. I acknowledge and make confession freely that the Revisers have retraced steps in a number of places and ejected Hort's readings sometimes even without the pro and con in a footnote, where Hort blindly followed a phantasma of evidence. But this text is still founded on too high a regard for B, and I pray for an entire reconsideration of the matter in the light of what follows.

The claim of W & H to have resurrected the texts of Origen certainly holds good except in certain places. But in doing so they far exceed Origen's own claim. Origen's citations are full of conflations, where he knew two recensions and incorporated both. If he was not able to judge which of these was original, why should he be a perfect judge of other double readings similarly situated but of which he chose one? Now W & H profess that they have not only restored the text of Origen but that they know that this is "Pre-Syrian"[2] and "Pre-Alexandrian" and, as represented by B, is "neutral" and fundamentally correct as opposed to all others. Their "selected readings," few and far between, can certainly not be considered proof of their contention, and we are prepared to challenge their assumption as to the supremacy of B. Meanwhile we would like to place on record again what Canon Cook had to say about the personality of Origen in connection with these matters, for that feature is of vital importance. The Church at large disagreed with Origen's conclusions. W & H after nearly 1700 years merely wished to replace us textually in the heart of an Alexandrian text, which after A.D. 450 or thereabouts fell into discredit and disuse. For Dr. Salmon says, "Giving to the common parent of B and Aleph as high antiquity as is claimed for it, still it will be distant by more than a century from the original autographs, and the attempts to recover the text of manuscripts which came to Alexandria in the second century may be but an elaborate locking of the stable door after the horse has been stolen."

And now hear what Canon Cook has to say about Origen: — "We go back one step further, a most critical

---

[2] This refers to Westcott and Hort's theory that there was a revision at Antioch in Syria which gave rise to the Traditional, Received, or Majority Text.

and important step, for it brings us at once into contact with the greatest name, the highest genius, the most influential person of all Christian antiquity. We come to Origen. And it is not disputed that Origen bestowed special pains upon every department of Biblical criticism and exegesis. His 'Hexapla' is a monument of stupendous industry and keen discernment; but his labors on the Old Testament were thwarted by his very imperfect knowledge of Hebrew, and by the tendency to mystic interpretations common in his own language, but in no other writer so fully developed or pushed to the same extremes.

"In his criticism of the New Testament Origen had greater advantages, and he used them with greater success. Every available source of information he studied carefully. Manuscripts and versions were before him; both manuscripts and versions he examined, and brought out the results of his researches with unrivaled power. But no one who considers the peculiar character of his genius, his subtlety, his restless curiosity, his audacity in speculation, his love of innovation, will be disposed to deny the extreme risk of adopting any conclusion, any reading, which rests on his authority, unless it is supported by the independent testimony of earlier or contemporary Fathers and Versions."

Hear also Bishop Marsh on the same subject (Lecture 11, edition 1838, page 482): "Whenever therefore grammatical interpretation produced a sense which in Origen's opinion was irrational or impossible, in other words irrational or impossible according to the philosophy which Origen had learnt at Alexandria, he then departed from the literal sense."

This sums up many other matters connected with Origen's treatment of textual matters, so that we do not necessarily recover Origen's manuscripts when we are inclined to follow Aleph and B, *but very likely only Origen himself.*

As to whether the Alexandrian School preserved the true text, or modified it by attempted improvement, is what we are to inquire into.

Hort's system involves dragging in readings of B whenever support can be found from another manuscript. Since Hort's day his true system thus demands and compels the acceptance of further "monstra" exhibited by B owing to support forthcoming since from other manuscripts or versions. I make free to prophesy that other documents so far unknown[3] will add to this list a further crop of vicious survivals which might give us eventually all of B's misreadings. The system is thus demonstrated to be unscientific in the extreme, notwithstanding the praise so fulsomely lavished on it by a certain school.

Toward the end of his great volume Hoskier wrote — In closing let me say that Burgon's position remains absolutely unshaken. He did not contend for acceptance of the "Textus Receptus," as has so often been scurrilously stated. He maintained that Aleph and B had been tampered with and revised and proved it in his *Causes of the Corruption of the Traditional Text.* He sought the truth wherever it might be recovered and did not stop at Origen's time. The material discovered since his day has not shaken his position at all. We seek the truth among all our witnesses, with unnecessary subservience to no one document or congeries of documents, deriving patently from a single recension. Nearly all revision appears to center in Egypt, and to suppose all the other documents wrong when opposed to these Egyptian documents is unsound and unscientific; for we must presuppose not only "Syrian" revision but a most foolish revision which did away with these "improvements" of the Egyptians and Alexandrians, or which destroyed the "neutral" text without rhyme or reason.

What Dean Burgon was chiefly concerned about was the lack of a scientific basis for our textual criticism. It is absolutely necessary to grasp this fact for a proper understanding of the whole matter. A scientific basis can only be obtained *after* we have made ourselves masters of a scientific knowledge of the real history of transmission,

---

[3] Hoskier shrewdly anticipated the discovery of some of the papyrus fragments which exhibit the same kind of defective text as B, and showed that this imperfect form of the text must have been in use in Egypt in the 4th century.

and of the interaction of the versions upon each other and of the versions upon the Greek texts.

It is now 25 years since Dean Burgon passed away,[4] and I ask myself what progress his opponents have made. The answer is that after 25 years they have discovered *some* flaws in the Hort textual theory and have partially dethroned B from the paramount position it occupied in the Hort text. There are further steps to be taken in this process, if I mistake not, and I hope that what I have written will tend further to clear the ground for a more intelligent view of the situation. The weight assigned by Burgon to Patristic testimony has been disallowed, but his indictment of B as a false witness is abundantly proved.

Reiteration of Hort's dicta by his followers is not proof. Let someone take the dozen "Alexandrian" readings of B which I have adduced — the existence of which in B was denied by Hort — and prove that they are in no wise Alexandrian. Then we can discuss the matter further. Let somebody explain how B comes to oppose the sub-apostolic Fathers, deliberately in places, if we are to accept Hort's assurance about B being "neutral." Until that is done, let us away with "dicta" and go by proof.

We have now completed the arraignment of Codex B in the gospels referring to a similar condition of the B text elsewhere and have presented the facts upon which the jury should base their verdict. My arguments have been cumulative rather than exhaustively elaborate. I could have elaborated and gone into much greater detail as to many matters simply mentioned or only sketched. I have preferred to write for those who can appreciate accumulative arguments which I hope I have at least outlined to their satisfaction. The verdict asked is whether B represents a "neutral" text or not. The claims put forward by us are that B does not exhibit a "neutral" text but is found to be tinged, as are other documents, with Coptic, Latin and Syriac colors and its testimony therefore is not of the paramount importance pre-supposed and claimed by Hort and by his followers. That B is guilty of laches, of a

---

[4] Dean Burgon passed away on August 4, 1888.

tendency to "improve," and of "sunstroke" amounting to doctrinal bias. That the maligned Textus Receptus served in large measure as the base which B tampered with and changed, and that the Church at large recognized all this until the year 1881 — when Hortism (in other words Alexandrianism) was allowed free play — and has not since retraced the path to sound traditions.

Upon the first page of this book I spoke of the "Hortian heresy." Upon this last page I would fain explain what it is that I accuse of being a heresy. The text printed by Westcott and Hort has been accepted as "the true text," and grammars, works on the synoptic problem, works on higher criticism, and others, have been grounded on this text. If the Hort text makes the evangelists appear inconsistent, then such and such an evangelist errs. Those who accept the W & H text are basing their accusations of untruth as to the Gospellists upon an Egyptian revision current 200 to 450 A.D. and abandoned between 500 to 1881, merely revived in our day and stamped as genuine.

A CRITICAL EXAMINATION OF THE
WESTCOTT-HORT TEXTUAL THEORY

Alfred Martin

Dr. Martin presented this dissertation to the faculty of the Graduate School of Dallas Theological Seminary in partial fulfillment of the requirements for the degree Doctor of Theology in May of 1951. Your editor has used significant and pertinent parts of this dissertation to compose this chapter. At present, Dr. Martin is Vice President of Moody Bible Institute in Chicago. In this compiler's humble opinion Dr. Martin has administered the coup de grace to the Westcott and Hort textual theory.

In the year 1881 there appeared in England two volumes called *The New Testament in the Original Greek,* the product of almost thirty years of work by two professors at Cambridge, Brooke Foss Westcott (later Bishop of Durham) and Fenton John Anthony Hort. The earlier of these volumes contained the text of the New Testament as constructed by the two editors according to their critical principles; the other contained a detailed statement of those principles from the pen of Hort.

This latter remarkable volume, called *Introduction—Appendix,* although permeated by an oracular tone, does not claim to present the final word on the subject. The conclusion expresses this well:

"Others assuredly in due time will prosecute the task with better resources of knowledge and skill, and amend the faults and defects of our processes and results. To be faithful to such light as could be enjoyed in our own day was the utmost that we could desire. How far we have fallen short of this standard, we are well aware: yet we are bold to say that none of the shortcomings are due to lack of anxious and watchful sincerity."[1]

It is hard to understand how, in spite of this modest disclaimer and of the assurances throughout the work that many conclusions are only tentative, the Westcott-Hort publication became almost immediately the standard of New Testament textual criticism. A writer in *The New Schaff-Herzog Encyclopedia,* discussing the Westcott-Hort theory in 1908, said: "Conscious agreement with it or conscious disagreement and qualification mark all work in this field since 1881."[2] After this long time, that is still almost literally true. The theory was hailed by many when it came forth as practically final, certainly definitive. It has been considered by some the acme in the textual criticism of the New Testament. Some of the followers of Westcott and Hort have been almost unreasoning in their devotion to the theory; and many people, even today, who have no idea what the Westcott-Hort theory is, or at best only a vague notion, accept the labors of those two scholars without question. During the past seventy years it has often been considered textual heresy to deviate from their position or to intimate that, sincere as they undoubtedly were, they may have been mistaken.

Most work in textual criticism today has at least a Hortian foundation; nevertheless there are fashions in criticism as in women's clothing, and the trend of scholars in more recent years has been away from the original Westcott-Hort position, as will be shown in a later chapter of this work. An amusing and amazing spectacle presents itself: many of the textbooks, books of Bible interpreta-

---

[1] *Introduction,* p. 323. The second edition of 1896 is referred to, but it does not differ from the first except in the addition of some supplementary notes.

[2] "Bible Text, II. The New Testament." *The New Schaff-Herzog Encyclopedia of Religious Knowledge,* Vol. II, p. 111.

tion, and innumerable secondary works go on repeating the Westcott-Hort dicta although the foundations have been seriously shaken even in the opinion of former Hortians and those who would logically be expected to be Hortians.

In spite of the notable work of Burgon, Hoskier, and others who supported them, the opponents of the Westcott-Hort theory have never had the hearing which they deserve. How many present-day students of the Greek New Testament ever heard of the two men just mentioned, and how many ever saw a copy of *The Revision Revised* or *Codex B and Its Allies,* to say nothing of actually reading these works? Hoskier says:

"Burgon tried to indicate a scientific method, and has barely had a hearing. Westcott and Hort indicated a less scientific method, because they seem to have *imagined* standards — which do not exist — and, marry! they have had a full hearing and a large following. Why? The reason is sadly obvious. The latter method is taking, easy, and at first sight plausible to the beginner. The former is horribly laborious, although precious in results."[3]

Consequently it will not be amiss after this interval to bring the controversy again into the light of day. It *is* a controversy; there can be no mistake about that. It will be seen in the subsequent discussion that the disagreement raged long before 1881 and that it is still raging. For it cannot be denied that the controversy is still alive; no amount of pontificating of present-day writers can obscure that fact. The reason for dwelling on this point is that today most writers, even though they differ from Westcott and Hort in conclusions, insist upon a Westcott-Hort point of departure and milieu. It is commonly said that the older controversy around the Textus Receptus is dead, but this cannot be true; for if it can be shown that Westcott and Hort were wrong in their basic premises, then it will be necessary to go back before Westcott and Hort and to take up the study afresh. If the direction is wrong, further supposed progress only leads farther from the truth.

---

[3] *Concerning the Text of the Apocalypse,* Vol. I, p. xlvii.

The thesis of this work is, then, that the Westcott-Hort theory is based upon false principles, follows fallacious methods, and is not worthy of the credence given to it by so many. This is a strong statement, but proof will follow.

Before the Westcott-Hort theory can be examined critically, there must be a clear understanding of what the theory is. A theory is usually propounded to account for some fact. The fact in this connection is that, of the more than four thousand manuscripts of the New Testament now extant (in a fragmentary, partial, or complete state), the great majority, perhaps as many as ninety or ninety-five per cent, are in substantial textual agreement. Nevertheless some of the oldest manuscripts known will differ markedly from the majority. The problem is to account not only for the agreement of the majority, but also for the deviations in other manuscripts as well as in versions and Fathers.

The Syrian text insisted upon by Westcott and Hort is said to be a full, smooth text, containing many "conflate" readings, that is, combinations of readings of two or more earlier texts. Westcott and Hort consider it to be worthless unless supported by "pre-Syrian" readings. Even if one did not know anything about New Testament textual criticism, one could see that this hypothesis eliminates at one stroke between ninety and ninety-five per cent of the evidence! Of course, if the theory is correct, and all the later manuscripts are copied from an "official" text, then they do lose their value as evidence. It will be shown, however, that there is *no proof* of the recensions which Westcott and Hort allege.

The paragraphs in the *Introduction* on "The neutral text and its preservation" are a model of obscurity and of theorizing but nonetheless of dogmatizing. There is absolutely no proof of the neutrality of this so-called Neutral Text. It is best represented by two uncial manuscripts of the fourth century, Vaticanus (B) and Sinaiticus (Aleph). The practical result of this classification is that Westcott and Hort relied most heavily on these two manuscripts, especially on B, as the foundation of their own text.

If the Westcott-Hort theory can be disproved, it can be

seen that the traditional text is closer to the original autographs than any other. The traditional text is not synonymous with the Received Text, but the latter does embody it in a rather corrupt form.

If it be objected that strong feeling obtrudes itself at times into the discussion, it can only be replied in extenuation that this is the kind of subject which engenders strong feeling. There are tremendous issues involved; the text of the Word of God is in question! How can one hold oneself mentally aloof? One is reminded of Burgon's statement in the preface to *The Revision Revised:*

"Earnestly have I desired, for many years past, to produce a systematic Treatise on this great subject. My aspiration all along has been, and still is, in place of the absolute Empiricism which has hitherto prevailed in Textual inquiry, to exhibit the logical outlines of what, I am persuaded, is destined to become a truly delightful Science. But I more than long — I fairly *ache* to have done with Controversy, and to be free to devote myself to the work of Interpretation. My apology for bestowing so large a portion of my time on Textual Criticism, is David's when he was reproached by his brethren for appearing on the field of battle, 'Is there not a cause?' "[4] Yes, there is a cause and it is a more important cause than many Bible students have yet realized. The writer is soundly convinced from years of reading and thinking upon this question that the Westcott-Hort theory is false and misleading!

If Origen's theology is any guide to his textual criticism, one would not be inclined to follow him very closely. His many deviations are well known, and his influence in promoting the "spiritualizing" method of Bible interpretation has done untold damage in the study of the Scriptures. Hort relied on him perhaps more than any Father, but that may have been because of the similarities between some of his readings and those of B and Aleph. A rather different estimate of him (Origen) was made by Burgon and Miller:

---

4 *The Revision Revised*, p. xxix.

"The influence which the writings of Origen exercised on the ancient Church is indeed extraordinary. The fame of his learning added to the splendour of his genius, his vast Biblical achievements and his real insight into the depth of Scripture, conciliated for him the admiration and regard of early Christendom. Let him be freely allowed the highest praise for the profundity of many of his utterances, the ingenuity of almost all. It must at the same time be admitted that he is bold in his speculations to the verge, and beyond the verge, of rashness; unwarrantedly confident in his assertions; deficient in sobriety; in his critical remarks even foolish. A prodigious reader as well as a prodigious writer, his words would have been of incalculable value, but that he seems to have been so saturated with the strange speculations of the early heretics, that he sometimes adopts their wild method; and in fact has not been reckoned among the orthodox Fathers of the Church."[5] It is manifest that Origen is not a safe guide in textual criticism any more than in theology.

One cannot say that the Textus Receptus, for example, is verbally inspired. It contains many plain and clear errors, as all schools of textual critics agree. But it embodies substantially the text which even Westcott and Hort admit was dominant in the church from the middle of the fourth century on. The text used by the Church Fathers from Chrysostom's time on was not materially different from the text of Erasmus and Stephanus. This is not a conclusive proof of the superiority of that text — far from it, but, taken in connection with other factors discussed in this dissertation, does it not present a strong presumption in favor of the reliability of this text? namely the Textus Receptus. It is hard to see how God would allow the true text to sink into virtual oblivion for fifteen hundred years only to have it brought to light again by two Cambridge professors who did not even believe it to be verbally inspired.

A Bible-believing Christian had better be careful what he says about the Textus Receptus, for the question is not at

---

5 *The Traditional Text of the Holy Gospels,* p. 162.

all the precise wording of that text, but rather a choice between two different kinds of texts, a fuller one and a shorter one. One need not believe in the infallibility of Erasmus, or his sanctity, or even his honesty; because he merely followed the type of text which was dominant in the manuscripts, although he probably was not aware of all the implications involved. He undoubtedly could have done much better than he did, but he also could have done a great deal worse. If some regret that the Vatican manuscript was not available to, or was not used by him, one may reply that it may yet be proved that the mercy of God kept him in his ignorance from following a depraved text that had been rejected by the church at large for at least a thousand years before his time.

The event for which Tischendorf is best known is his discovery of the Sinaitic Manuscript at the Monastery of St. Catherine on Mt. Sinai in 1859. He published his edition of this manuscript in 1862. Perhaps naturally, because of his discovery of it, he deferred too much to Aleph (the Sinaitic Manuscript). His eighth edition, published after the discovery of that manuscript, differs from his seventh in as many as 3369 places, to the scandal of the science of Comparative Criticism, as well as to his own grave discredit for discernment and consistency. Tregelles was a true believer in Christ who accepted without question the verbal inspiration of the Scriptures. He sincerely believed that in building a text on the fewer oldest authorities he was recovering the very words of inspiration. Burgon thus writes of him:

"Of the scrupulous accuracy, the indefatigable industry, the pious zeal of that estimable and devoted scholar, we speak not. All honour to his memory! As a specimen of conscientious labour, his edition of the New Testament (1857-72) passes praise, and will never lose its value. But it has only to be stated, that Tregelles effectually persuaded himself that 'eighty-nine ninethieths' of our extant manuscripts and other authorities may safely be rejected and lost sight of when we come to amend the text and try to restore it to its primitive purity — to make it plain that in Textual Criticism he must needs be regarded as an untrustworthy teacher."[6] Tregelles's influence was very great in leading British scholars of his time away from the Textus Receptus.

The Westcott-Hort theory, advanced somewhat tentatively by its original proponents, has been dominant in the field of New Testament textual criticism for almost the entire seventy years of its existence. There were, of course, able and powerful opponents of the theory, and it was not universally accepted all at once, but most of the opposing voices were still after a few years and the theory has prevailed. Because of this the earnest and scholarly men who wrote against it have almost been forgotten and their books are now difficult to find. Popular thinking scarcely recognizes the fact that there were opponents, so gigantic in stature have Westcott and Hort become.

The present generation of Bible students, having been reared on Westcott and Hort, have for the most part accepted the theory without independent or critical examination. To the average student of the Greek New Testament today it is unthinkable to question the theory at least in its basic premises. Even to imply that one believes the Textus Receptus to be nearer the original text than the Westcott-Hort text is, lays one open to the suspicion of gross ignorance or unmitigated bigotry. That is why this controversy needs to be aired again among Bible-believing Christians. There is little hope of convincing those who are unbelieving textual critics, but if believing Bible students had the evidence of both sides put before them, instead of one side only, there would not be so much blind following of Westcott and Hort.

Burgon was one of the greatest Greek scholars of his day and undoubtedly the greatest authority of the time on patristic quotations of the New Testament. His sixteen large manuscript volumes of an index to these quotations have never been published, but are in the British Museum. When the English Revised Version of the New Testament appeared in 1881, based to a considerable extent on the Westcott-Hort theory, he (Burgon) criticized it in a series

---

6 *The Revision Revised,* p. 22.

of three devastating articles in the *Quarterly Review*. Burgon's method has been largely misunderstood and sometimes misrepresented. He is often caricatured as a bigoted, ignorant upholder of the Textus Receptus who was blind to the niceties of scholarship. Westcott and Hort never took him seriously, but he was nevertheless an opponent to be reckoned with. Burgon held that there is absolutely no place for conjecture in the textual criticism of the New Testament.

Burgon's own statement of his system and method, as given in the preface to *The Revision Revised,* is to the point and worth quoting:

"What compels me to repeat this so often, is the impatient selfsufficiency of these last days, which is for breaking away from the old restraints; and for erecting the individual conscience into an authority from which there shall be no appeal. I know but too well how labourious is the scientific method which *I* advocate. . . . And yet it is the indispensable condition of progress in an unexplored region, that a few should thus labour, until a path has been cut through the forest — a road laid down — huts built — a *modus vivendi* established. In this department of sacred Science, men have been going on too long inventing their facts, and delivering themselves of oracular decrees, on the sole responsibility of their own inner consciousness. There is a great convenience in such a method certainly — a charming simplicity which is in a high degree attractive to flesh and blood. It dispenses with proof. It furnishes no evidence. It asserts when it ought to argue. It reiterates when it is called upon to explain. 'I am sir Oracle.' . . . This — which I venture to style the unscientific method — reached its culminating point when Professors Westcott and Hort recently put forth their Recension of the Greek Text. Their work is indeed quite a psychological curiosity. Incomprehensible to me is it how two able men of disciplined understanding can have seriously put forth the volume which they call *Introduction—Appendix.* It is the very *Reductio ad absurdum* of the uncritical method of the last fifty years.

"The method I persistently advocate in every case of a supposed doubtful Reading (I say it for the last time, and request that I may be no more misrepresented), is, that *an appeal should be unreservedly made to Catholic Antiquity;* and that the combined verdict of Manuscripts, Versions, Fathers, shall be regarded as decisive."[7]

Hoskier writes of Burgon in 1914 these words:

"Burgon's position remains absolutely unshaken. He did not contend for the acceptance of the Textus Receptus, as has so often been scurrilously stated. He maintained that Aleph and B had been tampered with and revised, and he proved it in his *Causes of Corruption.* He sought the truth wherever it might be recovered, and did not stop at Origen's time. The material discovered since his day has not shaken his position at all."[8]

This is a glimpse of the life and work of a man who opposed the Westcott-Hort theory and text with all his might. While his arguments were not generally accepted by his contemporaries, he was supremely confident of the rightness of his cause. Hoskier gives this interesting glimpse of him:

"Three and a half years ago [this was written in 1890] I was in Dean Burgon's study at Chichester. It was midnight, dark and cold without; he had just extinguished the lights, and it was dark, and getting cold within. We mounted the stairs to retire to rest, and his last words of the night have often rung in my ears since: 'As surely as it is dark now, and as certainly as the sun will rise tomorrow morning, so surely will the traditional text be vindicated and the views I have striven to express be accepted. I may not live to see it. Most likely I shall not. But it will come.' "[9]

Westcott and Hort had been working together on their text since 1853; in 1870 they printed a tentative edition for private distribution only. This they circulated under pledge of secrecy within the company of New Testament revisers, of which they were members (of which came the

---

[7] *Ibid.,* pp. xxix-xxxvii.

[8] *Codex B and Its Allies,* Vol. I, p. 415.

[9] H. C. Hoskier, *Collation of 604,* p. v.

Revised Version of 1881). It soon became evident that the New Testament committee was not going to be content merely to revise the Authorized Version, but was determined to revise the underlying Greek text radically. (Scrivener counted the number of changes in the underlying Greek text of the Revised Version from the Authorized Version as 5,788.) Hort became the leading spokesman for the views which he and Westcott advocated; Scrivener usually spoke for the other side. Most of the members of the committee were not textual critics, and were not at home in this area of discussion.

When the Revised Version of the New Testament was published in May, 1881, after more than ten years of revising sessions, there was intense interest in both England and America. It is difficult now to realize the enthusiasm of that day. A recent edition of a standard work describes the reception of the volume as unprecedented. Within four days after publication about two million copies are said to have been sold in England. On the morning of the American publication date (May 20) people were clamoring for copies before daybreak in New York and Philadelphia. On May 22 the Chicago *Tribune* and the Chicago *Times* published the entire New Testament in their issues. The Revision began with a tremendous popularity, but this popularity apparently did not spread to the masses and was not of long continuance. Scholars everywhere acclaimed it.

The fact that the Revised New Testament used a different underlying Greek text from that of the Authorized Version could be easily perceived, and the further fact became generally known through the subsequent controversy that Westcott and Hort had been extremely influential in effecting many of the changes. The two Cambridge professors had gone into the project of revision with the object of pressing for a revision of the accepted Greek text, and it was only natural that they should press their views with all their power in the sessions of the committee.

There is no intention in this work to disparage the intellect or the scholarship of Westcott and Hort. Their names are well known to all students of the Greek New

Testament, not only for their textual studies, but also for their exegetical work. No attempt will be made to list or discuss their voluminous writings, since there is no necessity of establishing this fact. Both men served for many years as professors at the University of Cambridge.

Hort was a man of great intellect, and his *Introduction,* if nothing else, would attest that fact. His involved development of the textual theory had plausibility and persuasiveness, and carries the reader along in his reasoning so that oftentimes the precarious nature of the factual basis of the theory is scarcely noticed. One can believe the premises to be utterly false and hence the conclusions invalid, and yet not fail to feel the force of Hort's powerful mind. There was, furthermore, the scholarship of at least fifty years behind the two Cambridge editors. The great and well-known names of Lachmann, Tischendorf, and Tregelles, to say nothing of the earlier Griesbach, stood back of the line of research that was continued by Westcott and Hort. Added to this was the fact that they were possessed with supreme self-confidence. If Hort was inclined at times to be timid and retiring, Westcott bolstered him up. They took little account of the views of those who opposed them. The Westcott-Hort method is certainly basically rationalistic, for it exalts the judgment of the individual critic. They were influenced either consciously or unconsciously by the liberal tendencies of their time. It was a period when the theory of evolution had been thrust before the popular attention with the publication of Darwin's *Origin of Species* in 1859. This theory had tremendous repercussions in every area of life. Both Westcott and Hort seem to have been theistic evolutionists.

It is clear, from Westcott's own statement, that he was what may be called a middle-of-the-road man. *Via media* was his watchword. Apparently Hort shared these views with him. Today they would be called probably moderate liberals. Westcott's son mentions more than once that his father was often considered "unorthodox," "unsound," or "unsafe."

When the company of New Testament revisers (for the

Revised Version) were ready to begin their work, a communion service was held in Westminster Abbey. A Unitarian member of the committee partook along with the others. There was serious criticism of this, and, in the words of Arthur Westcott, "The Revision was almost wrecked at the very outset." The upper house of the Convocation of Canterbury passed a resolution that no person who denied the deity of Christ should take part in the work. Westcott threatened to sever his connections with the project in these words to Hort: "If the Company accept the dictation of Convocation, my work must end." It may be argued that it is unfair and irrelevant to urge the liberal theological views of Westcott and Hort against their textual theory; but in reply it can be said that those views must inevitably have had some bearing upon their attitude toward the sacred text. One cannot help noticing parallels between the brilliant Westcott and Hort of the nineteenth century and the brilliant Origen, their favorite patristic authority, of the third century.

Hoskier has alluded to this situation in his *Codex B and Its Allies:*

"Finally observe that up to the time of Westcott and Hort the 'lower criticism' had kept itself quite apart from the so-called 'higher criticism.' Since the publication of Hort's text, however, and that of the Revisers, much of the heresy of our time has fallen back upon the supposed results acquired by the 'lower criticism' to bolster up their views."

Men who had long denied the infallibility of the Bible — and there were many such in the Church of England and in the independent churches — eagerly acclaimed a theory which they thought to be in harmony with their position. One cannot agree with all of Burgon's views, nor can one condone the erascibility and smugness, but one who believes the Bible cannot but rejoice in his love for God's Book and admire his masterly defense of verbal inspiration.

This is not to say that Burgon's theological views automatically make him right in textual criticism and that Westcott and Hort's theological views automatically make them wrong. In face of the fact, however, that they were all recognized and accomplished scholars, it ought to create a presumption of right on the side of one who fully upheld the Word of God. Not proof in itself, it nevertheless ought to make one cautious in examining the evidence. Those gigantic personalities merely crystallize the issue. It would be wrong and foolish to say that everyone who holds the Westcott-Hort textual theory is liberal in theology.

At precisely the time when liberalism was carrying the field in the English churches the theory of Westcott and Hort received wide acclaim. These are not isolated facts. Recent contributions on the subject — that is, in the present century — following mainly the Westcott-Hort principles and method, have been made largely by men who deny the inspiration of the Bible. Canon Streeter and Kirsopp Lake can be cited as only two outstanding examples in a list that could be greatly extended.

Textual criticism cannot be divorced entirely from theology. No matter how great a Greek scholar a man may be, or no matter how great an authority on the textual evidence, his conclusions must always be open to suspicion if he does not accept the Bible as the very Word of God.

As quoted previously, Burgon has shown the laborious nature of the method which he advocated. It involves exact collation of documents, minute examination of the evidence of manuscripts, versions, and Fathers on every disputed passage. Hoskier has expressed it in these words: "I rise from my complete examination [of 46 of the Apocalypse] with different feelings, and I record this merely to show how untrustworthy is partial examination. We read in Scrivener 'Hort collated the first five chapters' (of some manuscript) 'and sent his results to ——————. It is similar in text to B.' Such deductions are as stupid for our purpose as indeterminate. As a matter of fact the recension of the first five chapters of the Apocalypse itself frequently differs from that used for the remainder of the book in many manuscripts."[10]

---

[10] *Concerning the Text of the Apocalypse,* Vol. I, p. 128.

In contrast to Westcott and Hort's theorizing method, Scrivener in his *Plain Introduction* and Burgon and Miller in their *Traditional Text* and *Causes of Corruption* have outlined their inductive method. Hoskier advocated this method in all his works and demonstrated it in his monumental *Concerning the Text of the Apocalypse.*

Men are always seeking some self-evident principle that will explain everything. The Westcott-Hort theory is an attempt to find such a principle in New Testament textual criticism. This theory enabled the two editors to reject as of no value about ninety-five per cent of the available evidence, and, in effect, to make the text of Vaticanus the magic touchstone. If this is doubted, hear Hort's own words on the subject:

"Tried by the same tests as those just applied, B is found to hold a unique position. Its text is throughout Pre-Syrian, perhaps purely Pre-Syrian, at all events with hardly any, if any, quite clear exceptions. . . . The highest interest must already be seen to belong to a document of which thus far we know only that its text is not only Pre-Syrian but substantially free from Western and Alexandrian adulteration."[11]

No other writings were like the New Testament in the frequency of copyings made within a short time after their first appearing. This very multiplication of copies almost inevitably gave rise to a large number of corruptions of the text, most of them unintentional and most of them insignificant. It must be insisted, however, that intentional causes cannot safely be disregarded. The New Testament is different from other documents (it goes without saying that the Old Testament is also, but that is not now being considered) in that it is the infallible Word of God. This entails the fact that God will preserve the text against permanent or destructive error, although He does not guarantee the accuracy of any one manuscript. It means also that Satan will do everything in his power to corrupt the text; he put forth a series of mighty efforts almost at the very beginning through Marcion, Basilides, the Ebion-

---

[11] *Introduction,* pp. 150-51.

ites, the Valentinians, and many others. Burgon's word of caution about this is a wise one:

"I say it for the last time — of all such [intentional] causes of depravation the Greek Poets, Tragedians, Philosophers, Historians, neither knew nor could know anything. And it thus plainly appears that the Textual Criticism of the New Testament is to be handled by ourselves in an entirely different spirit from that of any other book."

Over and over again this same writer appeals for a realization that the New Testament is the Word of God and therefore must be handled in a different way from any other document. Decrying the tendency to look at New Testament textual criticism as a literary problem merely, Burgon stoutly avers, "The Holy Scriptures are not an arena for the exercise or display of the ingenuity of critics."[12]

There are, Hort says, two different kinds of internal evidence of readings, which must be distinguished sharply from one another. These are "intrinsic probability" and "transcriptional probability." The former inquires what the writer would most probably have written; the latter, which of two or more readings would most probably account for the origin of the other or others in successive stages of copying. Even such a cursory mention as this is sufficient to show that this kind of evidence is highly subjective. Hort freely admits this and concedes that "in dealing with this kind of evidence equally competent critics often arrive at contradictory conclusions as to the same variations."

The discussion of intrinsic probability, nevertheless, is the entering wedge for the theory, which is subjective throughout. In practice Westcott and Hort attach considerable value to intrinsic probability, especially as corroborative evidence. *But who can be the proper judge of what one of the New Testament writers would most probably have written?* There must be some standard. Could not Hort, brilliant man that he was, see that his conclusions

---

[12] *Traditional Text,* p. 27.

were entirely subjective and that the most that can be said for them is that they are possible? Hort says:

"The only safe order of procedure therefore is to start with the reading suggested by a strong genealogical presumption, if such there be: and then enquire whether the considerations suggested by other kinds of evidence agree with it, and if not, whether they are clear and strong enough to affect the *prima facie* claim of higher attestation."[13]

Note that word *presumption* and the phrase *if such there be*. All is speculation and uncertainty. Yet it is on this quicksand that Westcott and Hort erect their whole hypothesis of the posteriority of Syrian readings and the supremacy of the so-called Neutral Text.

Burgon's criticism of Westcott and Hort's conjectural emendations is apposite:

"For ourselves, what surprises us most is the fatal misapprehension they evince of the true office of Textual Criticism as applied to the New Testament. It never is to invent new Readings, but only to adjudicate between existing and conflicting ones. . . .

"May we be allowed to assure Dr. Hort that *'Conjectural Emendation' can be allowed no place whatever in the textual criticism of the New Testament?* He will no doubt disregard our counsel."[14]

No one assumes that this idea of conjectural emendation is basic to the Westcott-Hort theory; but it is an evidence of the subjective nature of the alleged proof. This vicious method has been carried to an absurd extreme by the modern followers of Westcott and Hort, some of whose work will be discussed in another chapter. Today it is taken for granted in most textual critical circles that the judgment of the critic is one of the main factors in textual criticism. That is to be expected from those who do not consider the Bible to be essentially different from any other book. The average textual critic starts with a

---

13 *Introduction*, p. 63.
14 *The Revision Revised*, p. 354.

prejudice against the Bible as the verbally inspired Word of God. How can one have confidence in his results?

Some of the principles and methods of Westcott and Hort have now been seen. Their starting principle that the textual criticism of the New Testament is to be conducted in exactly the same way as that of any other book, is utterly false, because the New Testament is the Word of God, and as such is subject both to Satanic attack and to the protection of God. Their principal method, an extreme reliance upon the internal evidence of readings, is fallacious and dangerous, because it makes the mind of the critic the arbiter of the text of the Word of God. It cannot justifiably be urged that Westcott and Hort's use of documentary evidence clears them of this charge of subjectivism, for they insist that documentary evidence is of no value unless it is genealogically interpreted.

The two central pillars of the Westcott-Hort temple are the Syrian recensions and the Neutral Text. If it can be shown that there were no such recensions (or, even if it cannot be shown that there were) and that the Neutral Text is not neutral, then the whole structure ought to topple as the temple of Dagon fell under the returning strength of Samson. It is generally acknowledged that the contribution of Westcott and Hort is in the realm of theory. That point is reiterated here, because so many have taken theory for fact. Is it any wonder that Hoskier exclaimed about the "most astonishing vogue" of this theory?

The main objection to be raised against the Westcott-Hort hypothesis of the Syrian recensions is that there is no record whatever in history of such occurrences. This is negative evidence, admittedly, and the argument from silence is often precarious; in a case like this, however, when the event was so momentous, the unbroken silence of history is disastrous to the theory. Many critics of Westcott and Hort, as well as many of their followers, have recognized this. Scrivener remarks:

"Dr. Hort's system, therefore, is entirely destitute of historical foundation. He does not so much as make a show of pretending to it: but then he would persuade us, as he has persuaded himself, that its substantial truth is proved by results; and for results of themselves to establish so very much, they must needs be unequivocal, and admit of no logical escape from the conclusions they lead up to. . . .

". . . With all our reverence for his [Hort's] genius, and gratitude for much that we have learnt from him in the course of our studies, we are compelled to repeat as emphatically as ever our strong conviction that the hypothesis to whose proof he has devoted so many labourious years, is destitute not only of historical foundation, but of all probability resulting from the internal goodness of the text which its adoption would force upon us."[15]

This is a clear, unimpassioned criticism from a learned contemporary of Westcott and Hort. There is no more proof today for the Syrian recensions than there was when these words were written. A further sweeping, although not unimpassioned, refutation came from the pen of Dean Burgon, who with his superb sense of satire reduced the whole hypothesis to an absurdity.

No matter how many heretics there were in the church in the third and fourth centuries, and there were many, they would not have dared to handle the text of Scripture in the way that Hort supposes. Even if they had dared to do so, they could not have succeeded with impunity. There would have been some writers who would have raged against them as Burgon did against Westcott and Hort in the nineteenth century. If there is no Syrian text — and there could be none without some such recension as Hort imagines — there is no Westcott-Hort theory. There is a traditional text, but it is not Syrian. If the Westcott-Hort theory of Syrian recensions and an official text were true, there would not be so much variety in the cursive manuscripts. Their differences indicate that they have been copied from different ancestors, which in turn have come from different ancestors. They could not all have come down through a single line of transmission. Westcott and

[15] Scrivener, *Plain Introduction,* Vol. II, pp. 291-92, 296.

Hort did not give much attention to the cursives and later uncials because they considered them valueless in recovering the true text; if they had given them more study they could not have held their theory of an official Syrian text.

The opponents of Westcott and Hort have not hesitated to impeach B, or Codex Vaticanus, as a fallible or false witness. It is clear that the traditional text and B cannot both be right, and if the traditional text is at least as old as B — Hort admits this — why should the authority of one manuscript be acknowledged against the host of manuscripts, versions, and Fathers which support the traditional text? Age alone cannot prove that a manuscript is correct. B and Aleph probably owe their preservation to the fact that they were written on vellum, whereas most other documents of that period were written on papyrus. Many students, including Tischendorf and Hort, have thought them to be two of the fifty copies which Eusebius had prepared under the order of Constantine for use in the churches of Constantinople. They are no doubt beautiful manuscripts, but their texts show scribal carelessness. B exhibits numerous places where the scribe has written the same word or phrase twice in succession. Aleph shows the marks of ten different correctors down through the centuries. Burgon's excoriation of Westcott and Hort's method cannot be considered too strong in the light of the facts concerning the character of these two manuscripts:

"Take away this one codex, and Dr. Hort's volume becomes absolutely without coherence, purpose, meaning. One-fifth of it is devoted to remarks on B and Aleph. The fable of 'the Syrian text' is invented solely for the glorification of B and Aleph — which are claimed, of course, to be '*Pre*-Syrian.' This fills 40 pages more. And thus it would appear that the Truth of Scripture has run a very narrow risk of being lost for ever to mankind. Dr. Hort contends that it more than half lay *perdu* on a forgotten shelf in the Vatican Library; Dr. Tischendorf, that it had been deposited in a waste-paper basket in the convent of St. Catherine at the foot of Mount Sinai, from which he rescued it on the 4th February, 1859 — neither, we venture to think, a very likely circumstance. We incline to believe that the Author of Scripture hath not by any means shown Himself so unmindful of the safety of the Deposit, as these distinguished gentlemen imagine."[16]

Naturally everyone would like to have the readings of the oldest manuscripts, but the oldest manuscripts are no longer in existence; for no autograph of the New Testament survives. There is undoubtedly divine wisdom in that; if men will go to such lengths to reverence a manuscript of the fourth century, would they not have made an idol of an autograph? It is generally known that the text was corrupted in the earliest centuries, sometimes deliberately by heretics. Students should be on their guard against considering as infallible any manuscript, no matter how old it may be. The readings which have the widest, the oldest, the most varied, the most continuous, the weightiest and most respectable attestations are to be taken as the true ones, not the *ipsissima verba* of any one or two or a few manuscripts.

There is absolutely no evidence that the so-called Neutral Text is the closest to the apostolic text, merely the assertion that this is so. Hort's veneration for the name of Origen does not carry weight with all scholars, for some would not trust that aberrant Father any more in textual criticism than they would in theology. One must not talk any longer about the "Neutral" Text unless one has studied Hoskier's *Codex B and Its Allies* and answered his arguments. He summarizes one of these arguments in this way:

"Reiteration of Hort's dicta by his followers is not proof. Let someone take the dozen 'Alexandrian' readings of B which I have adduced — the existence of which in B was denied by Hort — and prove that they are in no wise Alexandrian. Then we can discuss the matter further."[17]

The second volume of this significant work by Hoskier is concerned mainly with Sinaiticus and its divergences from Vaticanus. One's faith in the "Neutral" Text ought to be shaken or strained if one would pore over the many

---

16 *The Revision Revised,* pp. 342-43.

17 *Codex B and Its Allies,* p. 422.

pages which list in detail more than three thousand real differences between the texts of B and Aleph in the four Gospels alone! Hoskier says at the beginning of this volume, "In the light of the following huge lists let us never be told in future that either Aleph or B represents any form of 'Neutral' Text." He lists 656 differences in Matthew, 567 in Mark, 791 in Luke, and 1,022 in John (a total of 3,036 in the Gospels), and then shows by further lists at the back of the book that even these are not exhaustive. These are not theories, but facts which can be traced through more than three hundred pages of Hoskier's complicated collation.

Westcott and Hort's "question-begging nomenclature" has been shown to be worthless. They themselves admit that Western is not a correct designation. They adduce no definite manuscript support for their so-called Alexandrian. Their Neutral is conceded by most today to be a misnomer. Their Syrian, depending upon the fictional Syrian recensions, is most improper. As was stated at the beginning of this chapter, if there were no Syrian recensions and if the Neutral Text is not neutral, then the theory falls to the ground. In his recapitulation of genealogical evidence proper, Hort considers that he has established his propositions and that they are "absolutely certain."

In all of this discussion one is struck by that which has been mentioned earlier: the entire lack of consideration for the supernatural element in the Scripture. There is nothing of verbal inspiration; indeed there could not be, since Westcott and Hort disavowed that doctrine. There is no sense of the divine preservation of the text, which one ought to find in a discussion of this type by Christians.

Near the conclusion of this section occurs an amazing statement:

"It will not be out of place to add here a distinct expression of our belief that even among the numerous unquestionably spurious readings of the New Testament there are no signs of deliberate falsification of the text for dogmatic purposes."[18] How Hort can make such a

---

18 *Introduction,* p. 282.

statement as this in the face of patristic testimony is simply impossible to see.

The methods of Westcott and Hort sound plausible at first hearing, largely because of the persuasive and dogmatic presentation which Hort gives to them. Their application reveals their baselessness. "Conflation," the "Syrian recensions," the "Neutral Text," all are seen to be figments of the imagination of the two distinguished Cambridge professors. The whole genealogical method which they built up so elaborately over a period of almost thirty years is now called in question and the Neutral Text is no longer believed to be neutral.

Herman C. Hoskier (1864-1938) has been mentioned repeatedly. Born in London, educated in England, France, and Germany, he was engaged in the banking and brokerage business in New York as a young man, but retired from the business at the age of thirty-nine to give his time to his literary work. He was one of the few men courageous enough to stand against the tide in the present century. While he has been little listened to, he could not be wholly ignored even by those who disagreed violently with him, for his knowledge of documents and his scholarship were beyond question.

The great difficulty in New Testament textual criticism today, which makes it impossible for Bible-believing Christians to be sanguine about the results of present research, is the almost universally held view among critics of the relative nature of truth. Textual criticism has become more and more subjective since Westcott and Hort opened the door of subjectivism wide.

Thus far consideration has been given almost wholly to the theory underlying the Westcott-Hort text. It is necessary now to turn attention to the text itself. This text was acclaimed by Souter as "the greatest edition ever published,"[19] and castigated by Burgon as "a Text vastly more remote from the inspired autographs of the Evangelists than any which has appeared since the invention of printing."[20] This is in reality one of the best pieces of

---

[19] *Text and Canon of the New Testament,* p. 103.

[20] *The Revision Revised,* p. 25.

evidence for judging the theory. Here one finds the practical product of that involved ratiocination to which Hort devoted his *Introduction—Appendix.*

One cause for caution in the acceptance of either the Westcott-Hort theory or the text is that so few believing Bible students, even when they profess acceptance of the theory in principle and believe the Westcott-Hort text to be very close to the original, are wholly willing in practice to follow that text. It is well known that the chief point in which the Westcott-Hort ("Neutral") text differs from the traditional text is in the omission of certain passages, some rather lengthy and others quite brief. The two longest of these are Mark 16:9-20, which Westcott and Hort print in double brackets, and John 7:53—8:11, which they print in double brackets at the end of John. They do not consider either of these to be genuine Scripture. Now if one holds the Westcott-Hort theory and rejects these passages as spurious, one is at least consistent. But how many Christian Hortians do this? Such an approach to the problem as is being suggested may be called obscurantism or reaction or bigotry or any other name, but that does not alter the fact. Here is an interesting example from a respected, sound Bible teacher. Discussing the passage John 7:53—8:11, the so-called *Pericope de Adultera,* he writes:

"It is well known that the section of the Gospel according to John from 7:53 to 8:11 must be treated differently from the remainder of the text. In the first place, the manuscript authority behind it is too weak to permit us to regard it as a part of the original text. Westcott summarizes the point by stating, 'It is omitted by the oldest representatives of every kind of evidence (manuscripts, versions, Fathers).' . . . The evidence of vocabulary and of connectives is opposed to Johannine authorship."[21] Yet this same commentator writes nine printed pages upon the interpretation of the passage just as if he believed it to be Scripture. It either is Scripture or it

---

[21] E. F. Harrison, "Jesus and the Woman Taken in Adultery," *Bibliotheca Sacra,* Number 412 (Oct.-Dec. 1946), p. 431.

is not. If it is not, then it ought to be cast out utterly and not expounded as if it were.

What is it that causes Christian writers such as this to stop short of repudiating this passage and a number of similar ones? Is it tradition, or sentiment, as many would allege? Perhaps; one cannot say dogmatically. But is it not possibly the restraining influence of the Holy Spirit who bears testimony in this way to His Word?

The last twelve verses of the Gospel of Mark forms the subject of Burgon's formal entrance into the field of New Testament textual criticism, as mentioned earlier. Very few of the writers discuss his book or give more than passing attention to it, but as far as can be seen it has never been answered in detail. The scribe of B or Codex Vaticanus has given evidence that he was conscious of omission in that he has left an entire column blank immediately after Mark 16:8, a space large enough to contain the twelve verses.

Scrivener comments thus on Burgon's defense of this passage:

"Dean Burgon's brilliant monograph . . . has thrown a stream of light upon the controversy, nor does the joyous tone of his book misbecome one who is conscious of having triumphantly maintained a cause which is very precious to him. We may fairly say that his conclusions have in no essential point been shaken by the elaborate counter-plea of Dr. Hort. This whole paragraph is set apart by itself in the critical editions of Tischendorf and Tregelles. Besides this, it is placed within double brackets by Westcott and Hort, and followed by the wretched supplement derived from Codex L, annexed as an alternative reading. *Out of all the great manuscripts, the two oldest* (Aleph and B or Vaticanus) *stand alone in omitting verses 9-20 altogether.*"[22]

Burgon himself, addressing Bishop Ellicott, thus summarizes the evidence in favor of these twelve verses:

"*Your* ground for thus disallowing the last 12 verses of the second Gospel is, that B or Vaticanus and Aleph omit

_____

[22] Scrivener, *op. cit.*, Vol. II, p. 337.

them: — that a few late manuscripts exhibit a wretched alternative for them: — and that Eusebius says they were often awry. Now, *my* method on the contrary is to refer all such questions to 'the consentient testimony of the most ancient authorities.' And I invite you to note the result of such an appeal in the present instance. The verses in question I find are recognized,

"In the IInd century, — By the Old Latin — and Syriac Versions: — by Papias; Justin Martyr; — Irenaeus; — Tertullian.

"In the IIIrd century, — By the Coptic — and the Sahidic Versions: — by Hippolytus; — by Vincentius at the seventh council of Carthage; — by the 'Acta Pilati'; — and by the 'Apostolical Constitutions' in two places.

"In the IVth century, — By Cureton's Syriac and the Gothic Versions: — besides the Syriac Table of Canons; — Eusebius; — Marcarius Magnes; — Aphraates; — Didymus; — the Syriac 'Acts of the Apostles'; — Epiphanius; — Leontius; — Ephraem; — Ambrose; — Chrysostom; — Jerome; — Augustine."

This evidence is quoted at length from Burgon because he is the one who has made the most thorough study of this passage. Hort's answer is obvious: that this passage is very old, but is clearly a Western interpolation. B or Vaticanus (which testifies against itself by the inclusion of the blank column) and Aleph, whose character has already been discussed at some length, along with a statement of the latitudinarian Eusebius, who testifies on both sides of the question, are puffed up to what is considered to be a great weight of testimony. By the theory all so-called Western readings are disallowed and, as usual, practically all the evidence is thrown away without being faced. Swete, in his commentary on Mark admits that "the documentary testimony for the longer ending is over-whelming," but he rejects it nevertheless, partly if not mainly on internal grounds.

I Timothy 3:16. This famous passage has often been called the *crux criticorum*. It would be difficult to add to what Burgon has said in the seventy-six large pages which he devoted to it in *The Revision Revised*. Most people who talk about the "better reading" are totally unaware of this careful, closely reasoned argument.

These wise words of Burgon need to be taken to heart by more students of the New Testament:

"The one great Fact, which especially troubles him [Hort] and his joint Editor — (as well it may) — is *The Traditional Greek Text* of the New Testament Scriptures. Call this Text Erasmian or Complutensian, — the text of Stephens, or of Beza, or of the Elzevirs, — call it the 'Received,' or the *Traditional Greek Text,* or whatever other name you please; — the fact remains, that a Text has come down to us which is attested by a general consensus of ancient Copies, ancient Versions, ancient Fathers. This, at all events, is a point on which (happily) there exists entire conformity of opinion between Dr. Hort and ourselves. Our Readers cannot have yet forgotten his virtual admission that, — *Beyond all question the Textus Receptus* is *the dominant Graeco-Syrian Text* of A.D. 350 to A.D. 400."[23]

Since these dates go back to the time of the production of B and Aleph, why is their authority always flaunted by reason of their superior age? According to Westcott and Hort their mythical Syrian revisers were either so stupid that they did not recognize a good manuscript when they saw one, or so wicked that they deliberately fabricated a text which they well knew to be inferior.

The Westcott-Hort text has become a new Textus Receptus for the critically elite. Those who accuse the upholders of the traditional text of worshipping the old Textus Receptus had better look within themselves. The old Textus Receptus at least has a consensus of ancient testimony behind it, not just a few ancient authorities supported by a theory.

The Westcott-Hort theory has been examined and found wanting. The whole arrogant scheme of putting this study on a purely literary basis, without any acknowledgment of the corruption brought into the text in early days by willful and wicked men, and without any perception of

---

23 *The Revision Revised,* p. 269.

God's providential preservation of His Word down through the centuries, collapses when subjected to close scrutiny. Men would have seen this in the years immediately after 1881 if they had not been so committed to the liberal trends which were then gathering momentum. Burgon was a "voice crying in the wilderness" so far as most textual critics were concerned; yet there are those even today who attribute to his blast the quick drop in popularity of the English Revised Version, so closely identified with Westcott and Hort. Some did recognize the theory for what it is and would have none of it.

The Westcott-Hort theory holds the field in the opinions of so many people because it disposes of ninety-five per cent of the documentary evidence in such a clever way that they do not perceive the loss of it. "Good riddance," they say to all manuscripts, versions, and Fathers except a little handful (a handful incidentally which do not agree among themselves).

In an earlier chapter the Westcott and Hort theory was compared to a temple, the two chief columns of which were the "Syrian recensions" and the "Neutral Text." Certainly enough has been said to show that these columns were in reality made of air. Scarcely any scholar can be found today, even among those most favorable to Westcott and Hort, who will vouch for deliberate and authoritative Syrian recensions or who will call their Neutral Text neutral.

Is it possible to believe that a text actually fabricated in the fourth century rapidly became so dominant that practically no copies were made any longer of exemplars which contained the type of text found in B and Aleph, also of the fourth century? This is really asking too much. The subjective character of the evidence adduced by Westcott and Hort permeates their whole theory. Nowhere in their treatise have Westcott and Hort explained just what evidence there is to prove that the so-called Neutral Text is closest to the apostolic text. This colossal *petitio principii* has been set forth with such bold strokes that most people apparently never notice it. The mere fact that a little group of documents are found habitually to band themselves together in opposition to most of the rest does not in itself prove their superiority. Most people if faced with the issue in this way would say that common sense dictates otherwise. As Burgon repeatedly pointed out, Aleph and B are only two specimens of antiquity, not antiquity itself. When people insisted on having old readings, he was wont to reply that they ought to know that *all* readings are old.

In the light of what has been shown in the preceding chapters, Burgon's statement of the case in his famous reply to Bishop Ellicott was hardly too strong:

"Such builders are Drs. Westcott and Hort, — with whom (by your own avowal) you stand completely identified. I repeat (for I wish it to be distinctly understood and remembered) that what I assert concerning those Critics is, — not that their superstructure rests upon an insecure foundation; but that it rests on *no foundation at all.* My complaint is, — not that they are somewhat and frequently mistaken; but that they are mistaken entirely, and that they are mistaken *throughout.* There is no possibility of approximation between their mere assumptions and the results of my humble and laborious method of dealing with the Text of Scripture. We shall only then be able to begin to reason together with the slightest prospect of coming to any agreement, when they have unconditionally abandoned all their preconceived imaginations, and unreservedly scattered every one of their postulates to the four winds."[24]

It will not do to modify Westcott and Hort and to proceed from there. The only road to progress in New Testament textual criticism is repudiation of their theory and all its fruits. Most contemporary criticism is bankrupt and confused, the result of its liaison with liberal theology. A Bible-believing Christian can never be content to follow the leadership of those who do not recognize the Bible as the verbally inspired Word of God. The Textus Receptus is the starting-point for future research, because it embodies substantially and in a convenient form the traditional text.

---

[24] *Ibid.,* pp. 518-19.

Admitted, it will have to undergo extensive revision. It needs to be revised according to sound principles which will take account of all the evidence. Burgon's leading premise, in contrast to Westcott and Hort, is that textual criticism of the New Testament is not the same as that of any other work. Burgon says:

"That which distinguishes Sacred Science from every other Science which can be named is that it is Divine, and has to do with a Book which is inspired; that is, whose true Author is God. . . . It is chiefly from inattention to this circumstance that misconception prevails in that department of Sacred Science known as 'Textual Criticism.' "[25]

Having established this basic principle he shows that the issue can be narrowed down to this:

"Does the truth of the Text of Scripture dwell with the vast multitude of copies, uncial and cursive, concerning which nothing is more remarkable than the marvellous agreement which subsists between them? Or is it rather to be supposed that the truth abides exclusively with a very little handful of manuscripts, which at once differ from the great bulk of the witnesses, and — strange to say — also amongst themselves?"[26]

All these notes of truth used together will result in a far more scientific and far better method than that of Westcott and Hort. Christian students who accept the Bible as the verbally inspired Word of God need to interest themselves in the questions of textual criticism. This is not merely an academic matter which is only of passing interest to a few scholarly recluses. Burgon has pointed the way. Hoskier, as has been mentioned a number of times in the course of this dissertation, has made a noble beginning in the inductive processes that are required in this kind of work.

The question now is: "Who follows in their train?"

---

[25] Burgon and Miller, *The Traditional Text*, p. 9.
[26] *Ibid.*, pp. 16-17.

ABOUT THE AUTHOR OF
"OUR AUTHORIZED BIBLE VINDICATED"

David Otis Fuller

Benjamin G. Wilkinson, Ph.D. is all but unknown to the world of scholarship, but once his book is carefully considered it will be evident that here is a scholar of the first rank with a thorough knowledge of the subjects about which he wrote. Dr. Wilkinson taught for many years in a small and obscure Eastern college. For this excellent work which he produced he secured copyrights in both England and America back in 1930.

Someone has said, "There is no power on earth that can equal an idea ready to be born!" Dr. Wilkinson's book is not an idea but a cogent presentation of little known facts along with a thrilling review of the battle that began in Eden with Satan's skeptical question, "Yea, hath God said?" and has continued unabated until this present hour.

With such a surfeit of Bible translations and such profound confusion existing in Christian circles, Dr. Wilkinson's work will go a long way in bringing into proper focus and perspective the whole question of where final authority lies and just what we can trust with confidence in the midst of this multiplicity of versions.

Let Dr. Wilkinson tell us in his own words what prompted him to carry out such a research and what this has done for him in his own spiritual life:

"This volume is written in the fervent hope that it will confirm and establish faith in God's Word, which through the ages has been preserved inviolate. In these days when faith is weakening and the Bible is being torn apart, it is vital that we enter into fields which can yield up their evidence of how God, through the centuries, intervened to transmit to us a perfect Bible.

"Much of the material given in this book was collected in response to the needs of the author's classroom work. In pursuing this line of study, he has been astounded and thrilled to find in historical situations, where he least expected it, evidences of special intervention and special purposes of God with regard to His Holy Word. His faith in the inspiration of the Bible has been deeply strengthened as he has perceived how down through the ages God's true Bible has constantly triumphed over erroneous versions.

"With regard to the different versions, it is necessary, while confirming the glorious inspiration of the Bible, to warn the people against Bibles which include false books, and, especially at the present time, against the dangers of false readings in genuine books. There are versions of the Bible, prepared by men of scholarship, with certain books and readings we cannot accept. Such versions may be of use for reference or for comparison. In certain passages, they may give a clearer rendering. But it is unthinkable that those who use such versions would be unwilling to have the public informed of their dangers.

"This work has been written under great pressure. In addition to the author's tasks in the classroom and his evangelical work as pastor of a city church, he wrote this book in response to urgent requests. It may be possible that there are a few technical mistakes. The author has strong confidence, however, that the main lines of argument are timely, and that they stand on a firm foundation.

"Is it possible to know what is the true Word of God? The author sends forth this book with a fervent prayer that it may aid the earnest seeker after truth to find the answer to this all-important question."

OUR AUTHORIZED BIBLE VINDICATED

Benjamin G. Wilkinson

CHAPTER I

Fundamentally, Only Two Different Bibles

"There is the idea in the minds of some people that
scholarship demands the laying aside of the Authorized
Version of the Bible and taking up the latest Revised
Version. This is an idea, however, without any proper
basis. This Revised Version is in large part in line with
what is known as modernism, and is peculiarly acceptable
to those who think that any change, anywhere or in
anything, is progress. Those who have really investigated
the matter, and are in hearty sympathy with what is
evangelical, realize that this Revised Version is a part of
the movement to 'modernize' Christian thought and faith
and do away with the established truth."[1]

In one of our prominent publications, there appeared in
the winter of 1928, an article entitled, "Who Killed
Goliath?" and in the spring of 1929 an article named,
"The Dispute About Goliath." Attention was called to the
fact that in the American Revised Version,[2] II Samuel
21:19, we read that Elhanan killed Goliath. A special
cablegram from the "most learned and devout scholars" of

---

[1] *The Herald and Presbyter* (Presbyterian), July 16, 1924, p. 10.

[2] The revision referred to in this chapter is the American Standard Version
of 1901.

the Church of England said, in substance, that the Revised Version was correct, that Elhanan and not David killed Goliath; that there were many other things in the Bible which were the product of exaggeration, such as the story of Noah and the ark, of Jonah and the whale, of the Garden of Eden, and of the longevity of Methuselah. The first article says that these modern views have been held and taught in practically all American theological seminaries of standing, and that young ministers being graduated from them have rejected the old beliefs about these events whether the public knew it or not. This publication aroused a national interest and its office was "inundated," as the editor says, with letters as to whether this Revised Version is correct, or whether, as we have always believed, according to the Authorized Version, David killed Goliath.[3]

Is the American Revised Version correct on this point, or is the Bible that has led the Protestant world for three hundred years correct? Is the Revised Version correct in thousands of other changes made, or is the King James Version correct?

Back of this and other changes lie the motives and events which, in 1870, brought into existence the Committees which produced the Revised Versions — both the English and the American. During the three hundred and fifty years following the Reformation, repeated attempts were made to set aside the Greek New Testament, called the Received Text, from which the New Testament of the King James in English and other Protestant Bibles in other languages were translated. Many individual efforts produced different Greek New Testaments.

Likewise furious attacks were made upon the Old Testament in Hebrew, from which the King James and other Bibles had been translated. None of these assaults, however, met with any marked success until the Revision Committee was appointed by the southern half of the Church of England under the Archbishop of Canterbury, although the same church in the northern half of England

---

[3] *The Literary Digest*, December 29, 1928; March 9, 1929.

under the Archbishop of York, refused to be a party to the project. This Revision Committee, besides the changes in the Old Testament, made over 5,000 changes in the Received Text of the New Testament and so produced a new Greek New Testament. This permitted all the forces hostile to the Bible to gather themselves together and pour through the breach. Since then, the flood gates have been opened and we are now deluged with many different kinds of Greek New Testaments and with English Bibles translated from them, changed and mutilated in bewildering confusion.

Again, in the story of the dark hour when Jesus hung on the cross, the King James Bible declares that the darkness which was over the whole land from the sixth to the ninth hour was produced because the *sun was darkened.* This reason offers the Christian believer a testimony of the miraculous interposition of the Father in behalf of His Son, similar to the darkness which afflicted Egypt in the plagues upon that nation.

In the New Testament, as translated by Moffatt and also in certain other modern Bibles, we are told that the darkness was caused by an *eclipse of the sun.* Of course, a darkness caused by an eclipse of the sun is very ordinary; it is not a miracle. Moreover, Christ was crucified at the time of the Passover which always occurred when the moon was full. At the time of a full moon, no eclipse of the sun is possible. Now which of these two records in Greek did God write: the miraculous, as recorded in the King James Bible and which we have believed for three hundred years; or the unnatural and impossible, as recorded in Moffatt's translation? Moffatt and the Revisers both used the same manuscript.

Some of those who had part in these Revised and Modern Bibles were higher critics of the most pronounced type. At least one man sat on the Revision Committee of 1881 who had openly and in writing denied the Divinity of our Lord and Saviour Jesus Christ. On this account, their chairman of high standing absented himself almost from the first.[4]

"Since the publication of the revised New Testament, it has been frequently said that the changes of translation which the work contains are of little importance from a doctrinal point of view. . . . To the writer, any such statement appears to be in the most substantial sense contrary to the facts of the case."[5]

Life is bigger than logic. When it comes to the philosophy of life, scholarship and science are not the all which counts. It is as true today as in the days of Christ, that "the common people heard Him gladly." If it be a question of physics, of chemistry, of mathematics, or of mechanics, there scientists can speak with authority. But when it is a question of revelation, of spirituality, or of morality, the common people are as competent judges as are the product of the schools. And in great crises, history has frequently shown that they are safer.

Experience also determines issues. There are those among us now who would change the Constitution of the United States, saying: "Have we not men today who have as great intellect as Washington, Adams, Jefferson, and the others? Have we not much more light than they? Why must we be tied to what they taught?" We will not deny that there are men now living as brilliant as the founding fathers. But no men today ever went through the same experience as the framers of the Constitution. Those pioneers were yet witnesses of the vicious principles of the Dark Ages and their cruel results. They were called upon to suffer, to endure, to fight, that principles of a different nature might be established. Experience, not reading or philosophizing, had thoroughly wrought in them the glorious ideals incorporated into the fundamental document of the land.

---

[4] Samuel Hemphill, *A History of the Revised Version,* pp. 36, 37. The first chairman, Bishop Wilberforce, was replaced by Bishop Ellicott.

[5] Dr. G. Vance Smith, *Texts and Margins of the Revised New Testament,* p. 45. Dr. Smith was the Unitarian scholar referred to in the previous paragraph.

Experience can throw some light also upon the relative value of Bible versions. The King James Bible was translated when England was fighting her way out from Roman Catholicism to Protestantism;6 whereas, the Revised Version was born after fifty years (1833 — 1883) of terrific Romanizing campaigns, when one convulsion after another rocked the mental defenses of England and broke down the ascendency of the Protestant mentality in that empire. The King James Version was born of the Reformation; the Revised Versions and some modern Bibles were born of Higher Criticism and Romanizing activities, as this treatise will show.

We hear a great deal today about the Sunday Law of the Roman Emperor Constantine, 321 A.D. Why is it that we do not hear about the corrupt Bible which Constantine adopted and promulgated, the version which for 1800 years has been exploited by the forces of heresy and apostasy? This Bible, we regret to say, lies at the bottom of many versions which now flood the publishing houses, the schools, the churches, yes, many homes, and are bringing confusion and doubt to untold millions.

Down through the centuries, the pure Bible, the living Word of God, has often faced the descendants of this corrupt version, robed in splendor and seated on the throne of power. It has been a battle and a march, a battle and a march. God's Holy Word has always won; to its victories we owe the very existence of Christian civilization and all the happiness we now have and hope for in eternity. And now, once again, in these last days, the battle is being renewed, the affections and the control of the minds of men are being contended for by these two rival claimants.

Devotion to error can never produce true righteousness. Out of the present confusion of Bibles, I propose to trace the situation back to its origin, that our hearts may be full of praise and gratitude to God for the marvelous manner in

---

6 The KJV was the crowning fruit of a series of translations made in the Reformation period—Tyndale, Coverdale, Matthews, Geneva, and Bishops' Bible.

which He has given to us and preserved for us the Holy Scriptures.

The Hebrew Text of the Old Testament

For the present, the problem revolves mostly around the thousands of different readings in the Greek New Testament manuscripts. By the time of Christ, the Old Testament was in a settled condition. Since then, the Hebrew Scriptures had been carried down intact to the day of printing (about 1450 A.D.) by the unrivalled methods of the Jews in transmitting perfect Hebrew manuscripts. Whatever perplexing problems there are in connection with the Old Testament, these have largely been produced by translating it into Greek and uniting that translation to the Greek New Testament. It is around the problems of the Greek New Testament that the battle for centuries has been fought. We must, therefore, confine ourselves largely to the Christian Era; for the experience which befell the New Testament and the controversies that raged around it, also befell the Old Testament.

Moreover, the Revisers, themselves, would have no one think for an instant that they used any other manuscripts in revising the Old Testament than the Masoretic text, the only reliable Hebrew Bible. Dr. Ellicott, chairman of the English New Testament Committee, repeatedly recommends the story of the Old Testament Revision by Dr. Chambers. Dr. Chambers says:

"The more sober critics with one consent hold fast the Masoretic text. This has been the rule with the authors of the present revision. Their work is based throughout upon the traditional Hebrew. In difficult or doubtful places, where some corruption seems to have crept in or some accident to have befallen the manuscript, the testimony of the early versions is given in the margin, but never incorporated with the text."[7]

---

[7] Chambers, *Companion to the Revised Old Testament,* p. 74. Dr. Chambers was a member of the American O. T. Revision Committee.

The Apostasy of the Early Christian Church Prepares the Way for Corrupting the Manuscripts

Inspired by the unerring Spirit of God, chosen men brought forth the different books of the New Testament, these originally being written in Greek. For a few years, under the guidance of the noble apostles, believers in Christ were privileged to have the unadulterated Word of God.

But soon the scene changed; the fury of Satan, robbed of further opportunity to harass the Son of God, turned upon the written Word. Heretical sects, warring for supremacy, corrupted the manuscripts in order to further their ends. "Epiphanius, in his polemic treatise the 'Panarion,' describes not less than eighty heretical parties."[8] The Roman Catholics won. The true church fled into the wilderness, taking pure manuscripts with her.

When the Apostle Paul foretold the coming of the great apostasy in his sermon and later in his epistle to the Thessalonians, he declared that there would "come a falling away" (II Thess. 2:3); and then he added that the "mystery of iniquity doth already work" (II Thess. 2:7).

Later when Paul had gathered together, on his journey to Jerusalem, the bishops who were over the church of Ephesus, he said, "Of your own selves shall men arise, speaking perverse things, to draw away disciples after them. Therefore watch, and remember, that by the space of three years I ceased not to warn every one night and day with tears" (Acts 20:30, 31).

Though there are many important events in the life of the great apostle which have been left unrecorded, the Holy Spirit deemed it of high importance to put on record this prophecy, to warn us that even from among the elders or bishops there would arise perverse leadership. This prophecy would be fulfilled, and was fulfilled. Until we sense the importance of this great prediction of the Holy Spirit and come to recognize its colossal fulfillment, the Bible must in many things remain a sealed book.

---

[8] G. P. Fisher, *History of Christian Doctrine,* p. 19.

When Paul was warned of the coming apostasy, he aroused the Thessalonians not to be soon shaken or troubled in spirit "by letter as from us" (II Thess. 2:2). It would have been bold at any time to write a letter to a church and sign to it the apostle's name. But how daring must have been that iniquity which would commit that forgery even while the apostle was yet alive! Even in Paul's day, the apostasy was built on lawless acts.

Later in his labors, Paul specifically pointed out three ways in which the apostasy was working: (1) by exalting man's knowledge above the Bible; (2) by spiritualizing the Scriptures away; and (3) by substituting philosophy for revelation.

I — False Knowledge Exalted Above Scriptures

Of the first of these dangers we read as follows: "O Timothy, keep that which is committed to thy trust, avoiding profane and vain babblings, and oppositions of science falsely so called" (I Tim. 6:20).

The Greek word in this verse which is translated "science" is "gnosis." "Gnosis" means knowledge. The apostle condemned, not knowledge in general, but false knowledge. False teachers were placing their own interpretations on Christian truth by reading into it human ideas. This tendency grew and increased until a great system bearing the name of Christianity, known as Gnosticism, was established. To show that this religion was not a theory without an organization among men, but that it had communities and was widespread, I quote from Milman: "The later Gnostics were bolder, but more consistent innovators on the simple scheme of Christianity. . . . In all the great cities of the East in which Christianity had established its most flourishing communities, sprang up this rival which aspired to a still higher degree of knowledge than was revealed in the Gospel, and boasted that it soared almost as much above the vulgar Christianity as the vulgar paganism."[9]

---

[9] *History of Christianity*, Vol. II, p. 107.

The mysterious theories of these Gnostics have reappeared in the works of theologians of our day. The following words from the *Encyclopedia Americana* will prove the tendency of this doctrine to break out in our times. Note the place of "aeons" in their system: "There have been no Gnostic sects since the fifth century; but many of the principles of their system of emanations reappear in later philosophical systems, drawn from the same sources as theirs. Plato's lively representation had given to the idea of the Godhead, something substantial, which the Gnostics transferred to their aeons."[10]

In fact, the aeons system has found a treatment in the Revised Version. Bishop Westcott, who was one of the dominating minds of the English New Testament Revision Committee, advocates that the Revised New Testament be read in the light of the modern aeon theories of the Revisers. He comments thus on the revised reading of Eph. 3:21: "Some perhaps are even led to pause on the wonderful phrase in Eph. 3:21, margin, 'for all the generations of the age of the ages,' which is represented in English (A.V.) by 'to all generations forever and ever;' and to reflect on the vision so open of a vast aeon of which the elements are aeons unfolding, as it were, stage after stage, the manifold powers of one life fulfilled in many ways, each aeon the child (so to speak) of that which has gone before."[11]

J. H. Newman, the Oxford divine, who was made a Cardinal after he had left the Church of England for the Church of Rome, and whose doctrines, in whole or in part, were adopted by the majority of the Revisers, did more to influence the religion of the British Empire than any other man since the Reformation. He was invited to sit on the Revision Committee. Dr. S. Parkes Cadman speaks thus, referring to his Gnosticism:

"From the fathers, Newman also derived a speculative angelology which described the unseen universe as inhabited by hosts of intermediate beings who were spiritual

---

10 "Gnostics," *Encyclopedia Americana*, 1914.

11 B. F. Westcott, *Some Lessons of the Revised Version*, pp. 186, 187.

agents between God and creation. . . . Indeed, Newman's cosmogony was essentially Gnostic, and echoed the teachings of Cerinthus, who is best entitled to be considered as the link between the Judaizing and Gnostic sects."[12]

The following quotation from a magazine of authority gives a description of this modern species of Gnosticism which shows its Romanizing tendency. It also reveals how Bishop Westcott could hold this philosophy, while it names Dr. Philip Schaff, President of both American Committees of Revision, as even more an apostle of this modern Gnosticism: "The roads which lead to Rome are very numerous. . . . Another road, less frequented and less obvious, but not less dangerous, is the philosophical. There is a strong affinity between the speculative system of development, according to which every thing that is, is true and rational, and the Romish idea of a self-evolving infallible church. . . . No one can read the exhibitions of the Church and of theology written even by Protestants under the influence of the speculative philosophy, without seeing that little more than a change of terminology is required to turn such philosophy into Romanism. Many distinguished men have already in Germany passed, by this bridge, from philosophical skepticism to the Romish Church. A distinct class of the Romanizing portion of the Church of England belongs to this philosophical category. Dr. Nevin had entered this path long before Dr. Schaff came from Germany to point it out to him."[13]

II — Spiritualizing the Scriptures Away

The next outstanding phase of the coming apostasy — spiritualizing the Scriptures away — is predicted by the apostle:

"But shun profane and vain babblings: for they will increase unto more ungodliness. And their word will eat as doth a canker: of whom is Hymenaeus and Philetus; who concerning the truth have erred, saying that the resurrec-

12 *Three Religious Leaders of Oxford*, pp. 481, 482.
13 *Princeton Review*, January, 1854, pp. 152, 153.

tion is past already; and overthrow the faith of some" (II Tim. 2:16-18).

The Bible teaches the resurrection as a future event. One way these prominent teachers, full of vanity, could say that it was past, was to teach, as some of their descendants do today, that the resurrection is a spiritual process which takes place, say, at conversion. The prediction of the apostle was fulfilled in a great system of Bible spiritualizing or mystifying which subverted the primitive faith. Turning the Scripture into an allegory was a passion in those days. In our day, allegorizing is not only a passion, but is also a refuge from truth for many leaders with whom we have to do.

III — Substituting Philosophy for Scripture

The third way in which the apostasy came, was predicted by the apostle thus: "Beware lest any man spoil you through philosophy and vain deceit, after the tradition of men, after the rudiments of the world, and not after Christ" (Col. 2:8).

The philosophy condemned in this passage is not the philosophy found in the sacred Word, but the philosophy which is "after the tradition of men." Even before the days of Christ, the very existence of the Jewish religion was threatened by intellectual leaders of the Jews who were carried away with the subtleties and glamour of pagan philosophy. This same temptress quickly ensnared multitudes who bore the name of Christian.

"Greek philosophy exercised the greatest influence not only on the Christian mode of thought, but also through that on the institutions of the Church. In the completed church we find again the philosophic schools."[14]

The greatest enemies of the infant Christian church, therefore, were not found in the triumphant heathenism which filled the world, but in the rising flood of heresy which, under the name of Christianity, engulfed the truth for many years. This is what brought on the Dark Ages.

---

14 Harnack, *History of Dogma,* Vol. I, p. 128.

This rising flood, as we shall see, had multiplied in abundance copies of the Scriptures with bewildering changes in verses and passages within one hundred years after the death of John (100 A.D.). As Irenaeus said concerning Marcion, the Gnostic: "Wherefore also Marcion and his followers have betaken themselves to mutilating the Scriptures, not acknowledging some books at all; and, curtailing the Gospel according to Luke, and the epistles of Paul, they assert that these alone are authentic, which they have themselves shortened."[15]

Fundamentally, There Are Only Two Streams of Bibles

Anyone who is interested enough to read the vast volume of literature on this subject, will agree that down through the centuries there were only two streams of manuscripts.

The first stream which carried the Received Text in Hebrew and Greek, began with the apostolic churches, and reappearing at intervals down the Christian Era among enlightened believers, was protected by the wisdom and scholarship of the pure church in her different phases: precious manuscripts were preserved by such as the church at Pella in Palestine where Christians fled, when in 70 A.D. the Romans destroyed Jerusalem;[16] by the Syrian Church of Antioch which produced eminent scholarship; by the Italic Church in northern Italy; and also at the same time by the Gallic Church in southern France and by the Celtic Church in Great Britain; by the pre-Waldensian, the Waldensian, and the churches of the Reformation.

This first stream appears, with very little change, in the Protestant Bibles of many languages, and in English, in that Bible known as the King James Version, the one which has been in use for three hundred years in the English-speaking world. These manuscripts have in agreement with them, by far the vast majority of copies of the

---

15 *Ante-Nicene Fathers* (Scribner's), Vol. I, pp. 434, 435.

16 G. T. Stokes, *Acts of the Apostles,* Vol. II, p. 439.

original text. So vast is this majority that even the enemies of the Received Text admit that nineteen-twentieths of all Greek manuscripts are of this class.

The Old Latin texts, like the other versions, are of two kinds; both the Traditional Text and the forms of corruption find a place in them. Augustine wrote, "In the earliest days of the faith whenever any Greek codex fell into the hands of anyone who thought that he had a slight familiarity with Greek and Latin, he was bold enough to attempt to make a translation." The Old Latin evidence varies so much that it seems almost certain that several separate ancient translations from different Greek codices are represented by it. Much, but by no means all, of the Old Latin evidence is favourable to the Traditional Text.

The second stream is a small one of a very few manuscripts. These last manuscripts are represented:

(a) In Greek: — The Vatican MS., or Codex B, in the library at Rome; and the Sinaitic, or Codex Aleph, its brother. We will fully explain about these two manuscripts later.

(b) In Latin: — The Vulgate or Latin Bible of Jerome.

(c) In English: — The Jesuit Bible of 1582, which later with vast changes is seen in the Douay, or Catholic Bible.

(d) In English again: — In many modern Bibles which introduce practically all the Catholic readings of the Latin Vulgate which were rejected by the Protestants of the Reformation; among these, prominently, are the Revised Versions.

So the present controversy between the King James Bible in English and the modern versions is the same old contest fought out between the early church and rival sects; and later, between the Waldenses and the Papists from the fourth to the thirteenth centuries; and later still, between the Reformers and the Jesuits in the sixteenth century.

The Apostle Paul Prepares To Preserve the Truth Against Coming Apostasy

In his later years, the apostle Paul spent more time in

preparing the churches for the great future apostasy than in pushing the work farther on. He foresaw that this apostasy would arise in the West. Therefore, he spent years laboring to anchor the Gentile churches of Europe to the churches of Judea. The Jewish Christians had back of them 1500 years of training. Throughout the centuries God had so molded the Jewish mind that it grasped the idea of sin; of an invisible Godhead; of man's serious condition; of the need for a divine Redeemer.

But throughout these same centuries, the Gentile world had sunk lower and lower in frivolity, heathenism, and debauchery. It is worthy of notice that the apostle Paul wrote practically all of his epistles to the Gentile churches — to Corinth, to Rome, to Philippi, and so on. He wrote almost no letters to the Jewish Christians. Therefore, the great burden of his closing days was to anchor the Gentile churches of Europe to the Christian churches of Judea. In fact, it was to secure this end that he lost his life.

"St. Paul did his best to maintain his friendship and alliance with the Jerusalem Church. To put himself right with them, he traveled up to Jerusalem, when fresh fields and splendid prospects were opening up for him in the West. For this purpose he submitted to several days' restraint and attendance in the Temple, and the results vindicated his determination."[17]

This is how Paul used churches in Judea as a base: "For ye, brethren, became followers of the churches of God which in Judaea are in Christ Jesus: for ye also have suffered like things of your own countrymen, even as they have of the Jews" (I Thess. 2:14).

"There is not a word here of the church of Rome being the model after which the other churches were to be formed; it had no such preeminence — this honor belonged to the churches of Judea; it was according to them, not the church at Rome, that the Asiatic churches were modeled. The purest of all the apostolic churches was that of the Thessalonians, and this was formed after the Christian churches in Judea. Had any preeminence or authority

---

17 *Ibid.*

belonged to the church of Rome, the apostle would have proposed this as a model to all those which he formed, either in Judea, Asia Minor, Greece, or Italy."[18]

Early Corruption of Bible Manuscripts

The last of the apostles to pass away was John. His death is usually placed about 100 A.D. In his closing days, he cooperated in the collecting and forming of those writings we call the New Testament.[19] An ordinary careful reading of Acts, Chapter 15, will prove the scrupulous care with which the early church guarded her sacred writings. "And so well did God's true people through the ages agree on what was Scripture and what was not, that no general council of the church, until that of Trent (1645) dominated by the Jesuits, dared to say anything as to what books should comprise the Bible or what texts were or were not spurious."[20]

While John lived, heresy could make no serious headway. He had hardly passed away, however, before perverse teachers infested the Christian Church. The doom of heathenism, as a controlling force before the superior truths of Christianity, was soon foreseen by all. These years were times which saw the New Testament books corrupted in abundance.

Eusebius is witness to this fact. He also relates that the corrupted manuscripts were so prevalent that agreement between the copies was hopeless; and that those who were *corrupting* the Scriptures, claimed that they really were *correcting* them.[21]

When the warring sects had been consolidated under the iron hand of Constantine, this heretical potentate adopted the Bible which combined the contradictory versions into one, and so blended the various corruptions with the bulk

---

[18] Adam Clarke, *Commentary on the New Testament,* Vol. II, p. 544.

[19] Eusebius, *Eccles. History,* Book III, Chap. 24.

[20] Stanley, *Essays on Church and State,* p. 136.

[21] Eusebius, *Eccles. History,* Book V, Chap. 28.

of pure teachings as to give sanction to the great apostasy now seated on the throne of power.

Beginning shortly after the death of the apostle John, four names stand out in prominence whose teachings contributed both to the victorious heresy and to the final issuing of manuscripts of a corrupt New Testament. These names are (1) Justin Martyr, (2) Tatian, (3) Clement of Alexandria, and (4) Origen. We shall speak first of Justin Martyr.

The year in which the apostle John died, 100 A.D., is given as the date in which Justin Martyr was born. Justin, originally a pagan and of pagan parentage, afterward embraced Christianity and although he is said to have died at heathen hands for his religion, nevertheless, his teachings were of a heretical nature. Even as a Christian teacher, he continued to wear the robes of a pagan philosopher.

In the teachings of Justin Martyr, we begin to see how muddy the stream of pure Christian doctrine was running among the heretical sects fifty years after the death of the apostle John. It was in Tatian, Justin Martyr's pupil, that these regrettable doctrines were carried to alarming lengths, and by his hand committed to writing. After the death of Justin Martyr in Rome, Tatian returned to Palestine and embraced the Gnostic heresy. This same Tatian wrote a Harmony of the Gospels which was called the Diatessaron, meaning four in one. The Gospels were so notoriously corrupted by his hand that in later years a bishop of Syria, because of the errors, was obliged to throw out of his churches no less than two hundred copies of this Diatessaron, since church members were mistaking it for the true Gospel.

We come now to Tatian's pupil known as Clement of Alexandria, 200 A.D.[22] He went much further than Tatian in that he founded a school at Alexandria which instituted propaganda along these heretical lines. Clement expressly tells us that he would not hand down Christian teachings, pure and unmixed, but rather clothed with precepts of pagan philosophy. All the writings of the outstanding

---

[22] J. Hamlyn Hill, *The Diatessaron of Tatian*, p. 9.

heretical teachers were possessed by Clement, and he freely quoted from their corrupted manuscripts as if they were the pure words of Scripture.[23] His influence in the depravation of Christianity was tremendous. But his greatest contribution, undoubtedly, was the direction given to the studies and activities of Origen, his famous pupil.

When we come to Origen, we speak the name of him who did the most of all to create and give direction to the forces of apostasy down through the centuries. It was he who mightily influenced Jerome, the editor of the Latin Bible known as the Vulgate. Eusebius worshipped at the altar of Origen's teachings. He claims to have collected eight hundred of Origen's letters, to have used Origen's six-column Bible, the Hexapla, in his Biblical labors. Assisted by Pamphilus, he restored and preserved Origen's library. Origen's corrupted manuscripts of the Scriptures were well arranged and balanced with subtlety. The last one hundred years have seen much of the so-called scholarship of European and English Christianity dominated by the subtle and powerful influence of Origen.

Origen had so surrendered himself to the furore of turning all Bible events into allegories that he, himself, says, "The Scriptures are of little use to those who understand them as they are written."[24] In order to estimate Origen rightly, we must remember that as a pupil of Clement, he learned the teachings of the Gnostic heresy and like his master, lightly esteemed the historical basis of the Bible. As Schaff says, "His predilection for Plato (the pagan philosopher) led him into many grand and fascinating errors.[25] He made himself acquainted with the various heresies and studied under the heathen Ammonius Saccas, founder of Neo-Platonism.

He taught that the soul existed from eternity before it inhabited the body, and that after death, it migrated to a higher or a lower form of life according to the deeds done

---

23 Dean Burgon, *The Revision Revised,* p. 336.

24 "Origen," McClintock and Strong, *Encyclopedia.*

25 Schaff, *Church History,* Vol. II, p. 791.

in the body; and finally all would return to the state of pure intelligence, only to begin again the same cycles as before. He believed that the devils would be saved, and that the stars and planets had souls, and were, like men, on trial to learn perfection. In fact, he turned the whole Law and Gospel into an allegory.

Such was the man who from his day to this has dominated the endeavors of destructive textual critics. One of the greatest results of his life was that his teachings became the foundation of that system of education called Scholasticism, which guided the colleges of Latin Europe for nearly one thousand years during the Dark Ages.

Origenism flooded the Catholic Church through Jerome, the father of Latin Christianity. "I love . . . the name of Origen," says the most distinguished theologian of the Roman Catholic Church since 1850. "I will not listen to the notion that so great a soul was lost."[26]

A final word from the learned Scrivener will indicate how early and how deep were the corruptions of the sacred manuscripts: "It is no less true to fact than paradoxical in sound, that the worst corruptions to which the New Testament has ever been subjected, originated within a hundred years after it was composed; that Irenaeus (A.D. 150), and the African Fathers, and the whole Western, with a portion of the Syrian Church, used far inferior manuscripts to those employed by Stunica, or Erasmus, or Stephens thirteen centuries later, when moulding the Textus Receptus."[27]

The basis was laid to oppose a mutilated Bible to the true one. How these corruptions found their way down the centuries and reappear in our revised and modern Bibles, the following pages will tell.

---

[26] Newman, *Apologia, pro vita sua,* p. 282.

[27] Scrivener, *Introduction to New Testament Criticism,* 3rd Edition, p. 311.

CHAPTER II

The Bible Adopted by Constantine and the Pure Bible of the Waldenses

Constantine became emperor of Rome in 312 A.D. A little later he embraced the Christian faith for himself and for his empire. As this so-called first Christian emperor took the reins of the civil and spiritual world to bring about the amalgamation of paganism and Christianity, he found three types of manuscripts, or Bibles, vying for supremacy: the Textus Receptus[1] or Constantinopolitan, the Palestinian or Eusebio-Origen, and the Egyptian or Hesychian.[2] The adherents of each claimed superiority for their manuscript. Particularly was there earnest contention between the advocates of the Textus Receptus and those of the Eusebio-Origen text.[3] The defenders of the Textus Receptus were of the humbler class who earnestly sought to follow the early church. The Eusebio-Origen text was the product of the intermingling of the pure Word of God and Greek philosophy in the mind of Origen. It might be called the adaptation of the Word of God to Gnosticism.

---

[1] The title "Textus Receptus" was first given to the Traditional Text by Elzevir in 1633. In these chapters the name is given to the whole body of documents which preserve substantially the same kind of text.

[2] H. B. Swete, *Introduction to the Old Testament in Greek,* pp. 76-86.

[3] Hort, *Introduction,* p. 138.

As the Emperor Constantine embraced Christianity, it became necessary for him to choose which of these Bibles he would sanction. Quite naturally he preferred the one edited by Eusebius and written by Origen, the outstanding intellectual figure that had combined Christianity with Gnosticism in his philosophy, even as Constantine himself was the political genius that was seeking to unite Christianity with pagan Rome. Constantine regarded himself as the director and guardian of this anomalous world church, and as such he was responsible for selecting the Bible for the great Christian centers. His predilection was for the type of Bible whose readings would give him a basis for his imperialistic ideas of the great state church, with ritualistic ostentation and unlimited central power. The philosophy of Origen was well suited to serve Constantine's religio-political theocracy.

It is evident that the so-called Christian Emperor gave to the Papacy his endorsement of the Eusebio-Origen Bible. It was from this type of manuscript that Jerome translated the Latin Vulgate which became the authorized Catholic Bible for all time.

The Latin Vulgate, the Sinaiticus, the Vaticanus, the Hexapla, Jerome, Eusebius, and Origen, are terms for ideas that are inseparable in the minds of those who know. The type of Bible selected by Constantine has held the dominating influence at all times in the history of the Catholic Church. This Bible was different from the Bible of the Waldenses, and, as a result of this difference, the Waldenses were the object of hatred and cruel persecution, as we shall now show. In studying this history, we shall see how it was possible for the pure manuscripts, not only to live, but actually to gain the ascendancy in the face of powerful opposition.

A Channel of Communication from the Churches in Judea Carried Pure Manuscripts to the Primitive Christians in Western Lands

Attentive observers have repeatedly been astonished at the unusual phenomenon exhibited in the meteoric history of the Bible adopted by Constantine. Written in Greek, it was disseminated at a time when Bibles were scarce, owing to the unbridled fury of the pagan emperor, Diocletian. We should naturally think that it would therefore continue long. Such was not the case.

The echo of Diocletian's warfare against the Christians had hardly subsided, when Constantine assumed the imperial purple. Even as far as Great Britain, that far had the rage of Diocletian penetrated. One would naturally suppose that the Bible which had received the promotion of Constantine, especially when disseminated by that emperor who was the first to show favor to that religion of Jesus, would rapidly have spread everywhere in those days when imperial favor meant everything. The truth is, the opposite was the outcome. It flourished for a short space. The span of one generation sufficed to see it disappear from popular use as if it had been struck by some invisible and withering blast. We turn with amazement to discover the reason for this phenomenon.

This chapter will show that the Textus Receptus was the Bible in use in the Greek Empire, in the countries of Syrian Christianity, in northern Italy, in southern France, and in the British Isles in the second century. This was a full century and more before the Vaticanus and the Sinaiticus saw the light of day.[4] When the apostles of the Roman Catholic Church entered these countries in later centuries they found the people using the Textus Receptus; and it was not without difficulty and a struggle that they were able to displace it with their Latin Vulgate. This chapter will likewise show that the Textus Receptus belongs to the type of these early apostolic manuscripts that were brought from Judea, and its claim to priority over the Vaticanus and Sinaiticus will be established.

Early Greek Christianity — Which Bible?

First of all, the Textus Receptus was the Bible of early Eastern Christianity. Later it was adopted as the official

---

4 Burgon, *The Revision Revised*, p. 27.

text of the Greek Catholic Church. There were local reasons which contributed to this result. But, probably, far greater reasons will be found in the fact that the Received Text had authority enough to become, either in itself or by its translation, the Bible of the great Syrian Church; of the Waldensian Church of northern Italy; of the Gallic Church in southern France; and of the Celtic Church in Scotland and Ireland; as well as the official Bible of the Greek Catholic Church. All these churches, some earlier, some later, were in opposition to the Church of Rome and at a time when the Received Text and these Bibles of the Constantine type were rivals. They, as represented in their descendants, are rivals to this day. The Church of Rome built on the Eusebio-Origen type of Bible; these others built on the Received Text. Therefore, because they themselves believed that the Received Text was the true apostolic Bible, and further, because the Church of Rome arrogated to itself the power to choose a Bible which bore the marks of systematic depravation, we have the testimony of these five churches to the authenticity and the apostolicity of the Received Text. The following quotation from Dr. Hort is to prove that the Received Text was the Greek New Testament of the East. Note that Dr. Hort always calls it the Constantinopolitan or Antiochian text:

"It is no wonder that the traditional Constantinopolitan text, whether formally official or not, was the Antiochian text of the fourth century. It was equally natural that the text recognized at Constantinople should eventually become in practice the standard New Testament of the East."[5]

Early Syrian Christianity — Which Bible?

It was at Antioch, capital of Syria, that the believers were first called Christians. And as time rolled on, the Syrian-speaking Christians could be numbered by the thousands. It is generally admitted that the Bible was translated from the original languages into Syrian about

---

5 Hort, *Introduction*, p. 143. See also Burgon, *Revision Revised*, p. 134.

150 A.D.[6] This version is known as the Peshitto (the correct or simple). This Bible even today generally follows the Received Text.[7]

One authority tells us this — "The Peshitto in our days is found in use amongst the Nestorians, who have always kept it, by the Monophysites on the plains of Syria, the Christians of St. Thomas in Malabar, and by the Maronites, on the mountain terraces of Lebanon."[8]

Having presented the fact that the Bible of early Greek Christianity and early Syrian Christianity was not of the Eusebio-Origen or Vaticanus type, but the Received Text, we shall now show that the early Bible of northern Italy, of southern France, and of Great Britain was also the Received Text.

The type of Christianity which first was favored, then raised to leadership by Constantine was that of the Roman Papacy. But this was not the type of Christianity that first penetrated Syria, northern Italy, southern France, and Great Britain.[9] The ancient records of the first believers in Christ in those parts disclose a Christianity which is not Roman but apostolic. These lands were first penetrated by missionaries, not from Rome, but from Palestine and Asia Minor. And the Greek New Testament, the Received Text they brought with them, or its translation, was of the type from which the Protestant Bibles, such as the King James in English, and the Lutheran in German, were translated. We shall presently see that it differed greatly from the Eusebio-Origen Greek New Testament.

Early England — Which Bible?

Onward then pushed those heroic bands of evangelists to England, to southern France, and northern Italy. The Mediterranean was like the trunk of a tree with branches running out to these parts, the roots of the tree being in

---

6 *Ibid.*, p. 27, note.

7 *Ibid.*

8 Burgon and Miller, *The Traditional Text*, p. 128.

9 T. V. Moore, *The Culdee Church*, Chapters 3 and 4.

Judea or Asia Minor, from whence the sap flowed westward to fertilize the distant lands. History does not possess any record of heroism superior to the sacrifices and sufferings of the early Christians in the pagan West. The first believers of ancient Britain nobly held their ground when the pagan Anglo-Saxons descended on the land like a flood. Dean Stanley holds it against Augustine, the missionary sent by the Pope in 596 A.D. to convert England, that he treated with contempt the early Christian Britons.[10] Yes, more, he connived with the Anglo-Saxons in their frightful extermination of that pious people. And after Augustine's death, when those same pagan Anglo-Saxons so terrified the papal leaders in England that they fled back to Rome, it was the British Christians of Scotland who occupied the forsaken fields. It is evident from this that British Christianity did not come from Rome. Furthermore, Dr. Adam Clarke claims that the examination of Irish customs reveals that they have elements which were imported into Ireland from Asia Minor by early Christians.[11]

Since Italy, France, and Great Britain were once provinces of the Roman Empire, the first translations of the Bible by the early Christians in those parts were made into Latin. The early Latin translations were very dear to the hearts of these primitive churches, and as Rome did not send any missionaries toward the West before 250 A.D., the early Latin Bibles were well established before these churches came into conflict with Rome. Not only were such translations in existence long before the Vulgate was adopted by the Papacy, and well established, but the people for centuries refused to supplant their old Latin Bibles by the Vulgate. "The old Latin versions were used longest by the western Christians who would not bow to the authority of Rome — e.g., the Donatists; the Irish in Ireland, Britain, and the Continent; the Albigenses, etc."[12]

---

[10] Stanley, *Historic Memorials of Canterbury,* pp. 33, 34; quoted in Cathcart, *Ancient British and Irish Churches,* p. 12.

[11] Clarke, *Commentary on Matthew,* 1:18.

[12] Jacobus, *Catholic and Protestant Bibles Compared,* p. 200, n. 15.

God in His wisdom had invested these Latin versions by His Providence with a charm that outweighed the learned artificiality of Jerome's Vulgate. This is why they persisted through the centuries. A characteristic often overlooked in considering versions, and one that cannot be too greatly emphasized, needs to be pointed out in comparing the Latin Bible of the Waldenses, of the Gauls, and of the Celts with the later Vulgate. To bring before you the unusual charm of those Latin Bibles, I quote from the *Forum* of June, 1887:

"The old Italic version into the rude Low Latin of the second century held its own as long as Latin continued to be the language of the people. The critical version of Jerome never displaced it, and only replaced it when the Latin ceased to be a living language, and became the language of the learned. The Gothic version of Ulfilas, in the same way, held its own until the tongue in which it was written ceased to exist. Luther's Bible was the first genuine beginning of modern German literature. In Germany, as in England, many critical translations have been made, but they have fallen stillborn from the press. The reason of these facts seems to be this: that the languages into which these versions were made, were almost perfectly adapted to express the broad, generic simplicity of the original text. Microscopic accuracy of phrase and classical nicety of expression may be very well for the student in his closet, but they do not represent the human and Divine simplicity of the Scriptures to the mass of those for whom the Scriptures were written. To render that, the translator needs not only a simplicity of mind rarely to be found in companies of learned critics, but also a language possessing in some large measure that broad, simple, and generic character which we have seen to belong to the Hebrew and to the Greek of the New Testament. It was partly because the Low Latin of the second century, and the Gothic of Ulfilas, and the rude, strong German of Luther had that character in a remarkable degree, that they were capable of rendering the Scriptures with a faithfulness which guaranteed their permanence."[13]

13 Fulton, *Forum,* June, 1887.

For nine hundred years, we are told, the first Latin translations held their own after the Vulgate appeared. [14] The Vulgate was born about 380 A.D. Nine hundred years later brings us to about 1280 A.D. This accords well with the fact that at the famous Council of Toulouse, 1229 A.D., the Pope gave orders for the most terrible crusade to be waged against the simple Christians of southern France and northern Italy who would not bow to his power. Cruel, relentless, devastating, this war was waged, destroying the Bibles, books, and every vestige of documents telling the story of the Waldenses and Albigenses.

Since then, some authorities speak of the Waldenses as having their Bible, the Vulgate. We regret to dispute these claims. When we consider that the Waldenses were, so to speak, in their mountain fastnesses, on an island in the midst of a sea of nations using the Vulgate, it is no wonder that they knew and possessed the Vulgate. But the Italic, the earlier Latin, was their own Bible, the one for which they lived and suffered and died. Moreover, to the east was Constantinople, the center of Greek Catholicism, whose Bible was the Received Text; while a little farther east was the noble Syrian Church which also had the Received Text. In touch with these, northern Italy could easily verify her text.

It is clearly evident that the Latin Bible of early British Christianity was not the Latin Bible (Vulgate) of the Papacy. Furthermore, it was at such variance with the Vulgate as to engender strife. The following quotation from Dr. Von Dobschutz will verify these two facts: "When Pope Gregory found some Anglo-Saxon youths at the slave market of Rome and perceived that in the North there was still a pagan nation to be baptized, he sent one of his monks to England, and this monk, who was Saint Augustine, took with him the Bible and introduced it to the Anglo-Saxons, and one of his followers brought with him from Rome pictures showing the Biblical history, and decorated the walls of the church in the monastery of Wearmouth. We do not enter here into the difficult

---

14 Jacobus, *Catholic and Protestant Bibles*, p. 4.

question of the relations between this newly founded Anglo-Saxon church and the old Iro-Scottish church. Differences of Bible text had something to do with the pitiful struggles which arose between the churches and ended in the devastation of the older one."[15]

Famous in history among all centers of Bible knowledge and Bible Christianity was Iona, on the little island of Hy, off the northwest coast of Scotland. Its most historic figure was Columba. Upon this island rock, God breathed out His Holy Spirit and from this center, to the tribes of northern Europe. When Rome awoke to the necessity of sending out missionaries to extend her power, she found Great Britain and northern Europe already professing a Christianity whose origin could be traced back through Iona to Asia Minor. About 600 A.D. Rome sent missionaries to England and to Germany, to bring these simple Bible Christians under her dominion, as much as to subdue the pagans. D'Aubigne has furnished us this picture of Iona and her missions:

"D'Aubigne says that Columba esteemed the cross of Christ higher than the royal blood which flowed in his veins, and that *precious manuscripts were brought to Iona,* where a theological school was founded and the Word was studied. 'Ere long a missionary spirit breathed over this ocean rock, so justly named "the light of the Western world." ' British missionaries carried the light of the gospel to the Netherlands, France, Switzerland, Germany, yea, even into Italy, and did more for the conversion of central Europe than the half-enslaved Roman Church."[16]

Early France — Which Bible?

In southern France, when in 177 A.D. the Gallic Christians were frightfully massacred by the heathen, a record of their suffering was drawn up by the survivors and sent, not to the Pope of Rome, but to their brethren in

---

15 Von Dobschutz, *The Influence of the Bible on Civilization,* pp. 61, 62.
16 J. N. Andrews and L. R. Conradi, *History of the Sabbath,* pp. 581, 582.

Asia Minor.[17]   Milman claims that the French received their Christianity from Asia Minor.

These apostolic Christians in southern France were undoubtedly those who gave effective help in carrying the Gospel to Great Britain.[18] And as we have seen above, there was a long and bitter struggle between the Bible of the British Christians and the Bible which was brought later to England by the missionaries of Rome. And as there were really only two Bibles — the official version of Rome, and the Received Text — we may safely conclude that the Gallic (or French) Bible, as well as the Celtic (or British), were translations based on the Received Text. Neander claims as follows, that the first Christianity in England, came not from Rome, but from Asia Minor, probably through France:

"But the peculiarity of the later British church is evidence against its origin from Rome; for in many ritual matters it departed from the usage of the Romish Church, and agreed much more nearly with the churches of Asia Minor. It withstood, for a long time, the authority of the Romish Papacy. This circumstance would seem to indicate that the Britons had received their Christianity, either immediately, or through Gaul, from Asia Minor — a thing quite possible and easy, by means of the commercial intercourse. The later Anglo-Saxons, who opposed the spirit of ecclesiastical independence among the Britons, and endeavored to establish the church supremacy of Rome, were uniformly inclined to trace back the church establishments to a Roman origin; from which effort many false legends as well as this might have arisen."[19]

The Waldenses in Northern Italy — Which Bible?

That the messengers of God who carried manuscripts from the churches of Judea to the churches of northern

---

17 See Cathcart, *Ancient British and Irish Churches,* p. 16.

18 *Ibid.,* p. 17.

19 Neander, *History of the Christian Religion and Church,* Vol. 1, pp. 85, 86.

Italy and on, brought to the forerunners of the Waldenses a Bible different from the Bible of Roman Catholicism, I quote the following:

"The method which Allix has pursued, in his History of the Churches of Piedmont, is to show that in the ecclesiastical history of every century, from the fourth century, which he considers a period early enough for the enquirer after apostolical purity of doctrine, there are clear proofs that doctrines, unlike those which the Romish Church holds, and conformable to the belief of the Waldensian and Reformed Churches, were maintained by theologians of the north of Italy down to the period when the Waldenses first came into notice. Consequently the opinions of the Waldenses were not new to Europe in the eleventh or twelfth centuries, and there is nothing improbable in the tradition, that the Subalpine Church persevered in its integrity in an uninterrupted course from the first preaching of the Gospel in the valleys."[20]

There are many earlier historians who agree with this view (Allix, Leger, Gilly, Comba, Nolan). It is held that the pre-Waldensian Christians of northern Italy could not have had doctrines purer than Rome unless their Bible was purer than Rome's; that is, their Bible was not of Rome's falsified manuscripts.[21]

It is inspiring to bring to life again the outstanding history of an authority on this point. I mean Leger. This noble scholar of Waldensian blood was the apostle of his people in the terrible massacres of 1655, and labored intelligently to preserve their ancient records. His book, the *General History of the Evangelical Churches of the Piedmontese Valleys,* published in French in 1669, and called "scarce" in 1825, is the prized object of scholarly searchers. It is my good fortune to have that very book before me. Leger, when he calls Olivetan's French Bible of 1537 "entire and pure," says:

"I say 'pure' because all the ancient exemplars, which formerly were found among the Papists, were full of

---

[20] Gilly, *Waldensian Researches,* pp. 118, 119.

[21] Comba, *The Waldenses of Italy,* p. 188.

falsifications, which caused Beza to say in his book on Illustrious Men, in the chapter on the Vaudois, that one must confess it was by means of the Vaudois of the Valleys that France today has the Bible in her own language. This godly man, Olivetan, in the preface of his Bible, recognizes with thanks to God, that since the time of the apostles, or their immediate successors, the torch of the gospel has been lit among the Vaudois (or the dwellers in the Valleys of the Alps, two terms which mean the same), and has never since been extinguished."22

The Waldenses of northern Italy were foremost among the primitive Christians of Europe in their resistance of the Papacy. They not only sustained the weight of Rome's oppression but also they were successful in retaining the torch of truth until the Reformation took it from their hands and held it aloft to the world. Veritably they illustrated the prophecy of Revelation concerning the church which fled into the wilderness where she hath a place prepared of God (Revelation 12:6, 14). They rejected the mysterious doctrines, the hierarchal priesthood and the worldly titles of Rome, while they clung to the simplicity of the Bible.

The agents of the Papacy have done their utmost to calumniate their character, to destroy the records of their noble past, and to leave no trace of the cruel persecution they underwent. They went even further — they made use of words written against ancient heresies to strike out the name of the heretics and fill the blank space by inserting the name of the Waldenses. Just as if, in a book, written to record the lawless deeds of some bandit, like Jesse James, his name should be stricken out and the name of Abraham Lincoln substituted. The Jesuit Gretser in a book written against the heretics of the twelfth and thirteenth centuries, put the name Waldenses at the point where he struck out the name of these heretics.23

In the fourth century, Helvidius, a great scholar of northern Italy, accused Jerome, whom the Pope had

---

22 Leger, *General History of the Vaudois Churches,* p. 165.

23 Gilly, *Waldensian Researches,* p. 8, note.

empowered to form a Bible in Latin for Catholicism, with using corrupt Greek manuscripts. How could Helvidius have accused Jerome of employing corrupt Greek manuscripts if Helvidius had not had the pure Greek manuscripts? And so learned and so powerful in writing and teaching was Jovinian, the pupil of Helvidius, that it demanded three of Rome's most famous fathers — Augustine, Jerome, and Ambrose — to unite in opposing Jovinian's influence. Even then, it needed the condemnation of the Pope and the banishment of the Emperor to prevail. But Jovinian's followers lived on and made the way easier for Luther.

History does not afford a record of cruelty greater than that manifested by Rome toward the Waldenses. It is impossible to write fully the inspiring history of this persecuted people, whose origin goes back to apostolic days and whose history is ornamented with stories of gripping interest. Rome has obliterated the records. Dr. DeSanctis, many years a Catholic official at Rome, some time official Censor of the Inquisition and later a convert to Protestantism, thus reports the conversation of a Waldensian scholar as he points out to others the ruins of Palatine Hill, Rome:

" 'See,' said the Waldensian, 'a beautiful monument of ecclesiastical antiquity. These rough materials are the ruins of the two great Palatine libraries, one Greek and the other Latin, where the precious manuscripts of our ancestors were collected, and which Pope Gregory I, called the Great, caused to be burned.' "[24]

The destruction of Waldensian records beginning about 600 A.D. by Gregory I, was carried through with thoroughness by the secret agents of the Papacy.

"It is a singular thing," says Gilly, "that the destruction or rapine, which has been so fatal to Waldensian documents, should have pursued them even to the place of security, to which all, that remained, were consigned by Morland, in 1658, to the library of the University of Cambridge. The most ancient of these relics were ticketed

---

[24] DeSanctis, *Popery, Puseyism, Jesuitism,* p. 53.

in seven packets, distinguished by letters of the alphabet, from A to G. The whole of these were missing when I made inquiry for them in 1823.' "[25]

Ancient Documents of the Waldenses

There are modern writers who attempt to fix the beginning of the Waldenses from Peter Waldo, who began his work about 1175. This is a mistake. The historical name of this people as properly derived from the valleys where they lived, is Vaudois. Their enemies, however, ever sought to date their origin from Waldo. Waldo was an agent, evidently raised up of God to combat the errors of Rome. Gilly, who made extensive research concerning the Waldenses, pictures Waldo in his study at Lyon, France, with associates, a committee, "like the translators of our own Authorized Version."[26] Nevertheless the history of the Waldenses, or Vaudois, begins centuries before the days of Waldo.

There remains to us in the ancient Waldensian language, "The Noble Lesson" (*La Nobla Leycon*), written about the year 1100 A.D. which assigns the first opposition of the Waldenses to the Church of Rome to the days of Constantine the Great, when Sylvester was Pope. This may be gathered from the following extract:

"All the popes, which have been from Sylvester to the present time."[27]

Thus when Christianity, emerging from the long persecutions of pagan Rome, was raised to imperial favor by the Emperor Constantine, the Italic Church in northern Italy — later the Waldenses — is seen standing in opposition to papal Rome. Their Bible was of the family of the renowned Itala. It was that translation into Latin which represents the Received Text. Its very name, "Itala," is derived from the Italic district, the regions of the Vaudois.

---

[25] Gilly, *Waldensian Researches,* p. 80.

[26] Comba, *The Waldenses of Italy,* p. 169, note 596.

[27] *"Que tuit li papa, que foron de Silvestre en tro en aquest."* Gilly, *Excursions to the Piedmont,* Appendix II, p. 10.

Of the purity and reliability of this version, Augustine, speaking of different Latin Bibles (about 400 A.D.) says:
    "Now among translations themselves the Italian (Itala) is to be preferred to the others, for it keeps closer to the words without prejudice to clearness of expression."[28]

The old Waldensian liturgy which they used in their services down through the centuries contained "texts of Scripture of the ancient Version called the Italick."[29]

The Reformers held that the Waldensian Church was formed about 120 A.D., from which date on, they passed down from father to son the teachings they received from the apostles.[30] The Latin Bible, the Italic, was translated from the Greek not later than 157 A.D.[31] We are indebted to Beza, the renowned associate of Calvin, for the statement that the Italic Church dates from 120 A.D. From the illustrious group of scholars which gathered round Beza, 1590 A.D., we may understand how the Received Text was the bond of union between great historic churches.

As the sixteenth century is closing, we see in the beautiful Swiss city of Geneva, Beza, an outstanding champion of Protestantism, the scholar Cyril Lucar, later to become the head of the Greek Catholic Church, and Diodati, also a foremost scholar. As Beza astonishes and confounds the world by restoring manuscripts of that Greek New Testament from which the King James is translated, Diodati takes the same and translates into Italian a new and famous edition, adopted and circulated by the Waldenses.[32]

Leger, the Waldensian historian of his people, studied under Diodati at Geneva. He returned as pastor to the Waldenses and led them in their flight from the terrible massacre of 1655.[33] He prized as his choicest treasure the

---

[28] *Nicene and Post-Nicene Fathers,* Christian Lit. Ed., Vol. II, p. 542.

[29] Allix, *Churches of Piedmont,* 1690, p. 37.

[30] *Ibid.,* p. 177.

[31] Scrivener, *Introduction,* Vol. II, p. 43.

[32] "Waldenses," McClintock and Strong, *Encyclopedia.*

[33] Gilly, *Waldensian Researches,* pp. 79, 80.

Diodati Bible, the only worldly possession he was able to preserve. Cyril Lucar hastened to Alexandria where Codex A, the Alexandrian Manuscript,[34] was lying, and laid down his life to introduce the Reformation and the Reformers' pure light regarding the books of the Bible.

At the same time another group of scholars, bitterly hostile to the first group, were gathered at Rheims, France. There the Jesuits, assisted by Rome and backed by all the power of Spain, brought forth an English translation of the Vulgate. In its preface they expressly declared that the Vulgate had been translated in 1300 into Italian and in 1400 into French, "the sooner to shake out of the deceived people's hands, the false heretical translations of a sect called Waldenses." This proves that Waldensian Versions existed in 1300 and 1400. So the Vulgate was Rome's corrupt Scriptures against the Received Text; but the Received Text the New Testament of the apostles, of the Waldenses, and of the Reformers.

That Rome in early days corrupted the manuscripts while the Italic Church handed them down in their apostolic purity, Allix, the renowned scholar, testifies. He reports the following as Italic articles of faith: "They receive only, saith he, what is written in the Old and New Testament. They say, that the Popes of Rome, and other priests, have depraved the Scriptures by their doctrines and glosses."[35]

It is recognized that the Itala was translated from the Received Text (Syrian, Hort calls it); that the Vulgate is the Itala with the readings of the Received Text removed.[36]

Waldensian Bibles

Four Bibles produced under Waldensian influence touched the history of Calvin: namely, a Greek, a

---

[34] Cyril Lucar presented this manuscript to King Charles I of England in 1628. Because of his devotion to the Reformed Faith Lucar was hounded by the Jesuits, who brought about his death in 1638.

[35] Allix, *Churches of Piedmont,* pp. 288, 11.

[36] Kenyon, *Our Bible and the Ancient Manuscripts,* pp. 169, 170.

Waldensian vernacular, a French and an Italian. Calvin himself was led to his great work by Olivetan, a Waldensian. Thus was the Reformation brought to Calvin, that brilliant student of the Paris University. Farel, also a Waldensian, besought him to come to Geneva and open up a work there. Calvin felt that he should labor in Paris. According to Leger, Calvin recognized a relationship to the Calvins of the Valley of St. Martin, one of the Waldensian Valleys.[37]

Finally, persecution at Paris and the solicitation of Farel caused Calvin to settle at Geneva, where, with Beza, he brought out an edition of the Textus Receptus — the one the author now used in his college class rooms, as edited by Scrivener. Of Beza, Dr. Edgar says that he "astonished and confounded the world" with the Greek manuscripts he unearthed. This later edition of the Received Text is in reality a Greek New Testament brought out under Waldensian influence. Unquestionably, the leaders of the Reformation — German, French, and English — were convinced that the Received Text was the genuine New Testament, not only by its own irresistible history and internal evidence, but also because it matched with the Received Text which in Waldensian form came down from the days of the apostles.

The other three Bibles of Waldensian connection were due to three men who were at Geneva with Calvin, or when he died, with Beza, his successor, namely, Olivetan, Leger, and Diodati. How readily the two streams of descent of the Received Text, through the Greek East and the Waldensian West, ran together, is illustrated by the meeting of the Olivetan Bible and the Received Text. Olivetan, one of the most illustrious pastors of the Waldensian Valleys, a relative of Calvin, according to Leger,[38] and a splendid student, translated the New Testament into French. Leger bore testimony that the Olivetan Bible, which accorded with the Textus Receptus, was unlike the old manuscripts of the Papists, because they

---

[37] Leger, *History of the Vaudois,* p. 167.
[38] *Ibid.*

were full of falsification. Later, Calvin edited a second edition of the Olivetan Bible. The Olivetan in turn became the basis of the Geneva Bible[39] in English which was the leading version in England in 1611 when the King James appeared.

Diodati, who succeeded Beza in the chair of Theology at Geneva, translated the Received Text into Italian. This version was adopted by the Waldenses, although there was in use at that time a Waldensian Bible in their own peculiar language. This we know because Sir Samuel Morland, under the protection of Oliver Cromwell, received from Leger the Waldensian New Testament[40] which now lies in the Cambridge University library. After the devastating massacre of the Waldenses in 1655, Leger felt that he should collect and give into the hands of Sir Samuel Morland as many pieces of the ancient Waldensian literature as were available.

It is interesting to trace back the Waldensian Bible which Luther had before him when he translated the New Testament. Luther used the Tepl Bible, named from Tepl, Bohemia. This Tepl manuscript represented a translation of the Waldensian Bible into the German which was spoken before the days of the Reformation.[41] Of this remarkable manuscript, Comba says:

"When the manuscript of Tepl appeared, the attention of the learned was aroused by the fact that the text it presents corresponds word for word with that of the first three editions of the ancient German Bible. Then Louis Keller, an original writer, with the decided opinions of a layman and versed in the history of the sects of the Middle Ages, declared the Tepl manuscript to be Waldensian.

---

[39] The Geneva New Testament in English appeared in 1557, and the complete Bible in 1560.

[40] A copy was presented to the Pope at the Lateran Council of 1179. The Council of Toulouse condemned the version in 1229, and many copies were destroyed. The copy given to Morland was one of the few to survive. In many places this Romaunt version agrees with the old Italic against the Vulgate.

[41] Comba, *The Waldenses of Italy*, p. 191.

Another writer, Hermann Haupt, who belongs to the old Catholic party, supported his opinion vigorously."[42]

From Comba we also learn that the Tepl manuscript has an origin different from the version adopted by the Church of Rome; that it seems to agree rather with the Latin versions anterior to Jerome, the author of the Vulgate; and that Luther followed it in his translation, which probably is the reason why the Catholic Church reproved Luther for following the Waldenses.[43] Another peculiarity is its small size, which seems to single it out as one of those little books which the Waldensian evangelists carried with them hidden under their rough cloaks.[44] We have, therefore, an indication of how much the Reformation under Luther as well as Luther's Bible owed to the Waldenses.

Waldensian influence, both from the Waldensian Bibles and from Waldensian relationships, entered into the King James translation of 1611. Referring to the King James translators, one author speaks thus of a Waldensian Bible they used: "It is known that among modern versions they consulted was an Italian, and though no name is mentioned, there cannot be room for doubt that it was the elegant translation made with great ability from the original Scriptures by Giovanni Diodati, which had only recently (1607) appeared at Geneva."[45]

It is therefore evident that the translators of 1611 had before them four Bibles which had come under Waldensian influences: the Diodati in Italian, the Olivetan in French, the Lutheran in German, and the Genevan in English. We have every reason to believe that they had access to at least six Waldensian Bibles written in the old Waldensian vernacular.[46]

Dr. Nolan, who had already acquired fame for his Greek and Latin scholarship and researches into Egyptian chron-

---

[42] *Ibid.*, p. 190.

[43] *Ibid.*, p. 192.

[44] *Ibid.*, p. 191, note 679.

[45] Benjamin Warfield, *Collections of Opinions and Reviews,* Vol. II, p. 99.

[46] Including Dublin MS A[4]. No. 13, once the property of Archbishop Ussher, presented by King Charles II of England to the University of Dublin.

ology, and was a lecturer of note, spent twenty-eight years to trace back the Received Text to its apostolic origin. He was powerfully impressed to examine the history of the Waldensian Bible. He felt certain that researches in this direction would demonstrate that the Italic New Testament, or the New Testament of those primitive Christians of northern Italy whose lineal descendants the Waldenses were, would turn out to be the Received Text. He says:

"The author perceived, without any labor of inquiry, that it derived its name from that diocese, which has been termed the Italick, as contra-distinguished from the Roman. This is a supposition, which receives a sufficient confirmation from the fact, — that the principal copies of that version have been preserved in that diocese, the metropolitan church of which was situated in Milan. The circumstance is at present mentioned, as the author thence formed a hope, that some remains of the primitive Italick version might be found in the early translations made by the Waldenses, who were the lineal descendants of the Italick Church; and who have asserted their independence against the usurpations of the Church of Rome, and have ever enjoyed the free use of the Scriptures.

"In the search to which these considerations have led the author, his fondest expectations have been fully realized. It has furnished him with abundant proof on that point to which his inquiry was chiefly directed; as it has supplied him with the unequivocal testimony of a truly apostolical branch of the primitive church, that the celebrated text of the heavenly witnesses[47] was adopted in the version which prevailed in the Latin Church, previously to the introduction of the modern Vulgate."[48]

How the Bible Adopted by Constantine Was Set Aside

Where did this Vaudois Church amid the rugged peaks of the Alps secure these uncorrupted manuscripts? In the

---

[47] I John 5:7.

[48] Frederick Nolan, *Integrity of the Greek Vulgate,* pp. xvii, xviii.

silent watches of the night, along the lonely paths of Asia Minor where robbers and wild beasts lurked, might have been seen the noble missionaries carrying manuscripts, and verifying documents from the churches in Judea to encourage their struggling brethren under the iron heel of the Papacy. The sacrificing labors of the apostle Paul were bearing fruit. His wise plan to anchor the Gentile churches of Europe to the churches of Judea provided the channel of communications which defeated continually and finally the bewildering pressure of the Papacy. Or, as the learned Scrivener has beautifully put it:

"Wide as is the region which separates Syria from Gaul, there must have been in very early times some remote communication by which the stream of Eastern testimony, or tradition, like another Alpheus, rose up again with fresh strength to irrigate the regions of the distant West."[49]

We have it now revealed how Constantine's Hexapla Bible was successfully met. A powerful chain of churches, few in number compared with the manifold congregations of an apostate Christianity, but enriched with the eternal conviction of truth and with able scholars, stretched from Palestine to Scotland. If Rome in her own land was unable to beat down the testimony of apostolic Scriptures, how could she hope, in the Greek-speaking world of the distant and hostile East, to maintain the supremacy of her Greek Bible?

The Scriptures of the apostle John and his associates, the traditional text — the Textus Receptus, if you please — arose from the place of humiliation forced on it by Origen's Bible in the hands of Constantine and became the Received Text of Greek Christianity. And when the Greek East for one thousand years was completely shut off from the Latin West, the noble Waldenses in northern Italy still possessed in Latin the Received Text.

To Christians such as these, preserving apostolic Christianity, the world owes gratitude for the true text of the Bible. It is not true, as the Roman Church claims, that she gave the Bible to the world. What she gave was an impure

---

[49] Scrivener, *Introduction,* Vol. II, pp. 299, 300.

text, a text with thousands of verses so changed as to make way for her unscriptural doctrines. While upon those who possessed the veritable Word of God, she poured out through long centuries her stream of cruel persecution. Or, in the words of another writer:

"The Waldenses were among the first of the peoples of Europe to obtain a translation of the Holy Scriptures. Hundreds of years before the Reformation, they possessed the Bible in manuscript in their native tongue. They had the truth unadulterated, and this rendered them the special objects of hatred and persecution. . . . Here for a thousand years, witnesses for the truth maintained the ancient faith. . . . In a most wonderful manner it (the Word of Truth) was preserved uncorrupted through all the ages of darkness."

The struggle against the Bible adopted by Constantine was won. But another warfare, another plan to deluge the Latin West with a corrupt Latin Bible was preparing. We hasten to see how the world was saved from Jerome and his Origenism.

The two great families of Greek Bibles are well illustrated in the work of that outstanding scholar, Erasmus. Before he gave to the Reformation the New Testament in Greek, he divided all Greek manuscripts into two classes: those which agreed with the Received Text and those which agreed with the Vaticanus manuscript. [50]

The King James from the Received Text has been the Bible of the English-speaking world for 300 years. This has given the Received Text, and the Bibles translated from it into other tongues, standing and authority. At the same time, it neutralized the dangers of the Catholic manuscripts and the Bibles in other tongues translated from them.

[50] Nolan, *Inquiry*, p. 413.

CHAPTER III

The Reformers Reject the Bible of the Papacy

The Papacy, defeated in her hope to control the version of the Bible in the Greek world when the Greek New Testament favored by Constantine was driven into retirement, adopted two measures which kept Europe under its domination. First, the Papacy was against the flow of Greek language and literature to Western Europe. All the treasures of the classical past were held back in the Eastern Roman Empire, whose capital was Constantinople. For nearly one thousand years, the western part of Europe was a stranger to the Greek tongue. As Doctor Hort says:

"The West became exclusively Latin, as well as estranged from the East; with local exceptions, interesting in themselves and valuable to us but devoid of all extensive influence, the use and knowledge of the Greek language died out in Western Europe."[1]

When the use and knowledge of Greek died out in Western Europe, all the valuable Greek records, history, archaeology, literature, and science remained untranslated and unavailable to Western energies. No wonder, then, that this opposition to using the achievements of the past brought on the Dark Ages (476 A.D. to 1453 A.D.).

---

[1] Hort, *Introduction,* p. 142.

This darkness prevailed until the half-century preceding 1453 A.D. when refugees, fleeing from the Greek world threatened by the Turks, came west introducing Greek language and literature. After Constantinople fell in 1453, thousands of valuable manuscripts were secured by the cities and centers of learning in Europe. Europe awoke as from the dead, and sprang forth to newness of life. Columbus discovered America. Erasmus printed the Greek New Testament. Luther assailed the corruptions of the Latin Church. Revival of learning and the Reformation followed swiftly.

The second measure adopted by the Pope which held the Latin West in his power was to stretch out his hands to Jerome (about 400 A.D.), the monk of Bethlehem, reputed the greatest scholar of his age, and appeal to him to compose a Bible in Latin similar to the Bible adopted by Constantine in Greek. Jerome, the hermit of Palestine, whose learning was equaled only by his boundless vanity, responded with alacrity. Jerome was furnished with all the funds that he needed and was assisted by many scribes and copyists.

The Origenism of Jerome

By the time of Jerome, the barbarians from the north who later founded the kingdoms of modern Europe, such as England, France, Germany, Italy and other countries, were overrunning the Roman Empire. They cared nothing for the political monuments of the empire's greatness, for these they leveled to the dust. But they were overawed by the external pomp and ritual of the Roman Church. Giants in physique, they were children in learning. They had been trained from childhood to render full and immediate submission to their pagan gods. This same attitude of mind they bore toward the Papacy, as one by one they substituted the saints, the martyrs, and the images of Rome for their former forest gods. But there was danger that greater light might tear them away from Rome.

If, in Europe, these children fresh from the north were to be held in submission to such doctrines as the papal supremacy, transubstantiation, purgatory, celibacy of the priesthood, vigils, worship of relics, and the burning of daylight candles, the Papacy must offer, as a record of revelation, a Bible in Latin which would be as Origenistic as the Bible in Greek adopted by Constantine. Therefore, the Pope turned to Jerome to bring forth a new version in Latin.

Jerome was devotedly committed to the textual criticism of Origen, "an admirer of Origen's critical principles," as Swete says.[2] To be guided aright in his forthcoming translation, by models accounted standard in the semi-pagan Christianity of his day, Jerome repaired to the famous library of Eusebius and Pamphilus at Caesarea, where the voluminous manuscripts of Origen had been preserved.[3] Among these was a Greek Bible of the Vaticanus and Sinaiticus type.[4] Both these versions retained a number of the seven books which Protestants have rejected as being spurious. This may be seen by examining those manuscripts. These manuscripts of Origen influenced Jerome more in the New Testament than in the Old, since finally he used the Hebrew text in translating the Old Testament. Moreover, the Hebrew Bible did not have these spurious books. Jerome admitted that these seven books — Tobit, Wisdom, Judith, Baruch, Ecclesiasticus, 1st and 2nd Maccabees — did not belong with the other writings of the Bible. Nevertheless, the Papacy endorsed them, and they are found in the Latin Vulgate and in the Douay, its English translation.

The existence of those books in Origen's Bible is sufficient evidence to reveal that tradition and Scripture were on an equal footing in the mind of that Greek theologian. His other doctrines, such as purgatory and transubstantiation, had now become as essential to the imperialism of the Papacy as was the teaching that tradition had equal authority with the Scriptures. Doctor

---

2 Swete, *Introduction to Greek Old Testament,* p. 86.

3 Jacobus, *Catholic and Protestant Bibles,* p. 4.

4 Price, *Ancestry,* pp. 69, 70.

Adam Clarke indicates Origen as the first teacher of purgatory.

The Vulgate of Jerome

The Latin Bible of Jerome, commonly known as the Vulgate, held authoritative sway for one thousand years. The services of the Roman Church were held at that time in a language which still is the sacred language of the Catholic clergy, the Latin.

Jerome in his early years had been brought up with an enmity to the Received Text, then universally known as the Greek Vulgate.[5] The word Vulgate means "commonly used," or "current." This word Vulgate has been appropriated from the Bible to which it rightfully belongs, that is, to the Received Text, and given to the Latin Bible. In fact, it took hundreds of years before the common people would call Jerome's Latin Bible, the Vulgate. The very fact that in Jerome's day the Greek Bible, from which the King James is translated into English, was called the Vulgate, is proof in itself that, in the church of the living God, its authority was supreme. Diocletian (302-312 A.D.), the last in the unbroken line of pagan emperors, had furiously pursued every copy of it, to destroy it. The so-called first Christian emperor, Constantine, chief of heretical Christianity, now joined to the state, had ordered (331 A.D.) and under imperial authority and finances, had promulgated a rival Greek Bible. Nevertheless, so powerful was the Received Text that even until Jerome's day (383 A.D.) it was called the Vulgate.[6]

The hostility of Jerome to the Received Text made him necessary to the Papacy. The Papacy in the Latin world opposed the authority of the Greek Vulgate. Did it not see already this hated Greek Vulgate, long ago translated into Latin, read, preached from, and circulated by those Christians in northern Italy who refused to bow beneath its rule? For this reason it sought help from the great

---

5 Hort, *Introduction,* p. 138.

6 Swete, *Introduction,* pp. 85, 86.

reputation which Jerome enjoyed as a scholar. Moreover, Jerome had been taught the Scriptures by Gregory Nazianzen, who, in turn, had been at great pains with two other scholars of Caesarea to restore the library of Eusebius in that city. With that library Jerome was well acquainted; he describes himself as a great admirer of Eusebius. While studying with Gregory, he had translated from Greek into Latin the Chronicle of Eusebius. And let it be remembered, in turn, that Eusebius in publishing the Bible ordered by Constantine, had incorporated in it the manuscripts of Origen.[7]

In preparing the Latin Bible, Jerome would gladly have gone all the way in transmitting to us the corruptions in the text of Eusebius, but he did not dare. Great scholars of the West were already exposing him and the corrupted Greek manuscripts.[8] Jerome especially mentions Luke 2:33 (where the Received Text read: "And Joseph and his mother marvelled at those things which were spoken of him," while Jerome's text read: "His father and his mother marvelled," etc.) to say that the great scholar Helvidius, who from the circumstances of the case was probably a Vaudois, accused him of using corrupted Greek manuscripts.

Although endorsed and supported by the power of the Papacy, the Vulgate — which name we will now call Jerome's translation — did not gain immediate acceptance everywhere. It took nine hundred years to bring that about. Purer Latin Bibles than Jerome's had already a deep place in the affections of the West. Yet steadily through the years, the Catholic Church has uniformly rejected the Received Text wherever translated from the Greek into Latin and exalted Jerome's Vulgate. So that for one thousand years, Western Europe, with the exception of the Waldenses, Albigenses, and other bodies pronounced heretics by Rome, knew of no Bible but the Vulgate. As Father Simon, that monk who exercised so powerful an influence

---

7 Price, *Ancestry,* p. 70.

8 W. H. Green, *The Text of Old Testament,* p. 116; *Post-Nicene Fathers,* Vol. 6, p. 338.

on the textual criticism of the last century, says: "The Latins have had so great esteem for that father [Jerome] that for a thousand years they used no other version."9

Therefore, a millennium later, when Greek manuscripts and Greek learning were again general, the corrupt readings of the Vulgate were noted. Even Catholic scholars of repute, before Protestantism was fully under way, pointed out its thousands of errors. As Doctor Fulke in 1583 writing to a Catholic scholar, a Jesuit, says:

"Great friends of it and your doctrine, Lindanus, bishop of Ruremond, and Isidorus Clarius, monk of Casine, and bishop Fulginatensis: of which the former writeth a whole book, discussing how he would have the errors, vices, corruptions, additions, detractions, mutations, uncertainties, obscurities, pollutions, barbarisms, and solecisms of the vulgar Latin translation corrected and reformed; bringing many examples of every kind, in several chapters and sections: the other, Isidorus Clarius, giving a reason of his purpose, in castigation of the said vulgar Latin translation, confesseth that it was *full of errors almost innumerable;* which if he should have reformed all according to the Hebrew verity, he could not have set forth the vulgar edition, as his purpose was. Therefore in many places he retaineth the accustomed translation, but in his annotations admonisheth the reader, how it is in the Hebrew. And, notwithstanding this moderation, he acknowledgeth that about *eight thousand places* are by him so noted and corrected."10

Even Wycliffe's Translation was from the Vulgate

Wycliffe, that great hero of God, is universally called "The morning star of the Reformation." He did what he could and God greatly blessed. Wycliffe's translation of the Bible into English was two hundred years before the birth of Luther. It was taken from the Vulgate and, like its model, contained many errors. Therefore the Reformation

---

9 Quoted in Nolan, *Inquiry*, p. 33.
10 Fulke, *Defence of Translations of the Bible* (1583), p. 62.

lingered. Wycliffe, himself, nominally a Catholic to the last, had hoped that the needed reform would come within the Catholic Church. Darkness still enshrouded Western Europe and though bright stars shone out brilliantly for a while, only to disappear again into the night, the Reformation still lingered. Then appeared the translation into English of Tyndale from the pure Greek text of Erasmus.

Speaking of Tyndale, Demaus says:

"He was of course aware of the existence of Wycliffe's Version; but this, as a bald translation from the Vulgate into obsolete English, could not be of any assistance (even if he had possessed a copy) to one who was endeavoring, 'simply and faithfully, so far forth as God had given him the gift of knowledge and understanding' to render the New Testament from its original Greek into 'proper English.' "[11]

Again: "For, as became an accomplished Greek scholar, Tyndale was resolved to translate the New Testament from the original language, and not as Wycliffe had done, from the Latin Vulgate; and the only edition of the Greek text which had yet appeared, the only one at least likely to be in Tyndale's possession, was that issued by Erasmus at Basle."[12]

The Reformers Obliged To Reject Jerome's Vulgate

The Reformation did not make great progress until after the Received Text had been restored to the world. The Reformers were not satisfied with the Latin Vulgate.

The papal leaders did not comprehend the vast departure from the truth they had created when they had rejected the lead of the pure teachings of the Scriptures. The spurious books of the Vulgate opened the door for the mysterious and the dark doctrines which had confused the thinking of the ancients. The corrupt readings of the genuine books decreased the confidence of people in inspiration and increased the power of the priests. All were

---

[11] Demaus, *William Tyndale*, p. 105.

[12] *Ibid.*, p. 73.

left in a labyrinth of darkness from which there was no escape. According to Brooke, Cartwright, the famous Puritan scholar, described the Vulgate as follows:

"As to the Version adopted by the Rhemists [Cartwright's word for the Jesuits], Mr. Cartwright observed that all the soap and nitre they could collect would be insufficient to cleanse the Vulgate from the filth of blood in which it was originally conceived and had since collected in passing so long through the hands of unlearned monks, from which the Greek copies had altogether escaped."[13]

More than this, the Vulgate was the chief weapon relied upon to combat and destroy the Bible of the Waldenses. I quote from the preface of the New Testament translated by the Jesuits from the Vulgate into English, 1582 A.D.:

"It is almost three hundred years since James, Archbishop of Genoa, is said to have translated the Bible into Italian. More than two hundred years ago, in the days of Charles V the French king, was it put forth faithfully in French, the sooner to shake out of the deceived people's hands, the false heretical translations of a sect called Waldenses."

Such was the darkness and so many were the errors which the Reformers had to encounter as they started on their way. They welcomed the rising spirit of intelligence which shone forth in the new learning, but the priests loudly denounced it. They declared that the study of Greek was of the devil and prepared to destroy all who promoted it.[14] How entrenched was the situation may be seen in the following quotation of a letter written by Erasmus:

"Obedience (writes Erasmus) is so taught as to hide that there is any obedience due to God. Kings are to obey the Pope. Priests are to obey their bishops. Monks are to obey their abbots. Oaths are exacted, that want of submission may be punished as perjury. It may happen, it often does happen, that an abbot is a fool or a drunkard. He issues an

---

13 Brooke, *Memoir of Life of Cartwright*, p. 276.
14 Froude, *Life and Letters of Erasmus*, pp. 232, 233.

order to the brotherhood in the name of holy obedience. And what will such order be? An order to observe chastity? An order to be sober? An order to tell no lies? Not one of these things. It will be that a brother is not to learn Greek; he is not to seek to instruct himself. He may be a sot. He may go with prostitutes. He may be full of hatred and malice. He may never look inside the Scriptures. No matter. He has not broken any oath. He is an excellent member of the community. While if he disobeys such a command as this from an insolent superior there is stake or dungeon for him instantly."[15]

It was impossible, however, to hold back the ripening harvest. Throughout the centuries, the Waldenses and other faithful evangelicals had sown the seed. The fog was rolling away from the plains and hills of Europe. The pure Bible which long had sustained the faith of the Vaudois, was soon to be adopted by others so mighty that they would shake Europe from the Alps to the North Sea.

"The light had been spreading unobserved, and the Reformation was on the point of being anticipated. The demon Innocent III was the first to decry the streaks of day on the crest of the Alps. Horror-stricken, he started up, and began to thunder forth his pandemonium against a faith which had already subjugated provinces, and was threatening to dissolve the power of Rome in the very flush of her victory over the empire. In order to save the one-half of Europe from perishing by heresy, it was decreed that the other half should perish by the sword."[16]

It must be remembered that at the time (about 400 A.D.) when the Empire was breaking up into modern kingdoms, the pure Latin was breaking up into the Spanish Latin, the French Latin, the African Latin, and other dialects, the forerunners of many modern languages. Into all those different Latins the Bible had been translated, in whole or in part. Some of these, as the Bible of the Waldenses, had come mediately or immediately from the Received Text and had great influence.

---

[15] *Ibid.*, p. 64.
[16] Wylie, *The Papacy*, p. 92.

When the one thousand years had gone by, strains of new gladness were heard. Gradually these grew in crescendo until the whole choir of voices broke forth as Erasmus presented his first Greek New Testament at the feet of Europe. Then followed a full century of the greatest scholars of language and literature the world ever saw. Among them were Stephens and Beza, each contributing his part to establishing and fortifying the Received Text. The world stood amazed as these two last mentioned scholars brought forth from hidden recesses, old and valuable Greek manuscripts.

Erasmus Restores the Received Text

The Revival of Learning produced that giant intellect and scholar, Erasmus. It is a common proverb that "Erasmus laid the egg and Luther hatched it." The streams of Grecian learning were again flowing into the European plains, and a man of caliber was needed to draw from their best and bestow it upon the needy nations of the West. Endowed by nature with a mind that could do ten hours' work in one, Erasmus, during his mature years in the earlier part of the sixteenth century, was the intellectual giant of Europe. He was ever at work, visiting libraries, searching in every nook and corner for the profitable. He was ever collecting, comparing, writing and publishing. Europe was rocked from end to end by his books which exposed the ignorance of the monks, the superstitions of the priesthood, the bigotry, and the childish and coarse religion of the day. He classified the Greek manuscripts and read the Fathers.

It is customary even today with those who are bitter against the pure teachings of the Received Text, to sneer at Erasmus. No perversion of facts is too great to belittle his work. Yet while he lived, Europe was at his feet. Several times the King of England offered him any position in the kingdom, at his own price; the Emperor of Germany did the same. The Pope offered to make him a cardinal. This he steadfastly refused, as he would not compromise his conscience. In fact, had he been so minded, he perhaps could have made himself Pope. France and Spain sought him to become a dweller in their realm; while Holland prepared to claim him as her most distinguished citizen.

Book after book came from his hand. Faster and faster came the demands for his publications. But his crowning work was the New Testament in Greek. At last after one thousand years, the New Testament was printed (1516 A.D.) in the original tongue. Astonished and confounded, the world, deluged by superstitions, coarse traditions, and monkeries, read the pure story of the Gospels. The effect was marvelous. At once, all recognized the great value of this work which for over four hundred years (1516 to 1930) was to hold the dominant place in an era of Bibles. Translation after translation has been taken from it, such as the German, and the English, and others. Critics have tried to belittle the Greek manuscripts he used, but the enemies of Erasmus, or rather the enemies of the Received Text, have found insuperable difficulties withstanding their attacks. Writing to Peter Baberius August 13, 1521, Erasmus says:

"I did my best with the New Testament, but it provoked endless quarrels. Edward Lee pretended to have discovered 300 errors. They appointed a commission, which professed to have found bushels of them. Every dinner-table rang with the blunders of Erasmus. I required particulars, and could not have them."[17]

There were hundreds of manuscripts for Erasmus to examine, and he did; but he used only a few. What matters? The vast bulk of manuscripts in Greek are practically all the Received Text.[18] If the few Erasmus used were typical, that is, after he had thoroughly balanced the evidence of many and used a few which displayed that balance, did he not, with all the problems before him, arrive at practically the same result which only

---

[17] Froude, *Erasmus*, p. 267.

[18] They are, of course, not identical, but most of the variations are superficial; and in general character and content they represent the same kind of text.

could be arrived at today by a fair and comprehensive investigation?

Moreover, the text he chose had such an outstanding history in the Greek, the Syrian, and the Waldensian Churches, that it constituted an irresistible argument for and proof of God's providence. *God did not write a hundred Bibles; there is only one Bible, the others at best are only approximations. In other words the Greek New Testament of Erasmus, known as the Received Text, is none other than the Greek New Testament which successfully met the rage of its pagan and papal enemies.*

We are told that testimony from the ranks of our enemies constitutes the highest kind of evidence. The following statement which I now submit, is taken from the defense of their doings by two members of that body so hostile to the Greek New Testament of Erasmus — the Revisers of 1870-1881. This quotation shows that the manuscripts of Erasmus coincide with the great bulk of manuscripts.

"The manuscripts which Erasmus used, differ, for the most part, only in small and insignificant details from the bulk of the cursive manuscripts — that is to say, the manuscripts which are written in running hand and not in capital or (as they are technically called) uncial letters. The general character of their text is the same. By this observation the pedigree of the Received Text is carried up beyond the individual manuscripts used by Erasmus to a great body of manuscripts of which the earliest are assigned to the ninth century."

Then after quoting Doctor Hort, they draw this conclusion on his statement: "This remarkable statement completes the pedigree of the Received Text. That pedigree stretches back to a remote antiquity. The first ancestor of the Received Text was, as Dr. Hort is careful to remind us, at least contemporary with the oldest of our extant manuscripts, if not older than any one of them." [19]

---

[19] *Two Members of the New Testament Company on the Revisers and the Greek Text,* pp. 11, 12.

Tyndale's Towering Genius Is Used To Translate Erasmus into English

God, who foresaw the coming greatness of the English-speaking world, prepared in advance the agent who early would give direction to the course of its thinking. One man stands out silhouetted against the horizon above all others, as having stamped his genius upon English thought and upon the English language. That man was William Tyndale.

The Received Text in Greek, having through Erasmus reassumed its ascendancy in the West of Europe as it had always maintained it in the East, bequeathed its indispensable heritage to the English. It meant much that the right genius was engaged to clamp the English future within this heavenly mold. Providence never is wanting when the hour strikes. And the world at last is awakening fully to appreciate that William Tyndale is the true hero of the English Reformation.

The Spirit of God presided over Tyndale's calling and training. He early passed through Oxford and Cambridge Universities. He went from Oxford to Cambridge to learn Greek under Erasmus, who was teaching there from 1510 to 1514. Even after Erasmus returned to the Continent Tyndale kept informed on the revolutionizing productions which fell from that master's pen. Tyndale was not one of those students whose appetite for facts is omnivorous but who is unable to look down through a system. Knowledge to him was an organic whole in which, should discords come, created by illogical articulation, he would be able to detect quibblings at once. He had a natural aptitude for languages, but he did not shut himself into an airtight compartment with his results, to issue forth with some great conclusion which would chill the faith of the world. He had a soul. He felt everywhere the sweetness of the life of God, and he offered himself as a martyr, if only the Word of God might live.

Herman Buschius, a friend of Erasmus and one of the leaders in the revival of letters, spoke of Tyndale as "so skilled in seven languages, Hebrew, Greek, Latin, Italian, Spanish, English, French, that whichever he spoke you would suppose it his native tongue."[20] "Modern Catholic Versions are enormously indebted to Tyndale," says Dr. Jacobus. From the standpoint of English, not from the standpoint of doctrine, much work has been done to approximate the Douay to the King James.

When Tyndale left Cambridge, he accepted a position as tutor in the home of an influential landowner. Here his attacks upon the superstitions of Popery threw him into sharp discussions with a stagnant clergy, and brought down upon his head the wrath of the reactionaries. It was then, in disputing with a learned man who put the Pope's laws above God's laws, that he made his famous vow, "If God spare my life, ere many years, I will cause a boy that driveth a plough shall know more of the Scripture than thou doest."

From that moment until he was burnt at the stake, his life was one of continual sacrifice and persecution. The man who was to charm whole continents and bind them together as one in principle and purpose by his translation of God's Word, was compelled to build his masterpiece in a foreign land amid other tongues than his own. As Luther took the Greek New Testament of Erasmus and made the German language, so Tyndale took the same immortal gift of God and made the English language. Across the sea, he translated the New Testament and a large part of the Old Testament. Two-thirds of the Bible was translated into English by Tyndale, and what he did not translate was finished by those who worked with him and were under the spell of his genius. The Authorized Bible of the English language is Tyndale's, after his work passed through two or three revisions.

So instant and so powerful was the influence of Tyndale's gift upon England, that Catholicism, through those newly formed papal invincibles called the Jesuits, sprang to its feet and brought forth, in the form of a Jesuit New Testament, the most effective instrument of learning the Papacy, up to that time, had produced in the English language. This newly invented rival version advanced to the

---

[20] Demaus, *Life of Tyndale,* p. 130.

attack, and we are now called to consider how a crisis in the world's history was met when the Jesuit Bible became a challenge to Tyndale's translation.

CHAPTER IV

The Jesuits and the Jesuit Bible of 1582

The Catholic Church has 69 organizations of men, some of which have been in existence for over one thousand years. Of these we might name the Augustinians, the Benedictines, the Capuchins, the Dominicans, and so on. The Benedictines were founded about 540 A.D. Each order has many members, often reaching into the thousands, and tens of thousands. The Augustinians, for example (to which order Martin Luther belonged), numbered 35,000 in his day. The men of these orders never marry but live in communities or large fraternity houses known as monasteries, which are for men what the convents are for women. Each organization exists for a distinct line of endeavor, and each, in turn, is directly under the order of the Pope. They overrun all countries and constitute the army militant of the Papacy. The monks are called the regular clergy, while the priests, bishops, and others who conduct churches are called the secular clergy. Let us see why the Jesuits stand predominantly above all these, so that the general of the Jesuits has great authority within all the vast ranks of the Catholic clergy, regular and secular.

Within thirty-five years after Luther had nailed his theses upon the door of the Cathedral of Wittenberg, and launched his attacks upon the errors and corrupt practices of Rome, the Protestant Reformation was thoroughly established. The great contributing factor to this spiritual upheaval was the translation by Luther of the Greek New Testament of Erasmus into German. The medieval Papacy awakened from its superstitious lethargy to see that in one-third of a century, the Reformation had carried away two-thirds of Europe. Germany, England, the Scandinavian countries, Holland, and Switzerland had become Protestant. France, Poland, Bavaria, Austria, and Belgium were swinging that way.

In consternation, the Papacy looked around in every direction for help. If the Jesuits had not come forward and offered to save the situation, today there might not be a Catholic Church. What was the offer, and what were these weapons, the like of which man never before had forged?

The founder of the Jesuits was a Spaniard, Ignatius Loyola, whom the Catholic Church has canonized and made Saint Ignatius. He was a soldier in the war which King Ferdinand and Queen Isabella of Spain were waging to drive the Mohammedans out of Spain, about the time that Columbus discovered America.

Wounded at the siege of Pampeluna (1521 A.D.), so that his military career was over, Ignatius turned his thoughts to spiritual conquests and spiritual glory. Soon afterwards, he wrote the book called *Spiritual Exercises*, which did more than any other document to erect a new papal theocracy and to bring about the establishment of the infallibility of the Pope. In other words, Catholicism since the Reformation is a new Catholicism. It is more fanatical and more intolerant.

Ignatius Loyola came forward and must have said in substance to the Pope: "Let the Augustinians continue to provide monasteries of retreat for contemplative minds; let the Benedictines give themselves up to the field of literary endeavor; let the Dominicans retain their responsibility for maintaining the Inquisition; but we, the Jesuits, will capture the colleges and the universities. We will gain control of instruction in law, medicine, science, education, and so weed out from all books of instruction, anything injurious to Roman Catholicism. We will mold the thoughts and ideas of the youth. We will enroll ourselves as Protestant preachers and college professors in the different Protestant faiths. Sooner or later, we will undermine the authority of the Greek New Testament of Erasmus, and also of those Old Testament productions which have dared to raise their heads against tradition. And thus will we undermine the Protestant Reformation."

How well the Jesuits have succeeded, let the following pages tell. Soon the brains of the Catholic Church were to be found in that order. About 1582, when the Jesuit Bible was launched to destroy Tyndale's English Version, the Jesuits dominated 287 colleges and universities in Europe. Their complete system of education and of drilling was likened, in the constitution of the order itself, to the reducing of all its members to the placidity of a corpse, whereby the whole could be turned and returned at the will of the superior. We quote from their constitution:

"As for holy obedience, this virtue must be perfect in every point — in execution, in will, in intellect — doing what is enjoined with all celerity, spiritual joy, and perseverance; persuading ourselves that everything is just; suppressing every repugnant thought and judgment of one's own, in a certain obedience; . . . and let every one persuade himself that he who lives under obedience should be moved and directed, under Divine Providence, by his superior, just as if he were a corpse (*perinde ac si cadaver esset*), which allows itself to be moved and led in any direction."[1]

That which put an edge on the newly forged mentality was the unparalleled system of education impressed upon the pick of Catholic youth. The Pope, perforce, virtually threw open the ranks of the many millions of Catholic young men and told the Jesuits to go in and select the most intelligent. The initiation rites were such as to make a lifelong impression on the candidate for admission. He never would forget the first trial of his faith. Thus the youth are admitted under a test which virtually binds

---

[1] R. W. Thompson, *The Footprints of the Jesuits*, p. 51.

forever the will, if it has not already been enslaved. What matters to him? Eternal life is secure, and all is for the greater glory of God.

Then follow the long years of intense mental training, interspersed with periods of practice. They undergo the severest methods of quick and accurate learning. They will be, let us say, shut up in a room with a heavy Latin lesson, and expected to learn it in a given period of hours. Of the results achieved by means of this policy and the methods, Macaulay says:

"It was in the ears of the Jesuit that the powerful, the noble, and the beautiful, breathed the secret history of their lives. It was at the feet of the Jesuit that the youth of the higher and middle classes were brought up from childhood to manhood, from the first rudiments to the courses of rhetoric and philosophy. Literature and science, lately associated with infidelity or with heresy, now became the allies of orthodoxy.

"Dominant in the south of Europe, the great order soon went forth conquering and to conquer. In spite of oceans and deserts, of hunger and pestilence, of spies and penal laws, of dungeons and racks, of gibbets and quartering-blocks, Jesuits were to be found under every disguise, and in every country; scholars, physicians, merchants, serving men; in the hostile court of Sweden, in the old manor house of Cheshire, among the hovels of Connaught; arguing, instructing, consoling, stealing away the hearts of the young, animating the courage of the timid, holding up the crucifix before the eyes of the dying.

"Nor was it less their office to plot against the thrones and lives of the apostate kings, to spread evil rumors, to raise tumults, to inflame civil wars, to arm the hand of the assassin. Inflexible in nothing but in their fidelity to the Church, they were equally ready to appeal in her cause to the spirit of loyalty and to the spirit of freedom. Extreme doctrines of obedience and extreme doctrines of liberty, the right of rulers to misgovern the people, the right of every one of the people to plunge his knife in the heart of a bad ruler, were inculcated by the same man, according as he addressed himself to the subject of Philip or to the subject of Elizabeth."[2]

And again: "If Protestantism, or the semblance of Protestantism, showed itself in any quarter, it was instantly met, not by petty, teasing persecution, but by persecution of that sort which bows down and crushes all but a very few select spirits. Whoever was suspected of heresy, whatever his rank, his learning, or his reputation, knew that he must purge himself to the satisfaction of a severe and vigilant tribunal, or die by fire. Heretical books were sought out and destroyed with similar rigor."[3]

The Catholic Council of Trent (1545-1563) Called To Defeat the Reformation. How the Council Refused the Protestant Attitude Toward the Scriptures and Enthroned the Jesuit

"The Society came to exercise a marked influence to which their presence in the Council of Trent, as the Pope's theologians, gave signal testimony. It was a wise stroke of policy for the Papacy to entrust its cause in the Council so largely to the Jesuits."[4]

The Council of Trent was dominated by the Jesuits. This we must bear in mind as we study that Council. It is the leading characteristic of that assembly. "The great Convention dreaded by every Pope" was called by Paul III when he saw that such a council was imperative if the Reformation was to be checked. And when it did assemble, he so contrived the manipulation of the program and the attendance of the delegates, that the Jesuitical conception of a theocratic Papacy should be incorporated into the canons of the church.

So prominent had been the Reformers' denunciations of the abuses of the church, against her exactions, and against her shocking immoralities, that we would naturally expect that this council, which marks so great a turning point in

---

2 Macaulay, *Essays,* pp. 480, 481.

3 *Ibid.,* pp. 482, 483.

4 Hulme, *Renaissance and Reformation,* p. 428.

church history, would have promptly met the charges. But this it did not do. The very first propositions to be discussed at length and with intense interest were those relating to the Scriptures. This shows how fundamental to all reform, as well as to the great Reformation, is the determining power over Christian order and faith, of the disputed readings and the disputed books of the Bible. Moreover, these propositions denounced by the Council, which we give below, the Council did not draw up itself. They were taken from the writings of Luther. We thus see how fundamental to the faith of Protestantism is their acceptance; while their rejection constitutes the keystone to the superstitions and to the tyrannical theology of the Papacy. These four propositions which first engaged the attention of the Council, and which the Council condemned, are:

They Condemned: I — "That Holy Scriptures contained all things necessary for salvation, and that it was impious to place apostolic tradition on a level with Scripture."

They Condemned: II — "That certain books accepted as canonical in the Vulgate were apocryphal and not canonical."

They Condemned: III — "That Scripture must be studied in the original languages, and that there were errors in the Vulgate."

They Condemned: IV — "That the meaning of Scripture is plain, and that it can be understood without commentary with the help of Christ's Spirit."[5]

For eighteen long years the Council deliberated. The papal scholars determined what was the Catholic faith. During these eighteen years, the Papacy gathered up to itself what survived of Catholic territory. The Church of Rome consolidated her remaining forces and took her stand solidly on the grounds that tradition was of equal value with the Scriptures; that the seven apocryphal books of the Vulgate were as much Scripture as the other books; that those readings of the Vulgate in the accepted books, which differed from the Greek, were not errors, as Luther

[5] Froude, *The Council of Trent,* pp. 174, 175.

and the Reformers had said, but were authentic; and finally, that lay members of the church had no right to interpret the Scriptures apart from the Clergy.

The Jesuit Bible of 1582

The opening decrees of the Council of Trent had set the pace for centuries to come. They pointed out the line of battle which the Catholic reaction would wage against the Reformation. First undermine the Bible, then destroy the Protestant teaching and doctrine.

If we include the time spent in studying these questions before the opening session of the Council in 1545 until the Jesuit Bible made its first appearance in 1582,[6] fully forty years were passed in the preparation of the Jesuit students who were being drilled in these departments of learning. The first attack on the position of the Reformers regarding the Bible must soon come. It was clearly seen then, as it is now, that if confusion on the origin and authenticity of the Scriptures could be spread abroad in the world, the amazing certainty of the Reformers on these points, which had astonished and confounded the Papacy, could be broken down. In time the Reformation would be splintered to pieces, and driven as the chaff before the wind. The leadership in the battle for the Reformation was passing over from Germany to England.[7] Here it advanced mightily, helped greatly by the new version of Tyndale. Therefore, Jesuitical scholarship, with at least forty years of training, must bring forth in English a Jesuit Version capable of superseding the Bible of Tyndale. Could it be done?

Sixty years elapsed from the close of the Council of Trent (1563) to the landing of the Pilgrims in America. During those sixty years, England had been changing from a Catholic nation to a Bible-loving people. Since 1525,

---

6 The New Testament was published at Rheims in 1582, and the complete Bible at Douay in 1609. See page 151.

7 A. T. Innes, *Church and State*, p. 156.

when Tyndale's Bible appeared,[8] the Scriptures had obtained a wide circulation. As Tyndale foresaw, the influence of the Divine Word had weaned the people away from pomp and ceremony in religion. But this result had not been obtained without years of struggle. Spain, at that time, was not only the greatest nation in the world, but also was fanatically Catholic. All the new world belonged to Spain, she ruled the seas and dominated Europe. The Spanish sovereign and the Papacy united in their efforts to send into England bands of highly trained Jesuits. By these, plot after plot was hatched to place a Catholic ruler on England's throne.

At the same time, the Jesuits were acting to turn the English people from the Bible, back to Romanism. As a means to this end, they brought forth in English a Bible of their own. Let it always be borne in mind that the Bible adopted by Constantine was in Greek; that Jerome's Bible was in Latin; but that the Jesuit Bible was in English. If England could be retained in the Catholic column, Spain and England together would see to it that all America, north and south, would be Catholic. In fact, wherever the influence of the English-speaking race extended, Catholicism would reign. If this result were to be thwarted, it was necessary to meet the danger brought about by the Jesuit Version.

The Great Stir over the Jesuit Bible of 1582

So powerful was the swing toward Protestantism during the reign of Queen Elizabeth, and so strong the love for Tyndale's Version, that there was neither place nor Catholic scholarship enough in England to bring forth a Catholic Bible in strength. Priests were in prison for their plotting, and many had fled to the Continent. There they founded schools to train English youth and send them back to England as priests. Two of these colleges alone

---

[8] Tyndale's New Testament was published in 1525, his Pentateuch in 1530, and his amended edition of the New Testament in 1534.

sent over, in a few years, not less than three hundred priests.

The most prominent of these colleges, called seminaries, was at Rheims, France. Here the Jesuits assembled a company of learned scholars. From here they kept the Pope informed of the changes of the situation in England, and from here they directed the movements of Philip II of Spain as he prepared a great fleet to crush England and bring it back to the feet of the Pope.

The burning desire to give the common people the Holy Word of God was the reason why Tyndale had translated it into English. No such reason impelled the Jesuits at Rheims. In the preface of their Rheims New Testament, they state that it was not translated into English because it was necessary that the Bible should be in the mother tongue, or that God had appointed the Scriptures to be read by all; but from the special consideration of the state of their mother country. This translation was intended to do on the inside of England what the great navy of Philip II was to do on the outside. One was to be used as a moral attack, the other as a physical attack — both to reclaim England. The preface especially urged that those portions be committed to memory "which made most against heretics."

"The principal object of the Rhemish translators was not only to circulate their doctrines through the country, but also to depreciate as much as possible the English translations."9

The appearance of the Jesuit New Testament of 1582 produced consternation in England. It was understood at once to be a menace against the new English unity. It was to serve as a wedge between Protestants and Catholics. It was the product of unusual ability and years of learning. Immediately, the scholarship of England was astir. Queen Elizabeth sent forth the call for a David to meet this Goliath. Finding no one in her kingdom satisfactory to her, she sent to Geneva, where Calvin was building up his great work, and besought Beza, the co-worker of Calvin, to

_____

9 Brooke, *Cartwright,* p. 256.

undertake the task of answering the objectionable matter contained in this Jesuit Version. In this department of learning, Beza was easily recognized as chief. To the astonishment of the Queen, Beza modestly replied that her majesty had within her own realm a scholar more able to undertake the task than he. He referred to Thomas Cartwright, the great Puritan divine. Beza said, "The sun does not shine on a greater scholar than Cartwright."

Cartwright was a Puritan, and Elizabeth disliked the Puritans as much as she did the Catholics. She wanted an Episcopalian or a Presbyterian to undertake the answer. Cartwright was ignored. But time was passing and English Protestantism wanted Cartwright. The universities of Cambridge and Oxford, Episcopalian though they were, sent to Cartwright a ·request signed by their outstanding scholars.[10] Cartwright decided to undertake it. He reached out one arm and grasped all the power of the Latin manuscripts and testimony. He reached out his other arm and in it he embraced all the vast stores of Greek and Hebrew literature. With inescapable logic, he marshaled the facts of his vast learning and leveled blow after blow against this latest and most dangerous product of Catholic theology.[11]

Meanwhile, 136 great Spanish galleons, some armed with 50 cannons, were slowly sailing up the English Channel to make England Catholic. England had no ships. Elizabeth asked Parliament for 15 men-of-war — they voted 30. With these, assisted by harbor tugs under Drake, England sailed forth to meet the greatest fleet the world had ever seen. All England teemed with excitement. God helped: the Armada was crushed, and England became a great sea power.

The Rheims-Douay and the King James Version were published less than thirty years apart. Since then the King James has steadily held its own. The Rheims-Douay has been repeatedly changed to approximate the King James.

---

10 *Ibid.*, p. 260.

11 *English Hexapla*, pp. 98, 99; F. J. Firth, *The Holy Gospel,* pp. 17, 18.

The result is that the Douay of 1600 and that of 1900 are not the same in many ways.

"The New Testament was published at Rheims in 1582. The university was moved back to Douai in 1593, where the Old Testament was published in 1609-1610. This completed what is known as the original Douay Bible. There are said to have been two revisions of the Douay Old Testament and eight of the Douay New Testament, representing such an extent of verbal alterations, and modernized spelling that a Roman Catholic authority says, 'The version now in use has been so seriously altered that it can be scarcely considered identical with that which first went by the name of the Douay Bible,' and further that 'it never had any episcopal imprimatur, much less any papal approbation.'

"Although the Bibles in use at the present day by the Catholics of England and Ireland are popularly styled the Douay Version, they are most improperly so called; they are founded, with more or less alteration, on a series of revisions undertaken by Bishop Challoner in 1749-52. His object was to meet the practical want felt by the Catholics of his day of a Bible moderate in size and price, in readable English, and with notes more suitable to the time. . . . The changes introduced by him were so considerable that, according to Cardinal Newman, they 'almost amounted to a new translation.' So also, Cardinal Wiseman wrote, 'To call it any longer the Douay or Rhemish is an abuse of terms. It has been altered and modified until scarcely any verse remains as it was originally published. In nearly every case, Challoner's changes took the form approximating to the Authorized Version.' "[12]

Note the above quotations. Because if you seek to compare the Douay with the American Revised Version, you will find that the older, or first Douay of 1582, is more like it in Catholic readings than those editions of today, inasmuch as the 1582 Version had been doctored and redoctored. Yet, even in the later editions, you will find many of those corruptions which the Reformers

---

[12] "Douay Bible," *The Catholic Encyclopedia.*

denounced and which reappear in the American Revised Version.

A thousand years had passed before time permitted the trial of strength between the Greek Bible and the Latin. They had fairly met in the struggles of 1582 and the thirty years following in their respective English translations. The Vulgate yielded before the Received Text. The Latin was vanquished before the Greek; the mutilated version before the pure Word. The Jesuits were obliged to shift their line of battle. They saw, that armed only with the Latin, they could fight no longer. They therefore resolved to enter the field of the Greek and become superb masters of the Greek; only that they might meet the influence of the Greek. They knew that manuscripts in Greek, of the type from which the Bible adopted by Constantine had been taken, were awaiting them — manuscripts, moreover, which involved the Old Testament as well as the New. To use them to overthrow the Received Text would demand great training and almost Herculean labors, for the Received Text was apparently invincible.

But still more. Before they could get under way, the English champions of the Greek had moved up and consolidated their gains. Flushed with their glorious victory over the Jesuit Bible of 1582, and over the Spanish Armada of 1588, every energy pulsating with certainty and hope, English Protestantism brought forth a perfect masterpiece. They gave to the world what has been considered by hosts of scholars, the greatest version ever produced in any language, — The King James Bible, called "The Miracle of English Prose." This was not taken from the Latin in either the Old or the New Testament, but from the languages in which God originally wrote His Word, namely, from the Hebrew in the Old Testament and from the Greek in the New Testament.

The Jesuits had therefore before them a double task — both to supplant the authority of the Greek of the Received Text by another Greek New Testament, and then upon this mutilated foundation to bring forth a new English version which might retire the King James into the background. In other words, they must, before they could again give standing to the Vulgate, bring Protestantism to accept a mutilated Greek text and an English version based upon it.

The manuscripts from which the New Version must be taken would be like the Greek manuscripts which Jerome used in producing the Vulgate. The opponents of the King James Version would even do more. They would enter the field of the Old Testament, namely, the Hebrew, and, from the translations of it into Greek in the early centuries, seize whatever advantages they could. In other words, the Jesuits had put forth one Bible in English, that of 1582, as we have seen it; of course they could get out another.

CHAPTER V

The King James Bible Born Amid the Great Struggles over the Jesuit Version

The hour had arrived, and from the human point of view, conditions were perfect for God to bring forth a translation of the Bible which would sum up in itself the best of the ages. The Heavenly Father foresaw the opportunity of giving His Word to the inhabitants of earth by the coming of the British Empire with its dominions scattered throughout the world, and by the great American Republic, both speaking the English language.

Not only was the English language by 1611 in a more opportune condition than it had ever been before or ever would be again,[1] but the Hebrew and the Greek likewise had been brought up with the accumulated treasures of their materials to a splendid working point. The age was not distracted by the rush of mechanical and industrial achievements. Moreover linguistic scholarship was at its peak. Men of giant minds, supported by excellent physical health, had possessed in a splendid state of perfection a

---

[1] The translators wisely preserved what was good in the earlier translations, with the result that the language of our English Bible is *not* the language of the age in which the translators lived, but in its grand simplicity stands out in contrast to the ornate and often affected diction of the time.

knowledge of the languages and literature necessary for the ripest Biblical scholarship.

One hundred and fifty years of printing had permitted the Jewish rabbis to place at the disposal of scholars all the treasures in the Hebrew tongue which they had been accumulating for over two thousand years. In the words of the learned Professor E. C. Bissell:

"There ought to be no doubt that, in the text which we inherit from the Masoretes, and they from the Talmudists, and they in turn from a period when versions and paraphrases of the Scriptures in other languages now accessible to us were in common use — the same text being transmitted to this period from the time of Ezra under the peculiarly sacred seal of the Jewish canon — we have a substantially correct copy of the original documents, and one worthy of all confidence."[2]

We are told that the revival of Masoretic studies in more recent times was the result of the vast learning and energy of Buxtorf, of Basle.[3] He had given the benefits of his Hebrew accomplishments in time to be used by the translators of the King James Version. And we have the word of a leading Revisionist, highly recommended by Bishop Ellicott, that it is not to the credit of Christian scholarship that so little has been done in Hebrew researches during the past 300 years.[4]

What is true of the Hebrew is equally true of the Greek. The Unitarian scholar who sat on the English New Testament Revision Committee acknowledged that the Greek New Testament of Erasmus (1516) is as good as any.[5] It should be here pointed out that Stephens (1550), then Beza (1598), and Elzevir (1624) all subsequently printed editions of virtually the same Greek New Testa-

---

[2] Chambers, *Companion to Revised Old Testament,* pp. 63, 64.

[3] *A New Commentary by Bishop Gore and Others,* Part 1, p. 651.

[4] Chambers, *Companion to Revised Old Testament,* p. 66.

[5] Rev. G. Vance Smith, *Nineteenth Century,* July, 1881. Neither Vance Smith nor A. T. Robertson regarded the Received Text as the best text. Robertson says in the Preface to the first edition of his massive *Grammar of the Greek New Testament,* "The text of Westcott and Hort is followed in all essentials."

ment. Since the days of Elzevir it has been called the Received Text or Textus Receptus. Of it Dr. A. T. Robertson also says: "It should be stated at once that the Textus Receptus is not a bad text. It is not an heretical text. It is substantially correct."[6]

Again: "Erasmus seemed to feel that he had published the original Greek New Testament as it was written. . . . The third edition of Erasmus (1522) became the foundation of the Textus Receptus for Britain since it was followed by Stephens. There were 3300 copies of the first two editions of the Greek New Testament of Erasmus circulated. His work became the standard for three hundred years."[7]

This text is and has been for 300 years the best known and most widely used. It has behind it all the Protestant scholarship of nearly three centuries.[8] It ought to be pointed out that those who seem eager to attack the King James and the Greek text behind it, when the enormous difficulties of the Revised Greek Testament are pointed out, will claim the Revised Text is all right because it is like the Greek New Testament from which the King James was translated; on the other hand, when they are not called to account, they will say belittling things about the Received Text and the scholars who translated the King James Bible.

Better Condition of English Language in 1611

We are now come, however, to a very striking situation which is little observed and rarely mentioned by those who discuss the merits of the King James Bible. The English language in 1611 was in the very best condition to receive into its bosom the Old and New Testaments. Each word was broad, simple, and generic. That is to say, words were capable of containing in themselves not only their central

6 Robertson, *Introduction,* p. 21.

7 *Ibid.,* pp. 18, 19.

8 Excepting the architects of modern textual criticism, who have enthroned the few above the many manuscripts which preserve this text.

thoughts, but also all the different shades of meaning which were attached to that central thought.

Since then, words have lost that living, pliable breadth. Vast additions have been made to the English vocabulary during the past 300 years, so that several words are now necessary to convey the same meaning which formerly was conveyed by one. It will then be readily seen that while the English vocabulary has increased in quantity, nevertheless, single words have lost their many shades, combinations of words have become fixed, capable of only one meaning, and therefore less adaptable to receiving into English the thoughts of the Hebrew which likewise is a simple, broad, generic language. New Testament Greek, is, in this respect, like the Hebrew. When our English Bible was revised, the Revisers labored under the impression that the sacred writers of the Greek New Testament did not write in the everyday language of the common people. Since then the accumulated stores of archaeological findings have demonstrated that the language of the Greek New Testament was the language of the simple, ordinary people, rather than the language of scholars, and is flexible, broad, generic, like the English of the 1611 version. Or in the words of another:

"It is sometimes regretted that our modern English has lost, or very nearly lost, its power of inflection; but whatever may have been thus lost to the ear has been more than compensated to the sense, by our wealth of finely shaded auxiliary words. There is no differentiation of wish, will, condition, supposition, potentiality, or possibility representable in syllables of human speech, or conceivable to the mind of man, which cannot be precisely put in some form of our English verb.

"But here again, our power of precision has been purchased at a certain cost. For every form of our verbal combinations has now come to have its own peculiar and appropriate sense, and no other; so that, when we use any one of those forms, it is understood by the hearer or reader that we intend the special sense of that form, and of that alone. In this respect, as in the specific values of our synonyms, we encounter a self-evident difficulty in the literal translation of the Scriptures into modern English. For there is no such refinement of tense and mood in the Hebrew language; and, although the classical Greek was undoubtedly perfect in its inflections, the writers of the New Testament were either ignorant of its powers, or were not capable of using them correctly."[9]

The above writer then points out that the authors of the New Testament did not always use that tense of the Greek verb, called the aorist, in the same rigid, specific sense in which the Revisers claimed they had done. Undoubtedly, in a general way, the sacred writers understood the meaning of the aorist as distinguished from the perfect and imperfect; but they did not always use it so specifically as the Revisers claim.

Origin of the King James Version

After the life and death struggles with Spain, and the hard-fought battle to save the English people from the Jesuit Bible of 1582, victorious Protestantism took stock of its situation and organized for the new era which had evidently dawned. A thousand ministers, it is said, sent a petition, called the Millenary Petition, to King James who had now succeeded Elizabeth as sovereign. One author describes the petition as follows:

"The petition craved reformation of sundry abuses in the worship, ministry, revenues, and discipline of the national Church. . . . Among other of their demands, Dr. Reynolds, who was the chief speaker in their behalf, requested that there might be a new translation of the Bible, without note or comment."[10]

The strictest element of Protestantism, the Puritan, we conclude was at the bottom of this request for a new and accurate translation; and the Puritan element on the committee appointed was strong.[11]

---

[9] John Fulton, *Forum*, June, 1887. They delivered this message in words which were "God-breathed," and it was not the design of the Divine Author to use classical Greek as the medium of His revelation.

[10] McClure, *The Translators Revived*, pp. 57, 58.

[11] *Ibid.*, pp. 130, 131.

The language of the Jesuit Bible had stung the sensibilities and the scholarship of Protestants. In the preface of that book it had criticized and belittled the Bible of the Protestants. The Puritans felt that the corrupted version of the Rheimists was spreading poison among the people, even as formerly by withholding the Bible, Rome had starved the people.[12]

The Unrivaled Scholarship of the Reformers

The first three hundred years of the Reformation produced a grand array of scholars, who have never since been surpassed, if indeed they have been equaled. Melanchthon, the co-worker of Luther, was of so great scholarship that Erasmus expressed admiration for his attainments. By his organization of schools throughout Germany and by his valuable textbooks, he exercised for many years a more powerful influence than any other teacher. Hallam said that far above all others he was the founder of general learning throughout Europe. His Latin grammar was "almost universally adopted in Europe, running through fifty-one editions and continuing until 1734"; that is, for two hundred years it continued to be the textbook even in the Roman Catholic schools of Saxony. Here the names of others might be added: of Beza, the great scholar and co-worker of Calvin, of Bucer, of Cartwright, of the Swiss scholars of the Reformation, and of a host of others who were unsurpassed in learning in their day and have never been surpassed since.

It was said of one of the translators of the King James that "such was his skill in all languages, especially the Oriental, that had he been present at the confusion of tongues at Babel, he might have served as Interpreter-General."[13] In view of the vast stores of material which were available to verify the certainty of the Bible at the time of the Reformation, and the prodigious labors of the Reformers in this material for a century, it is very

---

12 Brooke, *Cartwright*, p. 274.
13 McClure, *The Translators Revived*, p. 87.

erroneous to think that they had not been sufficiently overhauled by 1611.

It is an exaggerated idea, much exploited by those who are attacking the Received Text, that we of the present have greater, as well as more valuable, sources of information than had the translators of 1611.[14] The Reformers themselves considered their sources of information perfect. Doctor Fulke says:

"But as for the Hebrew and Greek that now is, (it) may easily be proved to be the same that always hath been; neither is there any diversity in sentence, howsoever some copies, either through negligence of the writer, or by any other occasion, do vary from that which is commonly and most generally received in some letters, syllables, or words."[15]

We cannot censure the Reformers for considering their sources of information sufficient and authentic enough to settle in their minds the infallible inspiration of the Holy Scriptures, since we have a scholar of repute today rating their material as high as the material of the present. Doctor Jacobus thus indicates the relative value of information available to Jerome, to the translators of the King James, and to the Revisers of 1900:

"On the whole, the differences in the matter of the sources available in 390, 1590 and 1890 are not very serious."[16]

Alexandrinus, Vaticanus, and Sinaiticus

So much has been said about the Alexandrinus, Vaticanus, and Sinaitic Manuscripts being made available since 1611, that a candid examination ought to be given to see if it is all really as we have repeatedly been told.

---

[14] It is true that thousands of manuscripts have been brought to life since 1611, but it must be emphasized that the great majority of these are in substantial agreement with the Traditional Text underlying the Reformers' Bibles and the King James Version.

[15] Fulke, *Defence of Translations of the Bible* (1583), p. 73.

[16] Jacobus, *Catholic and Protestant Bibles*, p. 41.

The Alexandrinus Manuscript arrived in London in 1627, we are informed, just sixteen years too late for use by the translators of the King James. We would humbly inquire if a manuscript must dwell in the home town of scholars in order for them to have the use of its information? If so, then the Revisers of 1881 and 1901 were in a bad way. Who donated the Alexandrinus Manuscript to the British Government?[17] It was Cyril Lucar, the head of the Greek Catholic Church. Why did he do it? What was the history of the document before he did it? An answer to these inquiries opens up a very interesting chapter of history.

Cyril Lucar (1568-1638), born in the East, early embraced the principles of the Reformation, and for it, was pursued all his life by the Jesuits. He spent some time at Geneva with Beza and Calvin. When holding an important position in Lithuania, he opposed the union of the Greek Church there and in Poland with Rome. In 1602 he was elected Patriarch of Alexandria, Egypt, where the Alexandrinus Manuscript had been kept for years. It seems almost certain that this great Biblical scholar would have been acquainted with it. Thus he was in touch with this manuscript before the King James translators began work. Later he was elected the head of the Greek Catholic Church. He wrote a confession of faith which distinguished between the canonical and apocryphal books. He was thoroughly awake to the issues of textual criticism. These had been discussed repeatedly and to the smallest details at Geneva, where he had passed some time. Of Lucar one encyclopedia states:

"In 1602 Cyril succeeded Meletius as patriarch of Alexandria. While holding this position he carried on an active correspondence with David le Leu, de Wilhelm, and the Remonstrant Uytenbogaert of Holland; Abbot, Archbishop of Canterbury; Leger, professor of Geneva; the republic of Venice; the Swedish King Gustavus Adolphus; and his chancellor, Axel Oxenstierna. Many of these

---

17 The manuscript was entrusted by Cyril Lucar to the English ambassador Sir Thomas Rowe to pass on as a gift to King Charles I.

letters, written in different languages, are still extant. They show that Cyril was an earnest opponent of Rome, and a great admirer of the Protestant Reformation. He sent for all the important works, Protestant and Roman Catholic, published in the Western countries, and sent several young men to England to get a thorough theological education. The friends of Cyril in Constantinople, and among them the English, Dutch, and Swedish ambassadors, endeavored to elevate Cyril to the patriarchal see of Constantinople. . . .

"The Jesuits, in union with the agents of France, several times procured his banishment, while his friends, supported by the ambassadors of the Protestant powers in Constantinople, obtained, by means of large sums of money, his recall. During all these troubles, Cyril, with remarkable energy, pursued the great task of his life. In 1627 he obtained a printing press from England, and at once began to print his Confession of Faith and several catechisms. But before these documents were ready for publication, the printing establishment was destroyed by the Turkish Government at the instigation of the Jesuits. Cyril then sent his Confession of Faith to Geneva, where it appeared, in 1629, in the Latin language, under the true name of the author, and with a dedication to Cornelius de Haga. It created throughout Europe a profound sensation."[18]

We think enough has been given to show that the scholars of Europe and England, in particular, had ample opportunity to become fully acquainted by 1611 with the problems involved in the Alexandrinus Manuscript.

Let us pursue the matter a little further. The Catholic Encyclopaedia does not omit to tell us that the New Testament from Acts on, in Codex A (the Alexandrinus), agrees with the Vatican Manuscript. If the problems presented by the Alexandrinus Manuscript, and consequently by the Vaticanus, were so serious, why were we obliged to wait till 1881-1901 to learn of the glaring mistakes of the translators of the King James, when the

---

[18] "Cyril Lucar," McClintock and Strong, *Encyclopedia*, Vol. II, p. 635.

manuscript arrived in 1627?[19] The *Forum* informs us that 250 different versions of the Bible were tried in England between 1611 and now, but they all fell flat before the majesty of the King James. Were not the Alexandrinus and the Vaticanus able to aid these 250 versions, and overthrow the other Bible, resting, as the critics explain, on an insecure foundation?

The case with the Vaticanus and the Sinaiticus is no better. The problems presented by these two manuscripts were well known, not only to the translators of the King James, but also to Erasmus. We are told that the Old Testament portion of the Vaticanus has been printed since 1587.

"The third great edition is that commonly known as the 'Sixtine,' published at Rome in 1587 under Pope Sixtus V. . . . Substantially, the 'Sixtine' edition gives the text of B. . . . The 'Sixtine' served as the basis for most of the ordinary editions of the LXX for just three centuries." [20]

We are informed by another author that, if Erasmus had desired, he could have secured a transcript of this manuscript.[21] There was no necessity, however, for Erasmus to obtain a transcript because he was in correspondence with Professor Paulus Bombasius at Rome, who sent him such variant readings as he wished.[22]

"A correspondent of Erasmus in 1533 sent that scholar a number of selected readings from it [Codex B], as proof of its superiority to the Received Greek Text."[23]

Erasmus, however, rejected these varying readings of the Vatican Manuscript because he considered from the massive evidence of his day that the Received Text was correct.

---

[19] During this interval Walton (1657), Fell (1675), Mill (1707), Bengel (1734), Wetstein (1751), Griesbach, Scholz, Lachmann, and their successors expressed views of the text similar to those of the 1881-1901 Revisers; but their writings were not given the same wide publicity.

[20] Ottley, *Handbook of the Septuagint*, p. 64.

[21] Bissell, *Historic Origin of the Bible*, p. 84.

[22] S. P. Tregelles, *On the Printed Text of the Greek Testament*, p. 22.

[23] Kenyon, *Our Bible*, p. 133.

The story of the finding of the Sinaitic Manuscript by Tischendorf in a monastery at the foot of Mt. Sinai illustrates the history of some of these later manuscripts. Tischendorf was visiting this monastery in 1844 to look for these documents. He discovered in a basket, over forty pages of a Greek manuscript of the Bible. He was told that two other basket loads had been used for kindling. Later, in 1859, he again visited this monastery to search for other manuscripts. He was about to give up in despair and depart when he was told of a bundle of additional leaves of a Greek manuscript. When he examined the contents of this bundle, he saw them to be a reproduction of part of the Bible in Greek. He could not sleep that night. Great was the joy of those who were agitating for a revision of the Bible when they learned that the new find was similar to the Vaticanus, but differed greatly from the King James. Dr. Riddle informs us that the discovery of the Sinaiticus settled in its favor the agitation for revision.

Just a word on the two styles of manuscripts before we go further. Manuscripts are of two kinds — uncial and cursive. Uncials are written in large square letters much like our capital letters; cursives are of a free running hand.

We have already given authorities to show that the Sinaitic Manuscript is a brother of the Vaticanus. Practically all of the problems of any serious nature which are presented by the Sinaitic, are the problems of the Vaticanus. Therefore the translators of 1611 had available all the variant readings of these manuscripts and rejected them.

The following words from Dr. Kenrick, Catholic Bishop of Philadelphia, will support the conclusion that the translators of the King James knew the readings of Codices Aleph, A, B, C, D, where they differed from the Received Text and denounced them. Bishop Kenrick published an English translation of the Catholic Bible in 1849. I quote from the preface:

"Since the famous manuscripts of Rome, Alexandria, Cambridge, Paris, and Dublin, were examined . . . a verdict has been obtained in favor of the Vulgate.

"At the Reformation, the Greek Text, as it then stood,

was taken as a standard, in conformity to which the versions of the Reformers were generally made; whilst the Latin Vulgate was depreciated, or despised, as a mere version."[24]

In other words, the readings of these much boasted manuscripts, recently made available, are those of the Vulgate. The Reformers knew of these readings and rejected them, as well as the Vulgate.

Men of 1611 Had All the Material Necessary

Let us suppose, for the sake of argument, that the translators of 1611 did not have access to the problems of the Alexandrinus, the Sinaiticus, and the Vaticanus by direct contact with these uncials. It mattered little. They had other manuscripts accessible which presented all the same problems. We are indebted for the following information to Dr. F. C. Cook, editor of the *Speaker's Commentary,* chaplain to the Queen of England, who was invited to sit on the Revision Committee, but refused:

"That Textus Receptus was taken in the first instance, from late cursive manuscripts; but its readings are maintained only so far as they agree with the best ancient versions, with the earliest and best Greek and Latin Fathers, and with the vast majority of uncial and cursive manuscripts."[25]

It is then clear that among the cursive and uncial manuscripts which the Reformers possessed, the majority agreed with the Received Text; however, there were a few among these documents which belonged to the counterfeit family. These dissenting few presented all the problems which can be found in the Alexandrinus, the Vaticanus, and the Sinaiticus. In other words, the translators of the King James came to a diametrically opposite conclusion from that arrived at by the Revisers of 1881, although the men of 1611, as well as those of 1881, had before them

---

24 H. Cotton, quoted in *Rheims and Douay,* p. 155.

25 F. C. Cook, *Revised Version of the First Three Gospels,* p. 226.

the same problems and the same evidence. We shall present testimony on this from another authority:

"The popular notion seems to be, that we are indebted for our knowledge of the true texts of Scripture to the existing uncials entirely; and that the essence of the secret dwells exclusively with the four or five oldest of these uncials. By consequence, it is popularly supposed that since we are possessed of such uncial copies, we could afford to dispense with the testimony of the cursives altogether. A more complete misconception of the facts of the case can hardly be imagined. For the plain truth is *that all the phenomena exhibited by the uncial manuscripts* are reproduced by the cursive copies."[26]

We give a further testimony from another eminent authority: "Our experience among the Greek cursives proves to us that transmission has not been careless, and they do represent a wholesome traditional text in the passages involving doctrine and so forth."[27]

As to the large number of manuscripts in existence, we have every reason to believe that the Reformers were far better acquainted with them than later scholars. Doctor Jacobus in speaking of textual critics of 1582, says: "The present writer has been struck with the critical acumen shown at that date (1582), and the grasp of the relative value of the common Greek manuscripts and the Latin version."[28]

On the other hand, if more manuscripts have been made accessible since 1611, little use has been made of what we had before and of the majority of those made available since. The Revisers systematically ignored the whole world of manuscripts and relied practically on only three or four. As Dean Burgon says, "But nineteen-twentieths of those documents, for any use which has been made of them, might just as well be still lying in the monastic libraries from which they were obtained." We feel, therefore, that a mistaken picture of the case has been presented with

---

[26] Burgon and Miller, *The Traditional Text,* p. 202.

[27] H. C. Hoskier, *Concerning the Genesis of the Versions,* p. 416.

[28] Jacobus, *Catholic and Protestant Bibles,* p. 212.

reference to the material at the disposition of the translators of 1611 and concerning their ability to use that material.

Plans of Work Followed by the King James Translators

The forty-seven learned men appointed by King James to accomplish this important task were divided first into three companies: one worked at Cambridge, another at Oxford, and the third at Westminster. Each of these companies again split up into two. Thus, there were six companies working on six allotted portions of the Hebrew and Greek Bibles. Each member of each company worked individually on his task, then brought to each member of his committee the work he had accomplished. The committee all together went over that portion of the work translated.

Thus, when one company had come together, and had agreed on what should stand, after having compared their work, as soon as they had completed any one of the sacred books, they sent it to each of the other companies to be critically reviewed. If a later company, upon reviewing the book, found anything doubtful or unsatisfactory, they noted such places, with their reasons, and sent it back to the company whence it came. If there should be a disagreement, the matter was finally arranged at a general meeting of the chief persons of all the companies at the end of the work. It can be seen by this method that each part of the work was carefully gone over at least fourteen times.

It was further understood that if there was any special difficulty or obscurity, all the learned men of the land could be called upon by letter for their judgment. And finally each bishop kept the clergy of his diocese notified concerning the progress of the work, so that if any one felt constrained to send any particular observations, he was notified to do so.

How astonishingly different is this from the method employed by the Revisers of 1881! The Old Testament Committee met together and sat as one body secretly for ten years. The New Testament Committee did the same. This arrangement left the committee at the mercy of a determined triumvirate to lead the weak and to dominate the rest. All reports indicate that an iron rule of silence was imposed upon these Revisers during all that time. The public was kept in suspense all the long, weary ten years. And only after elaborate plans had been laid to throw the Revised Version all at once upon the market to effect a tremendous sale, did the world know what had gone on.

The Giants of Learning

No one can study the lives of those men who gave us the King James Bible without being impressed with their profound and varied learning.

"It is confidently expected," says McClure, "that the reader of these pages will yield to the conviction that all the colleges of Great Britain and America, even in this proud day of boastings, could not bring together the same number of divines equally qualified by learning and piety for the great undertaking. Few indeed are the living names worthy to be enrolled with those mighty men. It would be impossible to convene out of any one Christian denomination, or out of all, a body of translators on whom the whole Christ-community would bestow such confidence as is reposed upon that illustrious company or who would prove themselves as deserving of such confidence. Very many self-styled 'improved versions' of the Bible, or parts of it, have been paraded before the world, but the religious public has doomed them all without exception to utter neglect."[29]

The translators of the King James, moreover, had something beyond great scholarship and unusual skill. They had gone through a period of great suffering. They had offered their lives that the truths which they loved might live.[30] As the biographer of William Tyndale has

---

[29] McClure, *The Translators Revived*, p. 64.

[30] This is especially true of the earlier translators who labored in the reigns of Henry VIII and Mary. The King James translators built upon a foundation well and truly laid by the martyrs of the previous century.

aptly said, — "So Tyndale thought; but God had ordained that not in the learned leisure of a palace, but amid the dangers and privations of exile should the English Bible be produced. Other qualifications were necessary to make him a worthy translator of Holy Scripture than mere grammatical scholarship. . . . At the time he bitterly felt what seemed to be the total disappointment of all his hopes; but he afterwards learned to trace in what appeared a misfortune the fatherly guidance of God; and this very disappointment, which compelled him to seek his whole comfort in the Word of God, tended to qualify him for the worthy performance of his great work."[31]

Dr. Cheyne, in giving his history of the founders of higher criticism, while extolling highly the mental brilliancy of the celebrated Hebrew scholar, Gesenius, expresses his regrets for the frivolity of that scholar.[32] No such weakness was manifested in the scholarship of the Reformers.

"Reverence," says Doctor Chambers, "it is this more than any other one trait that gave to Luther and Tyndale their matchless skill and enduring preeminence as translators of the Bible."[33]

It is difficult for us in this present prosperous age to understand how heavily the heroes of Protestantism in those days were forced to lean upon the arm of God. We find them speaking and exhorting one another by the promises of the Lord, that He would appear in judgment against their enemies. For that reason they gave full credit to the doctrine of the Second Coming of Christ as taught in the Holy Scriptures. Passages of notable value which refer to this glorious hope were not wrenched from their forceful setting as we find them in the Revised Versions and some modern Bibles, but were set forth with a fullness of clearness and hope.

Something other than an acquaintanceship, more or less, with a crushing mass of intricate details in the Hebrew and

---

31 Demaus, *William Tyndale*, pp. 84, 85.

32 Cheyne, *Founders of Old Testament Criticism*, pp. 58, 59.

33 Chambers, *Companion To Revised Old Testament*, p. 53.

the Greek is necessary to be a successful translator of God's Holy Word. God's Holy Spirit must assist. There must exist that which enables the workman at this task to have not only a conception of the whole but also a *balanced* conception, so that there will be no conflicts created through lack of skill on the part of the translator. That the giants of 1611 produced this effect and injured no doctrine of the Lord by their labors, may be seen in these few words from Sir Edmund Beckett, as, according to Gladstone,[34] he convincingly reveals the failure of the Revised Version: "Not their least service, is their showing us how very seldom the Authorized Version is materially wrong, and that no doctrine has been misrepresented there."[35]

To show the unrivaled English language of the King James Bible, I quote from Doctor William Lyon Phelps, Professor of English Literature in Yale University: "Priests, atheists, skeptics, devotees, agnostics, and evangelists, are generally agreed that the Authorized Version of the English Bible is the best example of English literature that the world has ever seen. . . . Every one who has a thorough knowledge of the Bible may truly be called educated; and no other learning or culture, no matter how extensive or elegant, can, among Europeans and Americans, form a proper substitute. Western civilization is founded upon the Bible. . . . I thoroughly believe in a university education for both men and women; but I believe a knowledge of the Bible without a college course is more valuable than a college course without the Bible. . . .

"The Elizabethan period — a term loosely applied to the years between 1558 and 1642,[36] — is generally regarded as the most important era in English literature. Shakespeare and his mighty contemporaries brought the drama to the highest point in the world's history; lyrical poetry found supreme expression; Spenser's Faerie Queene was an

---

[34] Lathbury, *Ecclesiastical and Religious Correspondence of Gladstone,* Vol. II, p. 320.

[35] Edmund Beckett, *Revised New Testament,* p. 16.

[36] Queen Elizabeth died in 1603.

unique performance; Bacon's Essays have never been surpassed. But the crowning achievement of those spacious days was the Authorized Translation of the Bible, which appeared in 1611. Three centuries of English literature followed; but, although they have been crowded with poets and novelists and essayists, and although the teaching of the English language and literature now gives employment to many earnest men and women, the art of English composition reached its climax in the pages of the Bible. . . .

"Now, as the English-speaking people have the best Bible in the world, and as it is the most beautiful monument erected with the English alphabet, we ought to make the most of it, for it is an incomparably rich inheritance, free to all who can read. This means that we ought invariably in the church and on public occasions to use the Authorized Version; all others are inferior."[37]

This statement was made twenty years after the American Revised Version of 1901 appeared.

---

[37] *Ladies' Home Journal*, November, 1921.

OUR AUTHORIZED BIBLE VINDICATED

CHAPTER VI

Three Hundred Years of Attack upon the
King James Bible

"Wherever the so-called Counter-Reformation, started by the Jesuits, gained hold of the people, the vernacular was suppressed and the Bible kept from the laity. So eager were the Jesuits to destroy the authority of the Bible — the paper pope of the Protestants, as they contemptuously called it — that they even did not refrain from criticizing its genuineness and historical value."[1]

The opponents of the noble work of 1611 like to tell the story of how the great printing plants which publish the King James Bible have been obliged to go over it repeatedly to eliminate flaws of printing, to eliminate words which in time have changed in their meaning, or errors which have crept in through the years because of careless editing by different printing houses. They offer this as an evidence of the fallibility of the Authorized Version.

They seem to overlook the fact that this labor of necessity is an argument *for*, rather than *against*, the dependability of the translations. Had each word of the Bible been set in a cement cast, incapable of the slightest flexibility and been kept so throughout the ages, there

---

[1] Von Dobschutz, *The Influence of the Bible*, p. 136.

could have been no adaptability to the ever-changing structure of human language. The artificiality of such a plan would have eliminated the living action of the Holy Spirit and would accuse both man and the Holy Spirit of being without an intelligent care for the Divine treasure.

On this point the scholars of the Reformation made their position clear under three different aspects. First, they claimed that the Holy Scriptures had come down to them unimpaired throughout the centuries.[2] Second, they recognized that to reform any manifest oversight was not placing human hands on a Divine work and was not contrary to the mind of the Lord. Dr. Fulke says: "Nevertheless, whereinsoever Luther, Beza, or the English translators have reformed any of their former oversights, the matter is not so great, that it can make an heresy."[3]

And lastly, they contended that the Received Text, both in Hebrew and in Greek, as they had it in their day would so continue unto the end of time.[4]

In fact, a testimony no less can be drawn from the opponents of the Received Text. The higher critics, who have constructed such elaborate scaffolding, and who have built such great engines of war as their *apparatus criticus,* are obliged to describe the greatness and strength of the walls they are attacking in order to justify their war machine. On the Hebrew Old Testament, one of a group of the latest and most radical critics says:

"DeLagarde would trace all manuscripts back to a single archetype which he attributed to Rabbi Aquiba, who died in 135 A.D. Whether this hypothesis is a true one or not will probably never be known; it certainly represents the fact that from about his day variations of the consonantal text ceased almost entirely."[5]

While of the Greek New Testament, Dr. Hort, who was an opponent of the Received Text and who dominated the English New Testament Revision Committee, says: "An

---

2 "Semler," McClintock and Strong, *Encyclopedia.*

3 Fulke, *Defence of Translations of the Bible* (1583), p. 60.

4 Brooke, *Cartwright,* pp. 274, 275.

5 Gore, *A New Commentary,* Part I, p. 647.

overwhelming proportion of the text in all known cursive manuscripts except a few is, as a matter of fact, identical."6

Thus strong testimonies can be given not only to the Received Text, but also to the phenomenal ability of the manuscript scribes writing in different countries and in different ages to preserve an identical Bible in the overwhelming mass of manuscripts.

The large number of conflicting readings which higher critics have gathered must come from only a few manuscripts, since the overwhelming mass of manuscripts is identical.7

The phenomenon presented by this situation is so striking that we are pressed in spirit to inquire, Who are these who are so interested in urging on the world the finds of their criticism? All lawyers understand how necessary for a lawsuit it is to find someone "to press the case." Thousands of wills bequeath property which is distributed in a way different from the wishes of the testator because there are none interested enough to "press the case."

The King James Bible had hardly begun its career before the enemies commenced to fall upon it. Though it has been with us for three hundred years in splendid leadership — a striking phenomenon — nevertheless, as the years increase, the attacks become more furious. If the Book were a dangerous document, a source of corrupting influence and a nuisance, we would wonder why it has been necessary to assail it since it would naturally die of its own weakness. But when it is a Divine blessing of great worth, a faultless power of transforming influence, who can they be who are so stirred up as to deliver against it one assault after another?

Great theological seminaries, in many lands, led by accepted teachers of learning, are laboring constantly to

6 Hort, *Introduction,* p. 143.

7 There are numerous small variations, but the great majority of the documents give support to the Traditional Text and may thus be identified with it. It would be difficult to find even two "identical" manuscripts.

tear it to pieces. Point us out anywhere, any similar situation concerning the sacred books of any other religion, or even of Shakespeare, or of any other work of literature. Especially since 1814, when the Jesuits were restored by the order of the Pope — if they needed restoration — have the attacks on the Bible, by Catholic scholars and by other scholars who are Protestants in name, become bitter.

"For it must be said that the Roman Catholic or the Jesuitical system of argument — the work of the Jesuits from the sixteenth century to the present day — evinces an amount of learning and dexterity, a subtilty of reasoning, a sophistry, a plausibility combined, of which ordinary Christians have but little idea. . . . Those who do so [take the trouble to investigate] find that, if tried by the rules of right reasoning, the argument is defective, assuming points which should be proved; that it is logically false, being grounded in sophisms; that it rests in many cases on quotations which are not genuine . . . on passages which, when collated with the original, are proved to be wholly inefficacious as proofs."[8]

As time went on, this wave of higher criticism mounted higher and higher until it became an ocean surge inundating France, Germany, England, Scotland, the Scandinavian nations, and even Russia. "When the Privy Council of England handed down in 1864 its decision, breathlessly awaited everywhere, permitting those seven Church of England clergymen to retain their positions, who had ruthlessly attacked the inspiration of the Bible, a cry of horror went up from Protestant England; but 'the whole Catholic Church,' said Dean Stanley, 'is, as we have seen, with the Privy Council and against the modern dogmatists' (Stanley, *Essays*, p. 140). By modern dogmatists, he meant those who believe the Bible, and the Bible only."

The tide of higher criticism was soon seen to change its appearance and to menace the whole framework of fundamentalist thinking. The demand for revision became the order of the day. The crest was seen about 1870 in

---

8 William Palmer, *Narrative of Events on the Tracts,* p. 23.

France, Germany, England, and the Scandinavian countries.[9] Time-honored Bibles in these countries were radically overhauled and a new meaning was read into words
of Inspiration.

Three lines of results are strongly discernible as features
of the movement. First, "collation" became the watchword. Manuscripts were laid alongside of manuscripts to
detect various readings and to justify that reading which
the critic chose as the right one. With the majority of
workers, especially those whose ideas have stamped the
revision, it was astonishing to see how they turned away
from the overwhelming mass of manuscripts and invested
with tyrannical superiority a certain few documents, some
of them of a questionable character. Second, this wave of
revision was soon seen to be hostile to the Reformation.
There is something startlingly in common to be found in
the modernist who denies the element of the miraculous in
the Scriptures, and the Catholic Church which invests
tradition with an inspiration equal to the Bible. As a result,
it seems a desperately hard task to get justice done to the
Reformers or their product. As Dr. Demaus says:

"For many of the facts of Tyndale's life have been
disputed or distorted, through carelessness, through prejudice, and through the malice of that school of writers in
whose eyes the Reformation was a mistake, if not a crime,
and who conceive it to be their mission to revive all the old
calumnies that have ever been circulated against the
Reformers, supplementing them by new accusations of
their own invention."[10]

A third result of this tide of revision is that when our
time-honored Bibles are revised, the changes are generally
in favor of Rome. We are told that Bible revision is a step
forward; that new manuscripts have been made available
and advance has been made in archaeology, philology,
geography, and the apparatus of criticism. How does it
come then that we have been revised back into the arms of
Rome? If my conclusion is true, this so-called Bible

---

[9] Chambers, *Companion to Revised Old Testament,* pp. 13, 14.

[10] Demaus, *William Tyndale,* p. 13.

revision has become one of the deadliest of weapons in the hands of those who glorify the Dark Ages and who seek to bring Western nations back to the theological thinking which prevailed before the Reformation.

Some of the earliest critics in the field of collecting variant readings of the New Testament in Greek, were Mill and Bengel. We have Dr. Kenrick, Catholic Bishop of Philadelphia in 1849, as authority that they and others had examined these manuscripts recently exalted as superior, such as the Vaticanus, Alexandrinus, Beza, and Ephraem, and had pronounced in favor of the Vulgate, the Catholic Bible.[11]

Simon, Astruc, and Geddes, with those German critics, Eichhorn, Semler, and DeWette, who carried their work on further and deeper, stand forth as leaders and representatives in the period which stretches from the date of the King James (1611) to the outbreak of the French Revolution (1789). Simon and Eichhorn were co-authors of a Hebrew Dictionary.[12] These outstanding six — two French, one Scottish, and three German — with others of perhaps not equal prominence, began the work of discrediting the Received Text, both in the Hebrew and in the Greek, and of calling in question the generally accepted beliefs respecting the Bible which had prevailed in Protestant countries since the birth of the Reformation.

There was not much to do in France, since it was not a Protestant country; and the majority had not far to go to change their belief. There was not much done in England or Scotland because there a contrary mentality prevailed. The greatest inroads were made in Germany. Thus matters stood when in 1773 European nations arose and demanded that the Pope suppress the order of the Jesuits. It was too late, however, to smother the fury which sixteen years later broke forth in the French Revolution.

The upheaval which followed engaged the attention of all mankind for a quarter of a century. It was the period of indignation foreseen, as some scholars thought, by the

---

[11] H. Cotton, quoted in *Rheims and Douay*, p. 155.
[12] "Winer," McClintock and Strong, *Encyclopedia.*

prophet Daniel. As the armies of the Revolution and of Napoleon marched and counter-marched over the territories of Continental Europe, the foundations of the ancient regime were broken up. Even from the Vatican the cry arose, "Religion is destroyed." And when in 1812 Napoleon was taken prisoner, and the deluge had passed, men looked out upon a changed Europe. England had escaped invasion, although she had taken a leading part in the overthrow of Napoleon. France restored her Catholic monarchs — the Bourbons who "never learned anything and never forgot anything." In 1814 the Pope promptly restored the Jesuits.

Then followed in the Protestant world two outstanding currents of thought: first, on the part of many, a stronger expression of faith in the Holy Scriptures, especially in the great prophecies which seemed to be on the eve of fulfillment where they predict the coming of a new dispensation. The other current took the form of a reaction, a growing disbelief in the leadership of accepted Bible doctrines whose uselessness seemed proved by their apparent impotence in not preventing the French Revolution. And, as in the days before that outbreak, Germany, which had suffered the most, seemed to be fertile soil for a strong and rapid growth of higher criticism.

Griesbach and Mohler

Among the foremost of those who tore the Received Text to pieces in the Old Testament stand the Hollander, Kuenen, and the German scholars, Ewald and Wellhausen. Their findings, however, were confined to scholarly circles. The public were not moved by them, as their work appeared to be only negative. The two German critics who brought the hour of revision much nearer were the Protestant Griesbach and the Catholic Mohler. Mohler (1796-1838) did not spend his efforts on the text as did Griesbach, but he handled the points of difference in doctrine between the Protestants and the Catholics in such a way as to win over the Catholic mind to higher criticism and to throw open the door for Protestants who either loved higher criticism, or who, being disturbed by it, found in Catholicism a haven of refuge. Of him Hagenbach says: "Whatever vigorous vitality is possessed by the most recent Catholic theological science is due to the labors of this man."[13]

Kurtz states: "He sent rays of his spirit deep into the hearts and minds of hundreds of his enthusiastic pupils by his writings, addresses, and by his intercourses with them; and what the Roman Catholic Church of the present possesses of living scientific impulse and feeling was implanted, or at least revived and excited by him. . . . In fact, long as was the opposition which existed between both churches, no work from the camp of the Roman Catholics produced as much agitation and excitement in the camp of the Protestants as this."[14]

Or, as Maurice writes concerning Ward, one of the powerful leaders of the Oxford Movement: "Ward's notion of Lutheranism is taken, I feel pretty sure, from Mohler's very gross misrepresentations."[15]

Griesbach (1745-1812) attacked the Received Text of the New Testament in a new way. He did not stop at bringing to light and emphasizing the variant readings of the Greek manuscripts; he classified readings into three groups, and put all manuscripts under these groupings, giving them the names of "Constantinopolitan," or those of the Received Text, the "Alexandrian," and the "Western." While Griesbach used the Received Text as his measuring rod, nevertheless, the new Greek New Testament he brought forth by this measuring rod followed the Alexandrian manuscripts; that is, it followed Origen. His classification of the manuscripts was so novel and the result of such prodigious labors, that the critics everywhere hailed his Greek New Testament as the final word. It was not long, however, before other scholars took Griesbach's own theory of classification and proved him wrong.

---

13 Hagenbach, *Church History,* Vol. II, p. 446.

14 Kurtz, *History of the Reformation,* Vol. II, p. 391.

15 Maurice, *Life of T. D. Maurice,* Vol. I, p. 362.

The Gnosticism of German Theology
Invades England

By 1833 the issue was becoming clearly defined. It was Premillenarianism, that is, belief in the return of Christ before the millennium, or Liberalism; it was with regard to the Scriptures either literalism or allegorism. As Cadman says of the Evangelicals of that day:

"Their fatalism inclined many of them to Premillenarianism as a refuge from the approaching catastrophes of the present dispensation. . . . Famous divines strengthened and adorned the wider ranks of Evangelicalism, but few such were found within the pale of the Establishment. Robert Hall, John Foster, William Jay of Bath, Edward Irving, [16] the eccentric genius, and in Scotland, Thomas Chalmers, represented the vigor and fearlessness of an earlier day and maintained the excellence of Evangelical preaching."[17]

How deeply the conviction that the great prophecies which predicted the approaching end of the age had gripped the public mind can be seen in the great crowds which assembled to hear Edward Irving. They were so immense that he was constantly compelled to secure larger auditoriums. Even Carlyle could relate of his own father in 1832:

"I have heard him say in late years with an impressiveness which all his perceptions carried with them, that the lot of a poor man was growing worse and worse; that the world would not and could not last as it was; that mighty

[16] The Rev. Edward Irving, a Presbyterian minister in London, first attracted attention by a series of addresses asserting that the Apostolic gifts of healing and speaking with tongues were designed to continue in every age of the church. He and his followers also held heretical views of the human nature of Christ, which resulted in his deposition by the Presbytery from the office of minister. His adherents built a new church for him and the movement attracted a large number of people in England and in several European countries.

They drew up an elaborate ritual, instituted four "orders" of Apostles, Prophets, Evangelists and Pastors, adopted the Romish doctrine of transubstantiation, and assumed the name of the "Apostolic Catholic Church." In doctrine and ritual they approached nearer to Romanism than to any form of Protestantism.

[17] Cadman, *Three Religious Leaders*, pp. 416, 417.

changes of which none saw the end were on the way. To him, as one about to take his departure, the whole was but of secondary moment. He was looking toward 'a city that had foundations.' "18

Here was a faith in the Second Coming of Christ, at once Protestant and evangelical, which would resist any effort so to revise the Scriptures as to render them colorless, giving to them nothing more than a literary endorsement of plans of betterment, merely social or political. This faith was soon to be called upon to face a theology of an entirely different spirit. German religious thinking at that moment was taking on an aggressive attitude. Schleiermacher had captured the imagination of the age and would soon mold the theology of Oxford and Cambridge. Though he openly confessed himself a Protestant, nevertheless, like Origen of old, he sat at the feet of Clement, the old Alexandrian teacher of 190 A.D.

Clement's passion for allegorizing Scripture offered an easy escape from those obligations imposed upon the soul by a plain message of the Bible. Schleiermacher modernized Clement's philosophy and made it beautiful to the parlor philosophers of the day by imaginary analysis of the realm of spirit. It was the old Gnosticism revived, and would surely dissolve Protestantism wherever accepted and would introduce such terms into the Bible, if revision could be secured, as to rob the trumpet of a certain sound. The great prophecies of the Bible would become mere literary addresses to the people of bygone days, and unless counter-checked by the noble Scriptures of the Reformers, the result would be either atheism or papal infallibility.

If Schleiermacher did more to captivate and enthrall the religious thinking of the nineteenth century than any other one scholar, Coleridge, his contemporary, did as much to give aggressive motion to the thinking of England's youth of his day, who, hardly without exception, drank enthusiastically of his teachings. He had been to Germany and returned a fervent devotee of its theology and textual criticism. At Cambridge University he became the star

---

18 Froude, *Carlyle's Reminiscences,* p. 48.

around which grouped a constellation of leaders in thought. Thirwall, Westcott, Hort, Moulton, and Milligan, who were all later members of the English Revision Committees and whose writings betray the voice of the master, felt the impact of his doctrines.

"His influence upon his own age, and especially upon its younger men of genius, was greater than that of any other Englishman. . . . Coleridgeans may be found now among every class of English divines, from the Broad Church to the highest Puseyites," says McClintock and Strong's *Encyclopedia.*

The same article speaks of Coleridge as "Unitarian," "Metaphysical," a "Theologian," "Pantheistic," and says that "he identifies reason with the divine Logos," and that he holds "views of inspiration as low as the rationalists," and also holds views of the Trinity "no better than a refined, Platonized Sabellianism."

Lachmann, Tischendorf, and Tregelles

We have seen above how Lachmann, Tischendorf, and Tregelles fell under the influence of Cardinal Wiseman's theories. There are more recent scholars of textual criticism who pass over these three and leap from Griesbach to Westcott and Hort, claiming that the two latter simply carried out the beginnings of classification made by the former.[19] Nevertheless, since many writers bid us over and over again to look to Lachmann, Tischendorf, and Tregelles — until we hear of them morning, noon, and night — we would seek to give these laborious scholars all the praise justly due them, while we remember that there is a limit to all good things.

Lachmann's (1793-1851) bold determination to throw aside the Received Text and to construct a new Greek Testament from such manuscripts as he endorsed according to his own rules, has been the thing which endeared him to all who give no weight to the tremendous testimony of 1500 years of use of the Received Text. Yet

---

[19] Gore, *A New Commentary,* Part III, p. 720.

Lachmann's canon of criticism has been deserted by both Bishop Ellicott and Dr. Hort. Ellicott says, "Lachmann's text is really one based on little more than four manuscripts, and so is really more of a critical recension than a critical text." And again, "A text composed on the narrowest and most exclusive principles."[20] While Dr. Hort says:

"Not again, in dealing with so various and complex a body of documentary attestation, is there any real advantage in attempting, with Lachmann, to allow the distributions of a very small number of the most ancient existing documents to construct for themselves a provisional text."[21]

Tischendorf's (1815-1874) outstanding claim upon history is his discovery of the Sinaitic Manuscript in the convent at the foot of Mt. Sinai. Mankind is indebted to this prodigious worker for having published manuscripts not accessible to the average reader. Nevertheless, his discovery of Codex Aleph toppled over his judgment. Previous to that he had brought out seven different Greek New Testaments, declaring that the seventh was perfect and could not be superseded. Then, to the scandal of textual criticism, after he had found the Sinaitic Manuscript, he brought out his eighth Greek New Testament, which was different from his seventh in 3572 places![22] Moreover, he demonstrated how textual critics can artificially bring out Greek New Testaments when, at the request of a French publishing house, Firmin Didot, he edited an edition of the Greek Testament for Catholics, conforming it to the Latin Vulgate.[23]

Tregelles (1813-1875) followed Lachmann's principles by going back to what he considered the ancient manuscripts and, like him, he ignored the Received Text and the great mass of cursive manuscripts.[24] Of him, Ellicott says,

---

[20] Ellicott, *Considerations on Revision of the New Testament,* p. 46.

[21] Hort, *Introduction,* p. 288.

[22] Burgon and Miller, *Traditional Text,* p. 7.

[23] Ezra Abbott, *Unitarian Review,* March, 1875.

[24] Schaff, *Companion to Greek Testament,* p. 264.

"His critical principles, especially his general principles of estimating and regarding modern manuscripts, are now, perhaps justly, called in question by many competent scholars," and that his text "is rigid and mechanical, and sometimes fails to disclose that critical instinct and peculiar scholarly sagacity which is so much needed in the great and responsible work of constructing a critical text of the Greek Testament."[25]

In his splendid work which convinced Gladstone that the Revised Version was a failure, Sir Edmund Beckett says of the principles which controlled such men as Lachmann, Tischendorf, Tregelles, Westcott, and Hort in their modern canons of criticism:

"If two, or two-thirds of two dozen men steeped in Greek declare that they believe that he [John] ever wrote that he saw a vision with seven angels clothed in stone with golden girdles, which is the only honest translation of their Greek, and defend it with such arguments as these, I ... distrust their judgment on the 'preponderance of evidence' for new readings altogether, and all their modern canons of criticism, which profess to settle the relative value of manuscripts, with such results as this and many others."[26]

Such were the antecedent conditions preparing the way to draw England into entangling alliances, to de-Protestantize her national church and to advocate at a dangerous hour the necessity of revising the King James Bible. The Earl of Shaftesbury, foreseeing the dark future of such an attempt, said in May, 1856:

"When you are confused or perplexed by a variety of versions, you would be obliged to go to some learned pundit in whom you reposed confidence, and ask him which version he recommended; and when you had taken his version, you must be bound by his opinion. I hold this to be the greatest danger that now threatens us. It is a danger pressed upon us from Germany, and pressed upon us by the neological spirit of the age. I hold it to be far

---

[25] Ellicott, *Considerations on Revision of the New Testament,* pp. 47, 48.
[26] Beckett, *The Revised New Testament,* pp. 181, 182.

more dangerous than Tractarianism, or Popery, both of which I abhor from the bottom of my heart. This evil is tenfold more dangerous, tenfold more subtle than either of these, because you would be ten times more incapable of dealing with the gigantic mischief that would stand before you."[27]

The Polychrome Bible and the Shorter Bible

The results of this rising tide of higher criticism were the rejection of the Received Text and the mania for revision. It gave us, among other bizarre versions, the "Polychrome" and also the "Shorter Bible." The *Polychrome Bible* is generally an edition of the separate books of the Scriptures, each book having every page colored many times to represent the different writers.

Anyone who will take the pains to secure a copy of the "Shorter Bible" in the New Testament will recognize that about four thousand of the nearly eight thousand verses in that Scripture have been entirely blotted out. We offer the following quotation from the *United Presbyterian* of December 22, 1921, as a description of the "Shorter Bible":

"The preface further informs us that only about one-third of the Old Testament and two-thirds of the New Testament are possessed of this 'vital interest and practical value.' The Old Testament ritual and sacrificial system, with their deep lessons and their forward look to the atonement through the death of Christ are gone. As a result of this, the New Testament references to Christ as the fulfillment of the Old Testament sacrifices are omitted. Such verses as, 'Behold the Lamb of God which taketh away the sin of the world,' are gone.

"Whole books of the Old Testament are gone. Some of the richest portions of the books of the prophets are missing. From the New Testament they have omitted 4,000 verses. Other verses are cut in two, and a fragment left us, for which we are duly thankful. The great

---

[27] Bissell, *Origin of the Bible,* p. 355.

commission recorded in Matthew; the epistles of Titus, Jude, First and Second John, are entirely omitted, and but twenty-five verses of the second epistle of Timothy remain. The part of the third chapter of Romans which treats of human depravity, being 'of no practical value to the present age,' is omitted. Only one verse remains from the fourth chapter. The twenty-fourth chapter of Matthew and other passages upon which the premillenarians base their theory, are missing. All the passages which teach the atonement through the death of Christ are gone."

The campaigns of nearly three centuries against the Received Text did their work. The Greek New Testament of the Reformation was dethroned and with it the versions translated from it, whether English, German, French, or of any other language. It had been predicted that if the Revised Version were not of sufficient merit to be authorized and so displace the King James, confusion and division would be multiplied by a crop of unauthorized and sectarian translations.[28] The Polychrome, the Shorter Bible, and a large output of heterogeneous Bibles verify the prediction. No competitor has yet appeared able to create a standard comparable to the text which has held sway for 1800 years in the original tongue, and for 300 years in its English translation, the King James Version.

---

28 Schaff, *Bible Revision*, p. 20.

OUR AUTHORIZED BIBLE VINDICATED

CHAPTER VII

Westcott and Hort

It is interesting at this juncture to take a glance at Doctors Westcott and Hort, the dominating mentalities of the scheme of Revision, principally in that period of their lives before they sat on the Revision Committee. They were working together twenty years before Revision began, and swept the Revision Committee along with them after work commenced. Mainly from their own letters, partly from the comments of their respective sons, who collected and published their lives and letters, we shall here state the principles which affected their deeper lives.[1]

---

[1] The influence of Westcott, Lightfoot and Hort is clearly demonstrated in W. R. Glover Jr.'s book, *Evangelical Nonconformity and the Higher Criticism* (London, Independent Press, 1954). "Leaning heavily on the Cambridge trio as defenders of the faith, the English churches were led imperceptibly into a mildly critical view that prevented any serious shock from New Testament criticism ever developing" (p. 64). "In the early decades of higher criticism in England the nonconformists followed the intellectual leadership of the Anglicans—Westcott, Lightfoot and Hort" (p. 257). "In accepting the Cambridge defence against Strauss and Baier, the evangelicals accepted Higher Criticism in principle without being fully aware of what they had done" (p. 284).

Their Higher Criticism

Westcott writes to his fiancée, Advent Sunday, 1847:
"All stigmatize him [Dr. Hampden] as a 'heretic'. . . . If
he be condemned, what will become of me! . . . The battle
of the Inspiration of Scripture has yet to be fought, and
how earnestly I could pray that I might aid the truth in
that."[2]

Westcott's son comments, 1903: "My father . . . believed that the charges of being 'unsafe' and of 'German-
izing' brought against him were unjust."[3]

Hort writes to Rev. Rowland Williams, October 21,
1858: "Further I agree with them [authors of *Essays and
Reviews*] in condemning many leading specific doctrines
of the popular theology. . . . Evangelicals seem to me
perverted rather than untrue. There are, I fear, still more
serious differences between us on the subject of authority,
and especially the authority of the Bible."[4]

Hort writes to Rev. John Ellerton, April 3, 1860: "But
the book which has most engaged me is Darwin. Whatever
may be thought of it, it is a book that one is proud to be
contemporary with. . . . My feeling is strong that the
theory is unanswerable. If so, it opens up a new period."[5]

Their Mariolatry

Westcott writes from France to his fiancée, 1847:
"After leaving the monastery, we shaped our course to a
little oratory which we discovered on the summit of a
neighboring hill. . . . Fortunately we found the door open.
It is very small, with one kneeling-place; and behind a
screen was a 'Pieta' the size of life [i.e. a Virgin and dead
Christ] . . . . Had I been alone I could have knelt there for
hours."[6]

---

2 Westcott, *Life of Westcott*, Vol. I, pp. 94, 95.

3 *Ibid.*, Vol. I, p. 218.

4 Hort, *Life of Hort*, Vol. I, p. 400.

5 *Ibid.*, Vol. I, p. 416.

6 Westcott, *Life of Westcott*, Vol. I, p. 81.

Westcott writes to Archbishop Benson, November 17, 1865: "I wish I could see to what forgotten truth Mariolatry bears witness."[7]

Hort writes to Westcott: "I am very far from pretending to understand completely the oft-renewed vitality of Mariolatry."[8]

Hort writes to Westcott, October 17, 1865: "I have been persuaded for many years that Mary-worship and 'Jesus'-worship have very much in common in their causes and their results."[9]

Hort writes to Westcott: "But this last error can hardly be expelled till Protestants unlearn the crazy horror of the idea of priesthood."[10]

Hort writes to Dr. Lightfoot, October 26, 1867: "But you know I am a staunch sacerdotalist."[11]

Their Anti-Protestantism

Westcott wrote to the Archbishop of Canterbury: "It does not seem to me that the Vaudois claim an ecclesiastical recognition. The position of the small Protestant bodies on the Continent, is, no doubt, one of great difficulty. But our church can, I think, only deal with churches growing to fuller life."[12]

Hort writes to Westcott, September 23, 1864: "I believe Coleridge was quite right in saying that Christianity without a substantial church is vanity and disillusion; and I remember shocking you and Lightfoot not so long ago by expressing a belief that 'Protestantism' is only parenthetical and temporary."[13] "Perfect Catholicity has been nowhere since the Reformation."[14]

---

[7] *Ibid.,* Vol. II, p. 50.

[8] Hort, *Life of Hort,* Vol. II, p. 49.

[9] *Ibid.,* Vol. II, p. 50.

[10] *Ibid.,* Vol. II, p. 51.

[11] *Ibid.,* Vol. II, p. 86.

[12] Westcott, *Life of Westcott,* Vol. II, p. 53.

[13] Hort, *Life of Hort,* Vol. II, p. 30.

[14] *Ibid.,* Vol. II, p. 32.

Their Tendency to Evolution

Westcott writes to the Archbishop of Canterbury on Old Testament criticism, March 4, 1890: "No one now, I suppose, holds that the first three chapters of Genesis, for example, give a literal history — I could never understand how any one reading them with open eyes could think they did."[15]

Hort writes to Mr. John Ellerton: "I am inclined to think that no such state as 'Eden' (I mean the popular notion) ever existed, and that Adam's fall in no degree differed from the fall of each of his descendants, as Coleridge justly argues."[16]

Their Ritualism

We have already noticed Westcott's associated work with Archbishop Benson in protecting ritualism and giving the most striking blow which discouraged Protestantism.

Hort writes to Mr. John Ellerton, July 6, 1848: "The pure Romish view seems to me nearer, and more likely to lead to, the truth than the Evangelical. . . . We should bear in mind that that hard and unspiritual medieval crust which enveloped the doctrine of the sacraments in stormy times, though in measure it may have made it unprofitable to many men at that time, yet in God's providence preserved it inviolate and unscattered for future generations. . . . We dare not forsake the sacraments or God will forsake us."[17]

Their Papal Atonement Doctrine

Westcott writes to his wife, Good Friday, 1865: "This morning I went to hear the Hulsean Lecturer. He preached on the Atonement. . . . All he said was very good, but then he did not enter into the great difficulties of the notion of

---

[15] Westcott, *Life of Westcott,* Vol. II, p. 69.

[16] Hort, *Life of Hort,* Vol. I, p. 78.

[17] *Ibid.,* Vol. I, p. 76.

sacrifice and vicarious punishment. To me it is always most satisfactory to regard the Christian as in Christ — absolutely one with Him, and he does what Christ has done: Christ's actions become his, and Christ's life and death in some sense his life and death."[18]

Westcott believed that the death of Christ was of His human nature, not of His Divine nature, otherwise man could not do what Christ did in death. Dr. Hort agrees in the following letter to Westcott. Both rejected the atonement of the substitution of Christ for the sinner, or vicarious atonement; both denied that the death of Christ counted for anything as an atoning factor. They emphasized atonement through the Incarnation. This is the Catholic doctrine. It helps defend the Mass.

Hort writes to Westcott, October 15, 1860: "Today's post brought also your letter. . . . I entirely agree — correcting one word — with what you there say on the Atonement, having for many years believed that 'the absolute union of the Christian (or rather, of man) with Christ Himself' is the spiritual truth of which the popular doctrine of substitution is an immoral and material counterfeit. . . . Certainly nothing could be more unscriptural than the modern limiting of Christ's bearing our sins and sufferings to his death; but indeed that is only one aspect of an almost universal heresy."[19]

Their Collusion Previous to Revision

Westcott writes to Hort, May 28, 1870: "Your note came with one from Ellicott this morning. . . . Though I think that Convocation is not competent to initiate such a measure, yet I feel that as 'we three' are together it would be wrong not to 'make the best of it' as Lightfoot says. . . . There is some hope that alternative readings might find a place in the margin."[20]

Westcott writes to Lightfoot, June 4, 1870: "Ought we

---

18 Westcott, *Life of Westcott,* Vol. I, p. 231.

19 Hort, *Life of Hort,* Vol. I, p. 430.

20 Westcott, *Life of Westcott,* Vol. I, p. 390.

not to have a conference before the first meeting for Revision? There are many points on which it is important that we should be agreed."[21]

Westcott writes to Hort, July 1, 1870: "The Revision on the whole surprised me by prospects of hope. I suggested to Ellicott a plan of tabulating and circulating emendations before our meeting which may in the end prove valuable."[22]

Hort writes to Lightfoot: "It is, I think, difficult to measure the weight of acceptance won beforehand for the Revision by the single fact of our welcoming an Unitarian."[23]

Hort writes to Williams: "The errors and prejudices, which we agree in wishing to remove, can surely be more wholesomely and also more effectually reached by individual efforts of an indirect kind than by combined open assault. At present very many orthodox but rational men are being unawares acted on by influences which will assuredly bear good fruit in due time, if the process is allowed to go on quietly; and I cannot help fearing that a premature crisis would frighten back many into the merest traditionalism."[24]

Although these last words of Dr. Hort were written in 1858, nevertheless they reveal the method carried out by Westcott and himself as he said later, "I am rather in favor of indirect dealing." We have now before us the sentiments and purposes of the two men who entered the English New Testament Revision Committee and dominated it during the ten years of its strange work. We will now be obliged to take up the work of that Committee, to behold its battles and its methods, as well as to learn the crisis that was precipitated in the bosom of Protestantism.

---

[21] *Ibid.,* Vol. I, p. 391.

[22] *Ibid.,* Vol. I, pp. 392, 393.

[23] Hort, *Life of Hort,* Vol. II, p. 140.

[24] *Ibid.,* Vol. I, p. 400.

CHAPTER VIII

Revision at Last!

By the year 1870, so powerful had become the influence of the Oxford Movement, that a theological bias in favor of Rome was affecting men in high authority. Many of the most sacred institutions of Protestant England had been assailed and some of them had been completely changed. The attack on the Thirty-nine Articles by Tract 90, and the subversion of fundamental Protestant doctrines within the Church of England had been so bold and thorough, that an attempt to substitute a version which would theologically and legally discredit our common Protestant Version would not be a surprise.

The first demands for revision were made with moderation of language. "Nor can it be too distinctly or too emphatically affirmed that the reluctance of the public could never have been overcome but for the studious moderation and apparently rigid conservatism which the advocates of revision were careful to adopt."[1] Of course, the Tractarians were conscious of the strong hostility to their ritualism and said little in public about revision in order not to multiply the strength of their enemies.

The friends and devotees of the King James Bible

---

1 Hemphill, *History of the Revised Version*, p. 25.

naturally wished that certain retouches might be given the book which would replace words counted obsolete, bring about conformity to more modern rules of spelling and grammar, and correct what they considered a few plain and clear blemishes in the Received Text, so that its bitter opponents, who made use of these minor disadvantages to discredit the whole, might be answered. Nevertheless, universal fear and distrust of revision pervaded the public mind, who recognized in it, as Archbishop Trench said, "A question affecting . . . profoundly the whole moral and spiritual life of the English people," and the "vast and solemn issues depending on it."[2] Moreover, the composition of the Authorized Version was recognized by scholars as the miracle of English prose, unsurpassed in clearness, precision, and vigor. The English of the King James Bible was the most perfect, if not the only, example of a lost art. It may be said truthfully that literary men as well as theologians frowned on the revision enterprise.[3]

For years there had been a determined and aggressive campaign to take extensive liberties with the Received Text; and the Romanizing Movement in the universities of Oxford and Cambridge, both ritualistic and critical, had made it easy for hostile investigators to speak out with impunity. Lachmann had led the way by ignoring the great mass of manuscripts which favored the printed text and built his Greek New Testament, as Salmon says, of scanty material.[4] Tregelles, though English, "was an isolated worker, and failed to gain any large number of adherents."[5] Tischendorf, who had brought to light many new manuscripts and had done considerable collating, secured more authority as an editor than he deserved, and in spite of his vacillations in successive editions, became notorious in removing from the Sacred Text several passages hallowed by the veneration of centuries.[6]

---

[2] *Ibid.*, p. 24.

[3] *Ibid.*, p. 26.

[4] Salmon, *Some Criticisms,* p. 7.

[5] *Ibid.*, p. 8.

[6] *Ibid.*

The public would not have accepted the extreme, or, as some called it, "progressive" conclusions of these three. The names of Westcott and Hort were not prominently familiar at this time although they were Cambridge professors. Nevertheless, what was known of them was not such as to arouse distrust and apprehension. It was not until the work of revision was all over, that the world awoke to realize that Westcott and Hort had outdistanced Lachmann, Tischendorf, and Tregelles. As Salmon says, "Westcott and Hort's Greek Testament has been described as an epoch-making book; and quite as correctly as the same phrase has been applied to the work done by Darwin."[7]

The first efforts to secure revision were cautiously made in 1857 by five clergymen (three of whom, Ellicott, Moberly, and Humphrey, later were members of the New Testament Revision Committee), who put out a *Revised Version of John's Gospel.* Bishop Ellicott, who in the future was to be chairman of the New Testament Revision Committee, believed that there were clear tokens of corruptions in the Authorized Version.[8] Nevertheless, Ellicott's utterances, previous to Revision, revealed how utterly unprepared was the scholarship of the day to undertake it. Bishop Coxe, Episcopal, of Western New York, quotes Ellicott as saying about this time:

"Even critical editors of the stamp of Tischendorf have apparently not acquired even a rudimentary knowledge of several of the leading versions which they conspicuously quote. Nay, more, in many instances they have positively misrepresented the very readings which they have followed, and have allowed themselves to be misled by Latin translations which, as my notes will testify, are often sadly, and even perversely, incorrect."[9]

The triumvirate who constantly worked to bring things to a head, and who later sat on the Revision Committee, were Ellicott, Lightfoot, and Moulton. They found it

---

[7] *Ibid.,* p. 5.

[8] Ellicott, *Addresses,* p. 70.

[9] Bissell, *Origin of the Bible,* p. 357.

difficult to get the project on foot. Twice they had appealed to the Government in hopes that, as in the case of the King James in 1611, Queen Victoria would appoint a royal commission. They were refused.[10]

There was sufficient aggression in the Southern Convocation, which represented the Southern half of the Church of England, to vote Revision. But they lacked a leader. There was no outstanding name which would suffice in the public eye as a guarantee against the possible dangers. This difficulty, however, was at last overcome when Bishop Ellicott won over "that most versatile and picturesque personality in the English Church, Samuel Wilberforce, the silver-tongued Bishop of Oxford."[11]

He was the remaining son of the great Emancipator who was still with the Church of England; the two other sons, Henry and Robert, influenced by the Oxford Movement, had gone over to the Church of Rome. Dr. Wilberforce had rendered great service to the English Church in securing the resurrection of the Southern Convocation, which for a hundred years had not been permitted to act. "When Ellicott captured the persuasive Wilberforce, he captured Convocation, and revision suddenly came within the sphere of practical politics."[12]

First came the resolution, February 10, 1870, which expressed the desirability of revision of the Authorized Version of the New Testament: "Whether by marginal notes or otherwise, in all those passages where plain and clear errors, whether in the Hebrew or Greek text originally adopted by the translators, or in translation made from the same, shall, on due investigation, be found to exist."[13]

An amendment was passed to include the Old Testament. Then a committee of sixteen — eight from the Upper and eight from the Lower House — was appointed.

---

[10] *Historical Account of the Work of the American Committee of Revision,* pp. 3, 5.

[11] Hemphill, *History of the Revised Version,* p. 28.

[12] *Ibid.*

[13] W. F. Moulton, *The English Bible,* p. 215.

This committee solicited the participation of the Northern Convocation, but they declined to cooperate, saying that "the time was not favorable for Revision, and that the risk was greater than the probable gain."[14]

Later the Southern Convocation adopted the rules which ordered that Revision should touch the Greek text only where found necessary; should alter the language only where, in the judgment of most competent scholars, such change was necessary; and in such necessary changes, the style of the King James should be followed; and also, that Convocation should nominate a committee of its own members who would be at liberty to invite the cooperation of other scholars in the work of Revision. This committee when elected consisted of eighteen members. It divided into two bodies, one to represent the Old Testament and the other to represent the New. As the majority of the most vital questions which concern us involve New Testament Revision, we will follow the fortunes of that body in the main.

The seven members of this English New Testament Revision Committee sent out invitations which were accepted by eighteen others, bringing the full membership of the English New Testament Committee to the number of twenty-five. As we have seen before, Dr. Newman, who later became a cardinal, declined, as also did the leader of the Ritualistic Movement, Dr. Pusey.

It should be mentioned here also that Canon Cook, editor of the *Speaker's Commentary,* declined.

W. F. Moulton, a member of the committee who had spent some years in translating Winer's *Greek Grammar* from German into English, exercised a large influence in the selection of members. Dr. Moulton favored those modern rules appearing in Winer's work which, if followed in translating the Greek, would produce results different from that of the King James. How much Dr. Moulton was a devotee of the Vulgate may be seen in the following words from him:

"The Latin translation, being derived from manuscripts

---

14 *Ibid.,* p. 216.

more ancient than any we now possess, is frequently a witness of the highest value in regard to the Greek text which was current in the earliest times, and . . . its testimony is in many cases confirmed by Greek manuscripts which have been discovered or examined since the 16th century."[15]

From this it is evident that Dr. Moulton looked upon the Vulgate as a witness superior to the King James, and upon the Greek manuscripts which formed the base of the Vulgate as superior to the Greek manuscripts which formed the base of the King James. Furthermore, he said, speaking of the Jesuit New Testament of 1582, "The Rhemish Testament agrees with the best critical editions of the present day."[16] Dr. Moulton, therefore, not only believed the manuscripts which were recently discovered to be similar to the Greek manuscripts from which the Vulgate was translated, but he also looked upon the Greek New Testaments of Lachmann, Tischendorf, and Tregelles, built largely upon the same few manuscripts, as "the best critical editions." Since he exercised so large an influence in selecting the other members of the Committee, we can divine at the outset the attitude of mind which would likely prevail in the Revision Committee.

The Old Testament Committee also elected into its body other members which made the number in that company twenty-seven. Steps were now taken to secure cooperation from scholars in America. The whole matter was practically put in the hands of Dr. Philip Schaff of the Union Theological Seminary in New York City. Of Dr. Schaff's revolutionary influence on American theology through his bold Romanizing policy; of his trial for heresy; of his leadership in the American Oxford Movement, we will speak later. An appeal was made to the American Episcopal Church to take part in the Revision, but that body declined.[17]

Through the activities of Dr. Schaff, two American

---

15 *Ibid.*, p. 184.

16 *Ibid.*, p. 185.

17 Ellicott, *Addresses*, p. 39.

Committees were formed, the Old Testament Company having fourteen members, and the New Testament with thirteen. These worked under the disadvantage of being chosen upon the basis that they should live near New York City in order that meetings of the committee might be convenient. The American Committee had no deciding vote on points of revision. As soon as portions of the Holy Book were revised by the English committees, they were sent to the American committees for confirmation or amendment. If the suggestions returned by the American committees were acceptable to their English co-workers, they were adopted; otherwise they had no independent claim for insertion. In other words, the American committees were simply reviewing bodies.[18] In the long run, their differences were not many. They say: "The work then went on continuously in both countries, the English Companies revising, and the American Committees reviewing what was revised, and returning their suggestions. . . . When this list is fully considered, the general reader will, we think, be surprised to find that the differences are really of such little moment, and in very many cases will probably wonder that the American divines thought it worth while thus to formally record their dissent."[19]

Dr. Schaff, who was to America what Newman was to England, was president of both American Committees.[20]

The story of the English New Testament Revision Committee is a stormy one, because it was the battleground of the whole problem. That Committee finished its work three years before the Old Testament Company, and this latter body had three years to profit by the staggering onslaught which assailed the product of the New Testament Committee. Moreover, the American Revised Bible did not appear until twenty years after the work of the English New Testament Committee, so that the American

---

18 Hemphill, *History of the Revised Version,* p. 41.

19 *Historical Account of the Work of the American Committee of Revision,* pp. 10, 11.

20 *New Brunswick Review,* 1884, pp. 322, 282, 283.

Revisers had twenty years to understand the fate which would await their volume.

When the English New Testament Committee met, it was immediately apparent what was going to happen. Though for ten long years the iron rule of silence kept the public ignorant of what was going on behind closed doors, the story is now known. *The first meeting of the Committee found itself a divided body, the majority being determined to incorporate into the proposed revision the latest and most extreme higher criticism.* This majority was dominated and carried along by a triumvirate consisting of Hort, Westcott, and Lightfoot. The dominating mentality of this triumvirate was Dr. Hort. Before the Committee met, Westcott had written to Hort, "The rules though liberal are vague, and the interpretation of them will depend upon decided action at first."[21] They were determined at the outset to be greater than the rules, and to manipulate them.

The new members who had been elected into the body, and who had taken no part in drawing up the rules, threw these rules completely aside by interpreting them with the widest latitude. Moreover, Westcott and Hort, who had worked together before this for twenty years in bringing out a Greek New Testament constructed on principles which deviated the furthest ever yet known from the Received Text,[22] came prepared to effect a systematic change in the Protestant Bible. On this point Westcott wrote to Hort concerning Dr. Ellicott, the chairman: "The Bishop of Gloucester seems to me to be quite capable of accepting heartily and adopting personally a thorough scheme."[23]

And as we have previously seen, as early as 1851, before Westcott and Hort began their twenty years' labor on their Greek text, Hort wrote, "Think of that vile Textus Receptus."[24] In 1851, when he knew little of the Greek

---

[21] Hemphill, *History of the Revised Version,* p. 44.

[22] Salmon, *Some Criticisms,* pp. 10, 11.

[23] Westcott, *Life of Westcott,* Vol. I, p. 393.

[24] Hort, *Life of Hort,* Vol. I, p. 211.

New Testament, or of texts, he was dominated with the idea that the Received Text was "vile" and "villainous." The Received Text suffered fatal treatment at the hands of this master in debate.

We have spoken of Bishop Ellicott as the chairman. The first chairman was Bishop Wilberforce. One meeting, however, was sufficient for him. He wrote to an intimate friend, "What can be done in this most miserable business?"[25] Unable to bear the situation, he absented himself and never took part in the proceedings. His tragic death occurred three years later. One factor had disturbed him considerably — the presence of Dr. G. Vance Smith, the Unitarian scholar. In this, however, he shared the feelings of the people of England, who were scandalized at the sight of a Unitarian, who denied the Divinity of Christ, participating in a communion service held at the suggestion of Bishop Westcott in Westminster Abbey, immediately preceding their first meeting.

The minority in the Committee was represented principally by Dr. Scrivener, probably the foremost scholar of the day in the manuscripts of the Greek New Testament and the history of the Text. If we may believe the words of Chairman Ellicott, the countless divisions in the Committee over the Greek Text "was often a kind of critical duel between Dr. Hort and Dr. Scrivener."[26] Dr. Scrivener was continuously and systematically out-voted.

"Nor is it difficult to understand," says Dr. Hemphill, "that many of their less resolute and decided colleagues must often have been completely carried off their feet by the persuasiveness and resourcefulness, and zeal of Hort, backed by the great prestige of Lightfoot, the popular Canon of St. Paul's, and the quiet determination of Westcott, who set his face as a flint. In fact, it can hardly be doubted that Hort's was the strongest will of the whole Company, and his adroitness in debate was only equaled by his pertinacity."[27]

---

25 Hemphill, *History of the Revised Version*, p. 36.

26 Ellicott, *Addresses*, p. 61.

27 Hemphill, *History of the Revised Version*, pp. 49, 50.

The conflict was intense and ofttimes the result seemed dubious. Scrivener and his little band did their best to save the day. He might have resigned; but like Bishop Wilberforce, he neither wished to wreck the product of revision by a crushing public blow, nor did he wish to let it run wild by absenting himself. Dr. Hort wrote his wife as follows: "July 25, 1871. We have had some stiff battles today in Revision, though without any ill feeling, and usually with good success. But I, more than ever, felt how impossible it would be for me to absent myself."[28]

On the other hand, Westcott wrote: "March 22, 1886. I should be the last to rate highly textual criticism; but it is a little gift which from school days seemed to be committed to me."[29]

Concerning the battles within the Committee, Dr. Westcott writes: "May 24, 1871. We have had hard fighting during these last two days, and a battle-royal is announced for tomorrow."[30]

"January 27, 1875. Our work yesterday was positively distressing. . . . However, I shall try to keep heart today, and if we fail again I think that I shall fly, utterly despairing of the work."[31]

Same date. "Today our work has been a little better — only a little, but just enough to be endurable."[32]

The "ill-conceived and mismanaged" attempts of the Revision Committee of the Southern Convocation to bring in the contemplated radical changes[33] violated the rules that had been laid down for its control. Citations from ten out of the sixteen members of the Committee (sixteen was the average number in attendance) show that eleven members were fully determined to act upon the principle of exact and literal translation, which would permit them

---

[28] Hort, *Life of Hort,* Vol. II, p. 146.

[29] Westcott, *Life of Westcott,* Vol. II, p. 84.

[30] *Ibid.,* Vol. I, pp. 396, 397.

[31] *Ibid.*

[32] *Ibid.*

[33] Bissell, *Origin of the Bible,* p. 356.

to travel far beyond the instructions they had received. [34]
The Committee being assembled, the passage for consideration was read. Dr. Scrivener offered the evidence favoring the Received Text, while Dr. Hort took the other side. Then a vote was taken.[35] Settling the Greek Text occupied the largest portion of time both in England and in America.[36] The new Greek Testament upon which Westcott and Hort had been working for twenty years was, portion by portion, secretly committed into the hands of the Revision Committee.[37] Their Greek Text was strongly radical and revolutionary.[38] The Revisers followed the guidance of the two Cambridge editors, Westcott and Hort, who were constantly at their elbow, and whose radical Greek New Testament, deviating the furthest possible from the Received Text, is to all intents and purposes the Greek New Testament followed by the Revision Committee. [39] And this Greek text, in the main, follows the Vatican and Sinaiticus Manuscripts.[40]

Hort's partiality for the Vatican Manuscript was practically absolute.[41] We can almost hear him say, "The Vaticanus have I loved, but the Textus Receptus have I hated." As the Sinaiticus was the brother of the Vaticanus, wherever pages in the latter were missing, Hort used the former. He and Westcott considered that when the consensus of opinion of these two manuscripts favored a reading, that reading should be accepted as apostolic. [42] This attitude of mind involved thousands of changes in our time-honored Greek New Testament because a Greek Text formed upon the united opinion of Codex B and

---

[34] Hemphill, *History of the Revised Version,* pp. 67-70.

[35] Newth, *Revision,* p. 120.

[36] Ellicott, *Addresses,* p. 118.

[37] *Ibid.,* p. 56.

[38] Salmon, *Some Criticisms,* pp. 11, 12.

[39] Hemphill, *History of the Revised Version,* pp. 54, 55.

[40] Gore, *New Commentary,* Part III, p. 721.

[41] Hort, *Introduction,* p. 238.

[42] *Ibid.,* pp. 225, 251.

Codex Aleph would be different in thousands of places from the Received Text.

So the Revisers "went on changing until they had altered the Greek Text in 5337 places."[43] Dr. Scrivener, in the Committee sessions, constantly issued his warning of what would be the outcome if Hort's imaginary theories were accepted. In fact, nine-tenths of the countless divisions and textual struggles around that table in the Jerusalem Chamber arose over Hort's determination to base the Greek New Testament of the Revision on the Vatican Manuscript.[44] Nevertheless, the Received Text, by his own admission, had for 1400 years been the dominant Greek New Testament.[45]

It was of necessity that Westcott and Hort should take this position. Their own Greek New Testament upon which they had been working for twenty years was founded on Codex B and Codex Aleph, as the following quotations show: "If Westcott and Hort have failed, it is by an over-estimate of the Vatican Codex, to which (like Lachmann and Tregelles) they assign the supremacy, while Tischendorf may have given too much weight to the Sinaitic Codex."[46]

Dr. Cook, an authority in this field, also says: "I will ask the reader to compare these statements with the views set forth, authoritatively and repeatedly, by Dr. Hort in his 'Introduction,' especially in reference to the supreme excellence and unrivalled authority of the text of B — with which, indeed, the Greek text of Westcott and Hort is, with some unimportant exceptions, substantially identical, coinciding in more than nine-tenths of the passages which, as materially affecting the character of the synoptic Gospels, I have to discuss."[47]

Another quotation from Dr. Hoskier, an authority who

---

43 Everts, "The Westcott and Hort Text Under Fire," *Bibliotheca Sacra,* Jan., 1921.

44 Hemphill, *History of the Revised Version,* pp. 55, 56.

45 Hort, *Introduction,* p. 92.

46 Schaff, *Companion to the Greek Text, p. 277.*

47 Cook, *Revised Version,* p. 6.

worked in this field many years after the appearance of the Revised Version: "We always come back to B, as Westcott and Hort's text is practically B."[48]

Of course the minority members of the Revision Committee, and especially the world in general, did not know of the twenty years' effort of these two Cambridge professors to base their own Greek New Testament upon these two manuscripts. Hort's "excursion into cloudland," as one authority describes his fourth century revisions, was apparent to Dr. Scrivener, who uttered his protest. Here is his description of Hort's theory as Scrivener later published it:

"There is little hope for the stability of their imposing structure, if its foundations have been laid on the sandy ground of ingenious conjecture: and since barely the smallest vestige of historical evidence has ever been alleged in support of the views of these accomplished editors, their teaching must either be received as intuitively true, or dismissed from our consideration as precarious, and even visionary."[49]

As Westcott and Hort outnumbered Scrivener two to one, so their followers outnumbered the other side two to one; and Scrivener was systematically out-voted. As Professor Sanday writes: "They were thus able to make their views heard in the council chamber, and to support them with all the weight of their personal authority, while as yet the outer public had but partial access to them." [50]

As a consequence, the Greek New Testament upon which the Revised Version is based, is practically the Greek New Testament of Westcott and Hort. Dr. Schaff says: "The result is that in typographical accuracy the Greek Testament of Westcott and Hort is probably unsurpassed and that it harmonizes essentially with the text adopted by the Revisers."[51]

---

48 Hoskier, *Genesis of the Versions*, p. 416.

49 Scrivener, *Introduction*, Vol. II, p. 285.

50 W. Sanday, quoted in Hemphill, *History of the Revised Version*, p. 59.

51 Schaff, *Companion to the Greek Text*, p. 279.

The Revisers Professedly Liberal, Actually Narrow

We meet the paradox in the Revisers, as they sit assembled at their task, of men possessing high reputation for liberalism of thought, yet acting for a decade with extreme narrowness. Stanley, Thirlwall, Vaughan, Hort, Westcott, Moberly — men of leading intellect — would naturally be expected to be so broad as to give most sacred documents fair consideration. Dean Stanley had glorified the Church of England because within her ranks both ritualists and higher critics could officiate as well as the regular churchmen. When Bishop Colenso, of Natal, was on trial, amid great excitement throughout all England, for his destructive criticism of the first five books of Moses, Dean Stanley stood up among his religious peers and placed himself alongside of Colenso. He said:

"I might mention one who . . . has ventured to say that the Pentateuch is not the work of Moses; . . . who has ventured to say that the narratives of those historical incidents are colored not unfrequently by the necessary infirmities which belong to the human instruments by which they were conveyed — and that individual is the one who now addresses you. If you pronounce against the Bishop of Natal on grounds such as these, you must remember that there is one close at hand whom . . . you will be obliged to condemn."[52]

Bishop Thirlwall, of "princely intellect," had a well-known reputation for liberalism in theology. He introduced both the new theology of Schleiermacher and higher criticism into England. In fact, when Convocation yielded to public indignation so far as essentially to ask Dr. Smith, the Unitarian scholar, to resign, Bishop Thirlwall retired from the committee and refused to be placated until it was settled that Dr. Smith should remain.[53]

Evidence might be given to show liberalism in other

---

[52] Stanley, *Essays,* pp. 329, 330.

[53] Vance Smith received Holy Communion with his fellow-revisers in Westminster Abbey on June 22, 1870, and said afterwards that he did not join in reciting the Nicene Creed and did not compromise his principles as a Unitarian.

members. These men were honorably bound to do justice
to thousands of manuscripts if they assumed to recon-
struct a Greek Text. We are informed by Dr. Scrivener that
there are 2,864 cursive and uncial manuscripts of the New
Testament in whole or in part. Price says there are 112
uncials and 3,500 cursives. These represent many different
countries and different periods of time. Yet astonishing to
relate, the majority of the Revisers ignored these and
pinned their admiration and confidence practically to two
— the Vaticanus and Sinaiticus.

Doctor Moberly, Bishop of Salisbury, Bishop Westcott,
and Dr. G. Vance Smith came to the Committee with past
relationships that seriously compromised them. Bishop
Moberly "belonged to the Oxford Movement, and, it is
stated in Dean Church's 'Life and Letters' that he wrote a
most kind letter of approval to Mr. Newman as to the
famous Tract 90."[54] During the years when he was a
schoolmaster, the small attendance at times under his
instruction was credited to the fact that he was looked
upon as a Puseyite.[55] While with regard to Dr. Westcott,
his share in making the Ritualistic Movement a success has
been recognized.[56]

Dr. Vaughan, another member of the Revision Committee, was a close friend of Westcott.[57] The extreme
liberalism of Dr. G. Vance Smith, the Unitarian member of
the Committee, is well known through his book on the
Bible and Theology. This amounted practically to Chris-
tianized infidelity. Nevertheless, the worshipful attitude of
these men, as well as that of Lightfoot, Kennedy, and
Humphrey toward Codex B, was unparalleled in Biblical
history. The year 1870 was marked by the Papal declaration of infallibility. It has been well said that the blind
adherence of the Revisionists to the Vatican manuscript
proclaimed "the second infallible voice from the Vatican."

54 F. D. How, *Six Great Schoolmasters,* p. 69.

55 *Ibid.,* p. 82.

56 Kempson, *Church in Modern England,* p. 100.

57 How, *Six Great Schoolmasters,* pp. 179, 180.

The Ruthless Changes Which Resulted

Even the jots and tittles of the Bible are important. God has pronounced terrible woes upon the man who adds to or takes away from the volume of inspiration. The Revisers apparently felt no constraint on this point, for they made 36,000 changes in the English of the King James Version, and very nearly 6,000 in the Greek Text. Dr. Ellicott, in submitting the Revised Version to the Southern Convocation in 1881, declared that they had made between eight and nine changes in every five verses, and in about every ten verses three of these were made for critical purposes. [58] And for the most of these changes the Vatican and Sinaitic Manuscripts are responsible. As Canon Cook says: "By far the greatest number of innovations, including those which give the severest shocks to our minds, are adopted on the authority of two manuscripts, or even of one manuscript, against the distinct testimony of all other manuscripts, uncial and cursive. . . . The Vatican Codex . . . sometimes alone, generally in accord with the Sinaitic, is responsible for nine-tenths of the most striking innovations in the Revised Version." [59]

Wreckers, Not Builders

A force of builders do not approach their task with swords, spears, bombs, cannons, and other instruments of destruction. If the Greek New Testament of Westcott and Hort marks a new era, as we are repeatedly informed, then it was intended that the Revised Version would mark a new era. The appointees to the task of revision evidently approached their work with the intention of tearing down the framework of the teachings which sprang from the Received Text and of the institutions erected for the spread of such teachings.

The translators of 1611 organized themselves into six different companies. Each company allotted to each of its members a series of independent portions of the Bible to

[58] Ellicott, *Submission of Revised Version to Convocation,* p. 27.

[59] Cook, *Revised Version,* pp. 227, 231.

translate, so that all would act as checks and counter-checks on one another, in order that the truth might be transmitted. Above all, their interrelations were so preserved that the world would receive the gift of a masterpiece. Their units were organizations of construction.

On the other hand, the units of the 1881 Revision did not make for protection and independence, but rather for the suppression of individuality and freedom, and for tyrannical domination. The instruments of warfare which they brought to their task were new and untried rules for the discrimination of manuscripts; for attacking the verb; for attacking the article; for attacking the preposition, the pronoun, the intensive, Hebraisms, and parallelisms. The following quotations show that literal and critically exact quotations frequently fail to render properly the original meaning:

"The self-imposed rule of the Revisers," says the *Forum,* "required them invariably to translate the aoristic forms by their closest English equivalents; but the vast number of cases in which they have forsaken their own rule shows that it could not be followed without in effect changing the meaning of the original; and we may add that to whatever extent that rule has been slavishly followed, to that extent the broad sense of the original has been marred."[60]

One of the Revisers wrote, after the work was finished: "With reference to the rendering of the article, similar remarks may be made. As a rule, it is too often expressed. This sometimes injures the idiom of the English, and in truth impairs or misrepresents the force of the original." [61]

The obsession of the Revisionists for rendering literally Hebraisms and parallelisms has often left us with a doctrine seriously, if not fatally, weakened by their theory. "The printing in parallelisms spoils the uniformity

---

[60] *Forum,* June, 1887, p. 357.

[61] G. Vance Smith, *Nineteenth Century,* June, 1881. Thus the Unitarian member of the Revision Committee acknowledges that the Revision was at fault in this respect.

of the page too much and was not worth adopting, unless the parallelism was a good one."[62]

Probably no one act of Germany during the war of 1914-1918 brought down upon her more ill feeling than the bombing of Rheims Cathedral. We felt sad to see the building splintered and marred. It was the work of centuries. The Revisionists approached the beautiful cathedral of the King James Version and tunneled underneath in order that they might destroy the Received Text as its foundation, and slip into its place another composed of the Vatican and Sinaitic Manuscripts. In thousands of places the grandeur of the sacred building was chipped and splintered by the substitution of various readings. In the form of the Revised Version we no longer recognize the strong foundation and glorious features of the old edifice.

This is a case where a little means much. "If one wonders whether it is worth while," says Dr. Robertson, speaking of the Revision, "he must bear in mind that some of the passages in dispute are of great importance." The Bible should more probably be compared to a living organism. Touch a part and you spoil it all. To cut a vital artery in a man might be touching a very small point, but death would come as truly as if he were blown to pieces. Something more than a crushing mass of accumulated material is needed to produce a meritorious revision of God's Holy Book.

The Revisers' Greatest Crime

Ever since the Revised Version was printed, it has met with strong opposition. Its devotees reply that the King James met opposition when it was first published. There is a vast difference, however. Only one name of prominence can be cited as an opponent of the King James Version at its birth.[63] The Queen, all the Church of England — in fact,

---

62 *Ibid.*

63 Hugh Broughton, the Hebraist, who wrote—"Tell His Majesty I had rather be rent in pieces by wild horses, than any such translation, by my consent, should be urged on our churches."

all the Protestant world — was for it. On the other hand, royal authority twice refused to associate itself with the project of revision, as also did the northern half of the Church of England, the Episcopal Church of North America, besides a host of students and scholars of authority.

When God has taught us that "all Scripture is given by inspiration" of the Holy Spirit and that "men spake as they were moved by the Holy Ghost," the Holy Spirit must be credited with ability to transmit and preserve inviolate the Sacred Deposit. We cannot admit for a moment that the Received Text which, by the admission of its enemies themselves, has led the true people of God for centuries, can be whipped into fragments and set aside for a manuscript found in an out-of-the-way monastery, and for another of the same family which has lain, for man knows not how long, upon a shelf in the library of the Pope's palace. Both these documents are of uncertain ancestry, of questionable history, and of suspicious character. The Received Text was put for centuries in its position of leadership by Divine Providence, just as truly as the Star of Bethlehem was set in the heavens to guide the wise men. Neither was it the product of certain technical rules of textual criticism which some men have chosen in the last few decades to exalt as divine principles.

The change of one word in the Constitution of the United States, at least the transposition of two, could vitally affect thousands of people, millions of dollars, and many millions of acres of land. It took centuries of training to place within that document a combination of words which cannot be tampered with, without catastrophic results. It represents the mentality of a great people, and to change it would bring chaos into their well-ordered life.

Not of one nation only, but of all great nations, both ancient and modern, is the Bible the basis of the Constitution. It foretold the fall of Babylon; and when that empire had disappeared, the Bible survived. It announced beforehand the creation of the empires of Greece and Rome, and lived to tell their faults and why they failed. It warned succeeding kingdoms. All ages and continents have their life inwrought into the fabric of this Book. It is the handiwork of God through the centuries. Only those whose records are lifted high above suspicion can be accepted as qualified to touch it. Certainly no living being, or any number of them, ever had authority to make such astounding changes as were made by those men who were directly or indirectly influenced by the Oxford Movement.

The history of the Protestant world is inseparable from the Received Text. A single nation could break loose and plunge into anarchy and license. The Received Text shone high in the heavens to stabilize surrounding peoples. Even many nations at one time might fall under the shadow of some great revolutionary wave. But there stood the Received Text to fill their inner self with its moral majesty and call them back to law and order.

On what meat had Dr. Hort fed, when he dared, being only twenty-three years old, to call the Received Text "villainous" and "vile"? By his own confession he had at that time read little of the Greek New Testament, and knew nothing of texts and certainly nothing of Hebrew. What can be the most charitable estimate we can put upon that company of men who submitted to his lead, and would assure us in gentle words that they had done nothing, that there was really no great difference between the King James Bible and the Revised, while in another breath they reject as "villainous" and "vile" the Greek New Testament upon which the King James Bible is built? Did they belong to a superior race of beings, which entitled them to cast aside, as a thing of naught, the work of centuries? They gave us a Version which speaks with faltering tones, whose music is discordant. The Received Text is harmonious. It agrees with itself, it is self-proving, and it creeps into the affections of the heart.

When a company of men set out faithfully to translate genuine manuscripts in order to convey what God said, it is one thing. When a committee sets itself to revise or translate with ideas and a "scheme," it is another. But it may be objected that the translators of the King James were biased by their pro-Protestant views. The reader must judge whose bias he will accept — that of the influence of the Protestant Reformation, as heading up in the Authorized Version; or that of the influence of Darwinism, higher criticism, incipient modern religious liberalism, and a reversion to Rome, as heading up in the Revised Version. If we select the latter bias, we must remember that both higher criticism and Romanism reject the authority of the Bible as supreme.

The predominant ideas of the respective times of their births influenced and determined the essential characteristics of the Authorized and Revised Versions. The following chapters will establish the truthfulness of the position just stated.

OUR AUTHORIZED BIBLE VINDICATED

CHAPTER IX

The Rising Tide of Modernism and Modern Bibles

"The Revisers had a wonderful opportunity. They might have made a few changes and removed a few archaic expressions, and made the Authorized Version the most acceptable and beautiful and wonderful book of all time to come. But they wished ruthlessly to meddle. Some of them wanted to change doctrine. Some of them did not know good English literature when they saw it. . . . There were enough modernists among the Revisers to change the words of Scripture itself so as to throw doubt on the Scripture."[1]

Because of the changes which came about in the nineteenth century, there arose a new type of Protestantism and a new version of the Protestant Bible. This new kind of Protestantism was hostile to the fundamental doctrines of the Reformation. Previous to this there had been only two types of Bibles in the world, the Protestant and the Catholic. Now Protestants were asked to choose between the true Protestant Bible and one which reproduced readings rejected by the Reformers.

---

[1] *Herald and Presbyter,* July 16, 1924, p. 10.

A New Protestantism Which Is Not Protestant

The new Protestantism arose from the new doctrine concerning the Person of Christ. The deep love of all Christians for Christ makes them ready listeners to any teachings which seem to exalt Jesus and increase the glory of Christ. For this reason Protestants easily fell in with the new doctrines concerning Christ which were entirely different from those held by the Reformers. The new Protestantism rejected the sole authority of the Scriptures. They held that the church was instinct with a mysterious life which they called the Person of Christ.

They taught that this life came into all humanity when Jesus was manifest in the flesh; not simply the flesh of Jesus of Nazareth, but in the flesh of all humanity. They held that this life was progressive, and therefore, from time to time, it led the church to new doctrines. The Bible was secondary. This life was communicated through the sacraments, and the participants in the sacraments graduated from one experience to a higher experience. So Christ had two bodies — His own body in which divinity and humanity were united, and His "theanthropic" life common to all believers, which life constituted the body of the church, or Christ's second body.

This new Protestantism captured most of the Church of England, permeated other Protestant denominations in Great Britain, and flooded the theological seminaries of America. One college professor, alarmed at the atmosphere of paganism which had come into American universities and denominational colleges, investigated them and reported that "ninety per cent or more teach a false religion as well as a false science and a false philosophy."[2]

False science teaches the origin of the universe by organic development without God, and calls it evolution. German philosophy early taught the development of humanity through the self-evolution of the absolute spirit. The outstanding advocates of this latter philosophy, Schelling and Hegel, were admitted pantheists.[3] Their

2 "Confessions of a College Professor," *Sunday School Times,* p. 18.

3 *Princeton Review,* January, 1854, p. 168.

theory was applied to theology in the hands of Schleiermacher whose follower was Dr. Schaff, and whom Dr.
Schaff characterizes as "the greatest theological genius"
since the Reformation. He also said, "There is not to be
found now a single theologian of importance, in whom the
influence of his great mind is not more or less to be
traced."[4] The basis of Schleiermacher's philosophy and
theology was acknowledged by such men as Dorner to be
"thoroughly pantheistic."[5]

One definition of pantheism is the belief that "the
totality of the universe is God." God is in the grass, the
trees, the stones, earth, man, and in all. Pantheism
confounds God with matter. Gnosticism is essentially
pantheistic. "Dr. Schaff says there is 'a pantheistic feature
which runs through the whole system' of Popery."[6] Both
Gnosticism and Pantheism are at war with the first verse of
the Bible which reads, "In the beginning God created the
heaven and the earth." This verse places God before
matter, makes Him the Creator of matter, and hence apart
and distinguished from the material universe.

Modernism, or the new Protestantism, is essentially
pantheistic and therefore anti-Scriptural and anti-
Protestant. Schaff says that by following this new
theology, modern evangelical Germany is as widely separated from the Reformation as the Reformation was from
Roman Catholicism. The Reformers taught that every
child of God is in immediate contact with Christ and grows
in grace and the knowledge of God through the Word and
through the Spirit. The new theology taught that Christianity was not "a system of truth divinely revealed,
recorded in the Scriptures in a definite and complete form
for all ages," but that Christianity is Christ. The church is
the development of Christ very much as in this false
philosophy, the universe is the development of God. This,
of course, is pantheistic, though perhaps all who profess
this teaching are not avowed pantheists. The new theology

---

[4] *Princeton Review,* January, 1854, pp. 169, 170.

[5] *Princeton Review,* January, 1854, p. 170.

[6] *Princeton Review,* January, 1854, p. 167.

changed the Protestant conception of Christ; then very naturally it changed all the fundamental doctrines and consequently made the Bible secondary as the fountain of faith, while nominally giving to the Bible its customary usages. However, like the Gnostics of old, this new theology would not scruple to change sacred passages to support their theology.

The Glorification of the Vaticanus and Sinaiticus

Why was it that at so late a date as 1870 the Vatican and Sinaitic Manuscripts were brought forth and exalted to a place of supreme dictatorship in the work of revising the King James Bible? Especially when shocking corruptions of these documents betray a "systematic depravation"? On this Dean Burgon says: "The impurity of the texts exhibited by Codices B and Aleph is not a matter of opinion, but a matter of fact. These are two of the least trustworthy documents in existence. . . . Codices B and Aleph are, demonstrably, nothing else but specimens of the depraved class thus characterized."[7]

Dr. Salmon declares that Burgon "had probably handled and collated very many more manuscripts than either Westcott or Hort" and "was well entitled to rank as an expert."[8] Nevertheless, there has been a widespread effort to belittle Dean Burgon in his unanswerable indictment of the work of Revision. All assailants of the Received Text or their sympathizers feel so keenly the powerful exposures made by Dean Burgon that generally they labor to minimize his arguments.

Concerning the depravations of Codex Aleph, we have the further testimony of Dr. Scrivener. In 1864 he published *A Full Collation of the Codex Sinaiticus*. In the Introductions he makes it clear that this document was corrected by ten different scribes "at different periods." He tells of "the occurrence of so many different styles of handwriting, apparently due to penmen removed from

---

7 Burgon, *Revision Revised*, pp. 315, 316.
8 Salmon, *Some Criticisms*, p. 23.

each other by centuries, which deform by their corrections every page of this venerable-looking document." Codex Aleph is "covered with such alterations, brought in by at least ten different revisers, some of them systematically spread over every page."

Each of these manuscripts was made from the finest skins and was of rare beauty. "The Codex Sinaiticus of the fourth century is made of the finest skins of antelopes, the leaves being so large, that a single animal would furnish only two. . . . Its contemporary, the far-famed Codex Vaticanus, challenges universal admiration for the beauty of its vellum."[9]

Evidently these manuscripts had back of them royal gold. They were reasonably suspected to be two of the fifty Greek Bibles which the Emperor Constantine ordered at his own expense. Why should ten different scribes, through the centuries, have spread their corrections systematically over every page of the beautiful Sinaiticus? Evidently no owner of so costly a document would have permitted such disfigurements unless he considered the original Greek was not genuine and needed correcting.

As the Vaticanus and Sinaiticus are evidently the product of Gnosticism, what would be more natural than that the Catholicism of Cardinal Newman and the Gnosticism of his followers, who now flood the Protestant churches, would seek, by every means possible, to reinstate in leadership, Gnosticism's old title-papers, the Vaticanus and Sinaiticus?

The Gnosticism of the Revisers

Cardinal Newman believed that tradition and the Catholic Church were above the Bible. Westcott and Hort, great admirers of Newman, were on the Revision Committee in strong leadership. Dean Stanley believed that the Word of God did not dwell in the Bible alone, but that it dwelt in the sacred books of other religions as well.[10] Dr.

---

9 Scrivener, *Introduction*, Vol. I, p. 23.

10 Stanley, *Essays*, p. 124.

Schaff sat in the Parliament of Religions at the Chicago World's Fair, 1893, and was so happy among the Buddhists, Confucianists, Shintoists, and other world religions, that he said he would be willing to die among them.[11] The spirit of the Revisionists on both sides of the ocean was an effort to find the Word of God by the study of comparative religions.[12] This is the spirit of Gnosticism; it is not true faith in the inspiration and infallibility of the Bible.

Modern Bibles

How far the new theology has been adopted by the editors of the many different kinds of modern Bibles, is a question space does not permit us to pursue. In the main, all these new editions conform to the modern rules of textual criticism. We have already mentioned Fenton, Goodspeed, Moffatt, Moulton, Noyes, Rotherham, Weymouth, Twentieth Century, the Polychrome, and the Shorter Bible. To these the names of others might be added. The Ferrar Fenton translation opens thus in Genesis, first chapter: "By periods God created that which produced the Suns; then that which produced the Earth. . . . This was the close and the dawn of the first age."[13]

Here is plenty of scope for evolution, Gnosticism, and the aeon theory.

Another sensation was *A New Commentary,* by Bishop Gore, formerly of Oxford and a descendant of the Tractarians, and others. According to this publication David did not kill Goliath, Noah never had an ark, Jonah was not swallowed by a whale, the longevity of Methuselah was an impossibility, and certain Gospel miracles are regarded with skepticism.

---

[11] *Life of Schaff,* p. 486.

[12] G. F. Nolloth, *The Person of Our Lord,* p. 3.

[13] In his Introductory Note in the 1910 edition Fenton modestly asserts—"I contend that I am the only man who has ever applied real mental and literary criticism to the Sacred Scriptures."

"Every theological seminary of standing in this country, we are told," says one of the most widely read weeklies of America, "has been teaching for a quarter of a century almost everything contained in the new Commentary." [14]

Under these circumstances, how can these theological seminaries regard the Hebrew and the Greek of the Bible as dependable or attach to them any degree of inspiration?

When Doctors Westcott and Hort called "vile" and "villainous" the Received Text which, by the providence of God, was accounted an authority for 1800 years, they opened wide the door for individual and religious sects to bring forth new Bibles, solely upon their own authority.

It will be necessary to cite only two texts to show why the Protestants cannot use the Douay or Catholic Version in its present condition. Genesis 3:15 reads: "I will put enmities between thee and the woman, and thy seed and her seed: she shall crush thy head, and thou shalt lie in wait for her heel." This rendering opens the way to exalt the Virgin Mary as a redeemer instead of her Divine Seed.

Hebrews 11:21 reads: "By faith Jacob dying, blessed each of the sons of Joseph, and adored the top of his rod." What is this, if it is not image worship? One has only to read the 13th chapter of Daniel in the Douay, a chapter which does not exist in the King James, to be shocked at one of the corruptions of the Word of God, which the martyrs rejected. What becomes, then, of the statement that all versions are good, and that all versions contain the true, saving Word of God? The numerous modern Bibles, translated from the Westcott and Hort text, or from one built on similar principles are no better in many respects than the Douay.

Will not God hold us responsible for light and knowledge concerning His Word? Can we escape His condemnation, if we choose to exalt any version containing proved corruptions? Shall we not rather avoid putting these versions on a level with God's true Bible? And what is the practical result of this tide of modernism which has largely engulfed England and is sweeping the theological schools

---

[14] *Literary Digest,* December 29, 1928.

and popular Protestant churches in America? It renders such a modernist missionary useless in the foreign field. He will find that the heathen have been in possession of a philosophy like his for 3,000 years. He is no more certain of his ground than they are. It is sad to see the heathen world deprived of the Bread of Life because of modernism.

Uniformity in expressing the sacred language of the one God is highly essential. It would be confusion, not order, if we did not maintain uniformity of Bible language in our church services, in our colleges and in the memory work of our children. "For God is not the author of confusion, but of peace, as in all churches of the saints" (I Corinthians 14:33). It is not those who truly love the Word of God, who wish to multiply various versions, which they design shall be authorized for congregational use or exalted as authority for doctrine. Let the many versions be used as reference books, or books for study, but let us have a uniform standard version, namely, the venerated King James Version.

CHAPTER X

Conclusion

Barren rock, mountain solitude, and lonely wilderness have all contributed their brave sons to defend the Word of God, and, if need be, to die that it might be kept unadulterated. He who hath chosen the weak things of this world to confound the mighty, would not permit man to be robbed of that simplicity of the Divine Word which made the untampered Scriptures a peculiar treasure.

The moral law within the heart is compelling. One great philosopher felt this when he said, "There are two things in the universe which awe me: The glory of the heavens above and the majesty of the moral law within me." God did not leave mankind to struggle in ignorance with the awful impressiveness of the law within, without revealing Himself in His Word as the moral Governor of the universe. Only the supreme lessons of the Bible can reach the deeper feelings of the heart. The Bible is the absolute standard of right and wrong. In the Word dwells spiritual life the most perfect. Jesus said, "It is the spirit that quickeneth; the flesh profiteth nothing: the words that I speak unto you, they are spirit, and they are life" (John 6:63).

The Psalmist wrote: "Thou hast magnified thy word above all thy name." The created worlds magnify the exalted name of the Eternal. But God has magnified His

312

Word above all these. It is an unhappy hour when humanity lightly esteems the Bible; for there God reveals Himself more than through the material universe. A man is no better than his word; if one fails to command confidence, so does the other. Heaven and earth shall pass away, but God's Word shall never pass away.

In the Bible is revealed the standard by which we shall be tried when the judgment day comes. From the Garden of Eden until now, one standard and one only has been revealed. Inspiration declares that this revelation has been under the special protection of Him who has all power in heaven and in earth. "The words of the Lord are pure words," says the Psalmist, "as silver tried in a furnace of earth, purified seven times. Thou shalt keep them, O Lord, thou shalt preserve every one of them [margin] from this generation for ever" (Psalm 12:6, 7). Lonely mounds in distant lands mark the graves where fell those who forsook home and civilization that the Word of God might live.

We believe in Jesus Christ as the Divine Teacher, because, unlike Mohammed and others, He did not come unheralded. There were fifteen hundred years of prophecy pointing forward to His coming among men. A perfect transmission of these predictions was necessary if they were to be fulfilled in every specification.

There is nothing which so stirs men to the holiest living as the story of Jesus Christ. Yet only within the covers of the Bible is that story found. At the cost of great sufferings, God yielded up His Son. The history of the ages which prepared for this holy event, and the story of our Redeemer's life are all found within the same volume. These priceless records have been the object of God's infinite solicitude.

The Divine Saviour and the holy prophets and apostles spoke beforehand of events which would occur even to the end of time. Of what value would such a prophetic revelation be, if it were not to guide those who would pass through the predicted scenes, and if it were not to warn the wicked and encourage the good? This value, however, would be destroyed if the words foretelling the events, the meaning of the events, and the prediction of rewards and punishments were so tampered with that the force of the Divine utterance was destroyed. Moreover the fact that the Word could make such a prediction not only stamps the Word as divine but condemns as wicked, yes, points out as being the predicted apostasy, that system which would either tamper with the Word or make the Word secondary. The writing of the Word of God by Inspiration is no greater miracle than the miracle of its preservation.

The pathetic question of Pilate, "What is truth?" is not more pathetic than the error of those who say that only by balancing one version against another, or by examining the various manuscript readings — those of apostates as well as those of the faithful — can we arrive at approximate truth.

Left to ourselves we stumble through the darkness guided only by the little lamp of reason. But when we accept the Bible, a great light shines upon our path. History and prophecy unite to confirm our faith. Daniel the prophet and John the apostle point out the four great empires which succeeded one another — Babylon, Medo-Persia, Greece, and pagan Rome. After these arose a cruel, anti-Christian power, the Papacy, from whose terrible persecutions the church fled into the wilderness. As Daniel and John predicted, the Papacy trod underfoot the Truth, the Word of God. From false manuscripts she issued a volume which she chose to call a Bible, but added tradition and elevated it to a greater inspiration than the Scriptures themselves.

Eating the bread of poverty and dressed in the garments of penury, the church in the wilderness followed on to serve the Lord. She possessed the untampered manuscripts of holy revelation which discountenanced the claims of the Papacy. Among this little flock, stood out prominently the Waldenses. Generation after generation of skilled copyists handed down, unadulterated, the pure Word. Repeatedly their glorious truth spread far among the nations. In terror, the Papacy thundered at the monarchs of Europe to stamp out this heresy by the sword of steel. In vain the popish battalions drenched the plains of Europe with martyr blood. The Word lived, unconquered.

Let Gilly tell us how the Waldenses survived the fury of the Papacy:

"They occupy a mountain district, . . . and yet from this secluded spot, have they disseminated doctrines, whose influence is felt over the most refined and civilized part of Europe. They . . . speak the same language, have the same patriarchal habit, and simple virtues, and retain the same religion, which was known to exist there more than a thousand years ago.

"They profess to constitute the remains of the pure and primitive Christian church, and those who would question their claims cannot show either by history or tradition that they ever subscribed to the popish rituals, or bowed before any of the idols of the Roman Church. . . . They have seldom been free from persecution, or vexations and intolerant oppression, and yet nothing could ever induce them to conform, even outwardly, with the religion of the state.

"In short, there is no other way of explaining the political, moral, and religious phenomenon, which the Vaudois have continued to display for so many centuries, than by ascribing it to the manifest interposition of providence, which has chosen in them 'the weak things of this world to confound the things that are mighty.' "[1]

The Redeemer said: "Thy word is truth." Rome, the Papacy, did as the prophet Daniel wrote: she "cast down the truth to the ground." While Rome was cruelly persecuting the church in the wilderness, was she also the divinely appointed guardian of the true Word of God? God placed the answer to this question in prophecy. And now the Revised Version, built almost entirely on the Vatican Manuscript, kept in the Pope's library, and upon the Sinaiticus, found in a Catholic monastery[2] (types of manuscripts upon which the Vulgate was built), comes forward and proposes to set aside the text of our Authorized Bible.

---

[1] Gilly, *Excursions to Piedmont,* pp. 258, 259.

[2] The Convent of St. Catherine, of the "Holy Oriental Orthodox Apostolic Church."

The Authorized Version was translated in 1611, just before the Puritans departed from England,[3] so that they carried it with them across stormy seas to lay the foundation of one of the greatest governments the world has ever known. The Authorized Version of God's Holy Word had much to do with the laying of the foundation of our great country.

When the Bible was translated in 1611, God foresaw the wide, extended use of the English language; and, therefore, in our Authorized Bible, gave the best translation that has ever been made, not only in the English language, but as many scholars say, ever made in any language.

The original Scriptures were written by direct inspiration of God. This can hardly be said of any translation. Nevertheless, when apostasy had cast its dark shadow over the Western lands of opportunity, God raised up the men of 1611. They were true Protestants. Many of their friends and associates had already fallen before the sword of despotism while witnessing for the Holy Word. And in a marvelous way God worked to give us through them an English version from the genuine manuscripts. It grew and soon exercised a mighty influence upon the whole world. But this was an offense to the old systems of the past.

Then arose the pantheistic theology of Germany, the ritualistic Oxford Movement of England, and the Romanizing Mercersburg theology of America. Through the leaders of these movements, revised versions were brought forth, which were based on old manuscripts and versions long ago discarded by other scholars. These manuscripts and versions had been discarded because of the bewildering confusion which their uncertain message produced. In spite of all this, the new revised versions raised ancient but inferior manuscripts and versions to a place of unwarranted influence. Hence once again the true people of God are called upon to face this subtle and insidious program.

It is difficult for evangelical scholars to expose the systematic depravation without being misunderstood, and

---

[3] The "Pilgrim Fathers" sailed from Southampton in the "Mayflower" and landed in what is now Plymouth, Massachusetts, in December, 1620.

without being charged with attacking the genuine, while seeking to expose the erroneous mixed with the genuine. They recognize that these modern versions can be used as books of reference even if they cannot be put on a level with the Received Text.

Paul said, in Acts 17:28, "As certain also of your own poets have said, For we are also his offspring." Paul quoted good sayings from the pagan poets, but did not use these Greek writers as authority. It is as unthinkable to forbid excellent quotations from pagan and heathen scholars as it would be to place their writings on a level with the pure Word of God. Likewise, parts of modern versions edited by scholars may be used with care in considering Bible verses from another angle. This fact, however, is taken advantage of, to claim divine inspiration for all the rest, and sow confusion among the churches of believers.

Through the Reformation, the Received Text was again given to the Church. In the ages of twilight and gloom, the corrupt church did not think enough of the corrupt Bible to give it circulation. Since the Reformation, the Received Text, both in Hebrew and in Greek, has spread abroad throughout the world. Wherever it is accurately translated, regardless of whatever the language may be, it is as truly the Word of God as our own Authorized Bible. Nevertheless, in a remarkable way, God has honored the King James Version. It is the Bible of the 160,000,000 English-speaking people, whose tongue is spoken by more of the human race than any other. German and Russian are each the language of 100,000,000; while French is spoken by 70,000,000. The King James Version has been translated into many other languages. One writer claims 886. It is the Book of the human race. It is the author of vastly more missionary enterprises than any other version. It is God's missionary Book.

We shall need the Lord Jesus in the hour of death, we shall need Him in the morning of the resurrection. We should recognize our need of Him *now*. We partake of Him, not through some ceremony, wherein a mysterious life takes hold of us. When we receive by faith the written Word of God, the good pleasure of the Lord is upon us, and we partake of Him. Through this Word we receive the power of God, the same Word by which He upholds all things, by which He swings the mighty worlds and suns through the deeps of the stellar universe. This Word is able to save us and to keep us forever. This Word shall conduct us to our Father's throne on high. "The grass withereth, the flower fadeth: but the word of our God shall stand for ever."

"The starry firmament on high,
    And all the glories of the sky,
Yet shine not to thy praise, O Lord,
    So brightly as thy written Word.

"The hopes that holy Word supplies,
    Its truths divine and precepts wise,
In each a heavenly beam I see,
    And every beam conducts to Thee.

"Almighty Lord, the sun shall fail,
    The moon her borrowed glory veil,
And deepest reverence hush on high
    The joyful chorus of the sky.

"But fixed for everlasting years,
    Unmoved amid the wreck of spheres,
Thy Word shall shine in cloudless day,
    When heaven and earth have passed away."

APPENDIX
by Thomas R. Steinbach

I. Alphabetical Index
II. Scripture Index
III. Chronological Index

Millenary Petition, 248
Millennium, 270
Miller, Dr. E., 88, 128, 148, 158, 173, 198, 256, 273
Milligan, 272
Milman, 183, 203
Milon, 213
Minuscules, 26, 33, 89
"Miracle of English Prose," 242
Miracles, 309, 314
Miraculous, 266
Miriam, 73
Misnomer, 165
Missionary Book, 317
Missionary Enterprise, 317
Misunderstood, 316
Mizbeach, 69
Moab, 46, 53, 54
Moabites, 53
Moberly, Dr. 285, 296, 297
Modern Bibles, 178, 180
Modern criticism, 111, 118
Modernism, 176, 304, 306, 310
Modernist, 266, 304, 311
Modern school, 116
Modus vivendi, 152
Moffat, 178, 309
Mohammed, 66, 313
Mohammedans, 57, 232
Mohler, 268, 269
Moir, I.A., 29
Monastery, (231), 278, 301, 315
Monk of Bethlehem, 217
Monophysites, 198
"Monstra," 141
Montgomery, Dr. John Warwick, 8
Monuments, 45, 46, 53, (206)
Moody Bible Institute, 144
Moral attack, 239
Moral governor, 312
Moral law, 312
Morland, Sir Samuel, 206, 211
Morning of the resurrection, 317
"Morning star of the Reformation," 221
Moses, 296
Moulton, 272, 285-288, 309
Mount Sinai, 87, 94, 100, 150, 163, 254, 273
Mount Zion, 72, 75

Mysterious life, 305, 317
Mystery of iniquity, 182
Myth, 112, 113
"Mythical" tabernacle, 69

Nabatean Aramaic, 57
Nabunaid, 77
Nahum, 57
Napoleon, 66, 268
Naturalistic (critics), 7, 94, 101, 103, 104
Nazareth, 4, 305
Nazianzen, Gregory, 220
Neander, 203
Nebuchadnezzar, 53-55, 61, 62, 79
Necho, 54
Negroes, 79
Nehemiah, 57, 58, 75, 76, 81
Neo-Platonism, 192
Nestle-Aland, 27
Nestle's text, 29, 31
Nestorians, 198
Netherlands, 202
Neutrality, 134
"Neutral" texts, 106, 137-139, 141, 142, 147, 160, 161, 164-167, 171
Nevin, Dr., 185
New Commentary, A, 245, 263, 272, 293, 309, (310)
New Departure, 110
New dispensation, 268
New English Bible, 2
New Protestantism, 304-306, (309)
New Schaff-Herzog Encyclopedia, 145
New Testament in the Original Greek, 144
New Testament Studies, 29
New York City, 67, 154, 166, 288, 289
New York dailies, 66
New York State, 285
Newman, J.H., Cardinal, 184, 185, 241, (287), (289), (297), (308)
Nicene Creed, 296
Nile, 28
Nineteen-twentieths, 188, 256, (298)
Nine-tenths, 298
Nineveh, 62, 63
Nisibis, 130

SCRIPTURE INDEX

Chronological Index

INDEX